Education and Women's Work

SUNY Series on
WOMEN AND WORK

Joan Smith, Editor

Education and Women's Work

Female Schooling and the Division of Labor in Urban America, 1870–1930

John L. Rury

STATE UNIVERSITY OF NEW YORK PRESS

Cover photo courtesy of New York State Archives

Published by
State University of New York Press, Albany

For information, address State University of New York
Press, State University Plaza, Albany, N.Y. 12246

Production by Ruth East
Marketing by Bernadette LaManna

Library of Congress Cataloging-in-Publication Data

Rury, John L., 1951–
     Education and women's work : female schooling and the division of
labor in urban America, 1870–1930 / John L. Rury.
          p.   cm.   —   (SUNY series, women and work)
     Includes bibliographical references and index.
     ISBN 0-7914-0617-2 (alk. paper) .   — ISBN 0-7914-0618-0 (alk. paper
: pbk.)
          1. Women—Education (Secondary)—United States—History.
2. Women—Employment—United States—History. 3. United States-
-Social conditions—1865–1918. 4. United States—Social
conditions—1918–1932. I. Title. II. Series: SUNY series on women
and work.
     LC1755.R87   1991
     376'.63'0973—dc20
                                                                                90–38325
                                                                                CIP

10 9 8 7 6 5 4 3 2 1

To

Ellen, Aaron, and Derek

Contents

List of Tables

List of Figures

Foreword

The history of education is not rich in studies that combine an effusion of quantitative data, with equal portions of narrative elegance, biographical perspective, and attention to intellectual and spiritual as well as material dimensions. *Education and Women's Work* is such a book. The raw data alone tells us more about the connections between markets, politics, ideology, social structure, gender, and the evolution of education than any single history of progressive schooling preceding it. And it does so by combining careful analyses of statistical, demographic, and economic data, with equally careful readings of the moral, spiritual, intellectual, and biographical outpourings of the dazzling variety of human agents who formed the human networks within which the progressive high school was to acquire specific form and dimension. The voices of women, school reformers, industrialists, social scientists, and farmers; of African Americans, working-class Americans, rich Americans, and immigrants can be heard in this book.

Beyond the sheer force of its data, John Rury's interpretations are provocative and fundamental, creating new conceptual receptacles within which to re-examine the meaning of modernization, the evolution of opportunity, the power of economic, ideological, and political circumstance, and the peculiar dialectic between opportunity and constraint for women in education. Most important, perhaps, *Education and Women's Work* reveals the folly of trying to embed the history of education, the history of women, or the history of work simply—as a story of victims and victimizers, oppressors and liberators, material or spiritual hegemony, or even as is common these days, as a dialectic between markets and politics. As this book reveals, the history of education is much too complex for that.

Barbara Finkelstein
University of Maryland, College Park

Acknowledgments

In writing this book I have come to appreciate the extent to which scholarship is fundamentally a collective enterprise. This study began more than ten years ago as a doctoral thesis at the University of Wisconsin. It has since grown and matured, and has paralleled my continuing development as a historian and social scientist. In this process I have benefitted from the assistance and good will of countless other scholars, librarians, students and friends who have helped with research and with thinking about the issues associated with women's education and work. Consequently, whatever merit this study possesses is largely due to what I have learned from others. Its shortcomings reflect my own disabilities as a student. Unfortunately, I can only identify a few of the most helpful people herein; I apologize to anyone whom I may have overlooked.

My greatest debt as a historian is to Carl Kaestle, who supervised the early stages of this study as my dissertation advisor and has been a continuing source of advice and encouragement in the years hence. Carl introduced me to the excitement of "social science history" when it was still a new field and to the social history of American education. The very shape of the book reflects his influence. In more recent years David Tyack and Elizabeth Hansot have proven to be especially valuable friends and critics, pointing out problems of interpretation and style and sharing their own work on the history of women's education (even though we do not agree on everything). Barbara Finkelstein provided invaluable advice for revision in the latter stages of the study's evolution, particularly regarding matters of interpretation. To John Sharpless goes responsibility for introducing me to women's history and to the problem of understanding education and women's work at the turn of the century. He and Michael Olneck taught me much about quantitative analysis at the dissertation phase of this study, in addition to providing advice about other questions. David Angus, Jeffrey Mirel, and Maris Vinovskis were stimulating colleagues and critics as I set about expanding and revising the study several years later. Other friends and colleagues who read the manuscript or particular chapters and offered comments at different points include Geraldine Clifford, Nancy Green, Jane Hunter, Harvey Kantor, Herbert Kliebard, and Maxine Seller. I also received helpful comments from several anonymous readers.

I have had the good fortune to receive financial assistance for this study from a number of sources. My dissertation was supported by a contract from the National Institute of Education from 1979 to 1981, when much of the research for chapters 3, 4, and 5 was completed. A Spencer Fellowship from the National Academy of Education during the 1986–87 academic year supported research for chapters 1 and 2, and time for revision of the other chapters in the study. Smaller research grants from the Spencer Foundation (administered through Ohio State University) and the Schlesinger Library at Radcliffe College also helped with the research.

I utilized collections of documents and other materials at the State Historical Society of Wisconsin, the Bentley Historical Library (in Ann Arbor), the Ruether Library (Wayne State University), and the Schlesinger Library (Radcliffe College). I used books and additional materials from other libraries at the University of Wisconsin, the University of Michigan, Ohio State University, Wayne State University, the Gutman Library (Harvard University), De Paul University, the University of Chicago, and the University of Illinois libraries at Chicago and Urbana. Librarians at each of these institutions were unfailingly helpful collaborators in my research.

There were yet other sources of assistance as well. Colleagues, administrators, and friends (not necessarily exclusive categories) at my various workplaces over the past decade—the History Department at Wayne State University, the Humanities Division at Antioch College, the College of Education at Ohio State University, and the School for New Learning at DePaul University—have been helpful sources of support for my work on this project. Without their encouragement and understanding, this book would have taken much longer to write. I was designated a visiting scholar by the University of Michigan during my fellowship year, allowing me use of libraries and computer time. Data used in the individual level analyses in chapter 2 were provided by the Inter-university Consortium for Political and Social Research (ICPSR). Carol Wasson typed the dissertation chapters that formed the starting point for this book. (I prepared the new chapters and subsequent revisions of the old chapters on a word processor.)

I would like to thank the following individuals and institutions for permission to use various items: The Bentley Historical Library at the University of Michigan, the Ruether Library at Wayne State University, and the Schlesinger Library at Radcliffe College (for diaries and other personal documents of nineteenth-century women); The University of Chicago Press (for material from George Counts, *The Selective Character of American Secondary Education*, published in 1921); The Women's Educational and Industrial Union in Boston (for material from the 1914 study, *Women in Office Service*); Michael B. Katz and the *History of Education Quarterly* (for material from "Youth and Early Industrialization in a Canadian City: A Multivariate Analysis," published in 1978 in the *History of Education Quarterly*); and Carl F. Kaestle and Cambridge University Press (for material from *Education and Social Change in Nineteenth Century Massachusetts*, published in 1979). Portions of chapter 4 first appeared in 1984 in the *History of Education Quarterly*, and the information in Table A.7 appeared in *Urban Education* in 1988 and is used herein with permission of Sage Publications. The picture on the front cover is used with permission of the New York State Library.

Lois Patton, Ruth East, and other members of the editorial staff at the State University of New York Press have been a great source of assistance in the difficult process of seeing this work through to completion. Lois Patton deserves special recognition for shepherding the book through an extended review process.

The people who have been closest to this project, though often not by choice, have been my wife and children, Ellen Kennedy and Aaron and Derek Rury. Ellen's contribution started at the very beginning, when she assisted with data collection for the dissertation. Since then she has given me valuable advice about various sections of the book and has been a steady source of support—in every sense of the term—throughout its gestation. For their part, Aaron and Derek have occasionally complained about my monopolizing the family computer and about wanting me outside to play ball, but they also have come to understand dad's need to do his work at home. Without my family's support this study simply would not have been possible. The book's dedication to them is just a small token of my gratitude and affection.

Introduction

Between the end of the Civil War and the advent of the Great Depression, the lives of American women changed profoundly. It was a process of change marked by considerable conflict and one that received much attention from contemporaries. "I have no patience with the modern dilettantism that would withhold from a woman any respectable gainful calling," a judge in Newburgh, New York, declared at a graduation ceremony in 1896. "Today from the Newburgh Academy to Vassar, to Wellesley, to Harvard, the road is open to her. There is no distinction of sex."[1] Apart from the obvious hyperbole in these remarks (sex differences, of course, continued to be important in American life), this view contained a good deal of prescience in the 1890s. It was an era when female roles were expanding, and many observers agreed that the time had come for women to play a larger part in public affairs. The next several decades would prove them right. Women became socially and politically active, advocating political reform and social improvement. Their legal status changed as well. They secured the right to vote, a host of new laws liberalized their obligations as marriage partners, and a controversial body of legislation gave them special protection as workers. But these were only the most obvious changes in women's lives. Many other things changed as well, including—as suggested in the judge's remarks cited above—the schools they attended and the work they performed.

This study examines the development of women's secondary education in the years between the Civil War and the Great Depression.[2] Its focus is decidedly urban. It was in the nation's cities, after all, that the most important changes occurred in women's roles, particularly regarding education. The high school was an urban institu-

1

tion, even though it appeared in many different kinds of cities, large and small. And the very context of education was distinctive in the cities. As other historians have noted, the cities were focal points of social change. For many women at this time, city life became symbolic of new opportunities and challenges. The United States was becoming an urban nation, with an increasingly urban culture, and the most important changes in both education and women's lives occured first in the cities.[3]

Education and urbanization notwithstanding, perhaps the single most important development in women's lives during the six decades following 1870 was a set of sweeping changes in women's work. The rate of female labor force participation in the United States increased from less than 15 to nearly 25 percent in these years, such that by 1930 almost one out of every four American workers was a woman. Taking jobs as typists, clerks, teachers, and telephone operators, as well as traditionally female jobs in manufacturing and domestic service, women rapidly expanded the range of positions open to them as well.[4] Not surprisingly, these changes raised troublesome questions about women's roles in society and initiated a good deal of controversy. "For the past fifty years," wrote one commentator in 1929, "there have been many 'scare' headlines and perturbed fathers, mothers, preachers, teachers and reformers, ready to tell of dire consequences to follow the entrance of women into new occupations."[5] There is little evidence, however, that such objections in any way slowed or otherwise affected the pace of these changes. As Barbara Bergmann has noted, the growth of female labor force participation in this period (and since then) was inexorable. And as Bergmann also points out, a host of important changes in women's status and social roles have followed in the wake of changing patterns of women's work.[6] Even today it is commonplace to remark how the movement of women out of the home and into the work force has had important implications for many aspects of American life. It is little wonder, in that case, that the transformation of women's work at the turn of the century—part of an ongoing change in female roles—was accompanied by a set of important changes in women's education.

The focal point of this study, accordingly, is the changing relationship of women's work and education. Education and work are closely linked under most circumstances, of course, but the relationship between women's secondary education and women's work was especially striking in the decades following 1870. This is partly because of the peculiar quality of women's work. In the nineteenth century most American women worked outside the wage labor force, usually as homemakers in their own households. Those women who did work in the paid labor force, moreover, were restricted to a rather narrow range of occupations, most of which did not require formal education. The only important exception to this was women employed as teachers, though it is not clear that much formal education was required of teachers in many parts of the country at this time. As female labor force participation grew around the turn of the century, however, the range of jobs open to women expanded substantially. And many of these new positions required relatively high levels of schooling. If women had not been well educated—comparatively speaking—it is not clear that these jobs would have been available to them (and women without schooling generally were excluded from such positions). In other words, education may have helped to prepare women for a new set of occupational roles at a critical period in American social and economic history. Accordingly, the study of women's education in the late nineteenth- and early twentieth-century United States offers a unique opportunity to examine the relationship between formal schooling and the development of paid labor in a modern industrial society.[7]

Opportunity and Constraint

The development of women's education and work in the half century or so following the Civil War was marked by a curious dialectic of opportunity and constraint. These elements are both a part of any social change, of course, but in the case of American women their interaction was especially notable. This is perhaps most evident in the timing of changes in education and work. Widening receptivity to women in education, it seems, was not always accompanied by growing opportunities in women's work. And when female work roles changed most dramatically, opening up new areas of employment, women's education appears to have become more restrictive. In both cases forces of opportunity and constraint seem to have maintained a delicate balance that prevented any single set of changes from becoming too sweeping. The result was a transformation of women's roles which was incremental and delimited, despite its relatively rapid pace, and decidedly not revolutionary—regardless of contemporary anxieties to the contrary.

Perhaps the easiest way to describe the general relationship between education and women's work at this time—and the shifting interplay of opportunity and constraint—is to depict the way in which these aspects of women's lives changed chronologically. The development of women's schooling and female labor force participation proceeded in a series of distinct steps, starting with the early growth of women's education. This study examines each of these stages separately in five rather broad chapters, each dealing with a related set of issues in the development of women's education and work. By and large, the organization of the book is chronological. The first two chapters deal with women's education and work in the nineteenth century, and the second three are concerned primarily with events after 1900. Each chapter is also thematic, however, and focuses on a particular set of issues in each of these periods.

The story begins in the years following the Civil War, when few middle-class women worked outside their homes and most did not go to high school. In the next several decades, however, larger numbers of young women began attending secondary schools. This was a period of great promise for young middle-class white women in American society. By 1900 women high school graduates outnumbered their male classmates by a 2 to 1 margin, and female college enrollments had started to grow faster than those for men. As a group, women may have had more education than men.

This does not mean, however, that forces of constraint were altogether absent in education. This set of changes was accompanied by a vigorous debate among educators and scientists about whether education was a benefit to young women. Even so, these concerns do not seem to have affected the decision of many teenage girls to attend school. The continuing growth of female enrollments in this period proved to be the most telling answer to the critics of women's education. Not only did women attend school in astounding numbers, they also did quite well. This general process of expansion in women's secondary education, and all of the controversy that accompanied it, is the topic of chapter 1.

Regardless of high school enrollments, however, there were definite limits to the extent of opportunity for American women in the nineteenth century. Most did not go to school to get a job. In fact, relatively few middle-class women worked outside of their homes at this time. Chapter 2 explores the reasons why young women attended high schools. Most of them, it appears, simply enjoyed school and valued education as a general preparation for life rather than as training for a particular job. As such, these educated women constituted a rather large and underutilized reservoir of skilled labor in the general population. It is little wonder, given this, that they became more active in matters of political and social reform at this time. Many middle-class women believed it their responsibility to pursue such ends precisely because of their education and background. At the same time, however, many of them recognized that they also could perform—if they wanted to—many of the remunerative tasks that their male classmates had undertaken after leaving high school. By its very nature, the coeducational high school of the nineteenth century broached the question of women working, even if most educated women decided not to.

Of course, barriers to female employment eventually gave way in the face of demand from employers and the willingness (in some cases, eagerness) of young women to take on new occupational roles. Beginning in the 1890s, women began to move into a range of new occupations. Most of these positions were white-collar jobs—the most important being clerical work in offices and teaching in public schools. The appearance of these employment opportunities was linked to the growth of corporate enterprise and government in this period, which generated an unprecedented demand for clerical workers, teachers, and social service personnel. Chapter 3 considers the relationship of these changes to women's education in the opening decades of the twentieth century. In particular, it examines the ways in which schools prepared women for the new jobs then open to them. Most of these positions, after all, required relatively high levels of formal education. Schooling, it seems, became an essential condition for employment in many areas of women's work in the twentieth century.

Regardless of their educational qualifications, however, women apparently proved a capable and willing labor force. They eagerly responded to opportunities to work in the growing service economy, sometimes against the advice of parents and educators who wanted them to do more traditionally female kinds of work. Altogether, female labor force participation increased by about 65 percent between 1870 and 1930, and the rate of growth was even more dramatic among younger women—who comprised the largest number of female workers at this time. The result was a remarkable change in the lives of American women in the space of about five decades. Once limited to a narrow domestic sphere of activities and volunteer work in a variety of social contexts, by 1920 young women in the United States could choose from a number of different occupational roles before they were married. In more than a figurative sense, women had left the home for the workplace—even if many of them eventually returned to their traditional domestic roles after marriage. Much of the promise of the latter nineteenth century, it may have seemed, had been fulfilled.

At the same time that a new openness in employment appeared, however, new patterns of constraint were evident in the nation's schools. The Progressive movement in education—along with the rapid transformation of women's work—inspired a host of educational reforms in the early twentieth century designed both to help women become better workers and to make them better wives and homemakers. These changes are the topic of chapter 4. The vocational education movement which swept through American high schools in these years helped create a gender-segregated curriculum in secondary education. While boys studied industrial subjects and principles of business, young women studied home economics and stenography. The growth of female labor force participation, itself partly an outgrowth of improvements in women's education, exerted a telling influence on the evolution of female schooling. By the third decade of the twentieth century, young men and women in high schools often pursued different courses of study designed to prepare them for their separate responsibilities in the social order. Women's work had entered the high school, and the result was a new gender-specific curriculum. The new occupations women entered after the turn of the century became sex typed, and a highly developed array of institutional constraints began to take form in women's education.

The interaction between education and work in women's lives, in that case, was rather complex and included elements of both openness and limitation. The growth of women's education and the changes in women's work in this period were linked in a number of ways, some of which are easier to identify than others. As indicated above, for instance, the development of female secondary education preceded the movement of women into the new white-collar jobs (clerical, teaching, and social work) they took up in the 1890s and afterward. Most of these jobs, after all, required at least a moderate degree of literary preparation and often demanded a cultural orientation that many employers associated with formal education. On the other hand, the process was also cyclical. The rapid transformation—and growth—of female employment inspired the development of several new curricula for women in the nation's secondary schools, including female industrial education, office education, and home economics. The development of these courses was directly linked to the perception that women were performing a host of new tasks, and that their traditional domestic roles consequently were in danger of erosion. Education, in short, helped make it possible for women to move into a number of new jobs, and the growth of female labor force participation led educators to develop new courses of study specifically designed for women likely to enter the work force.

The relationship of education and women's work, accordingly, changed dramatically between 1870 and 1930. In terms of women's experiences in secondary schools, this span of time can be divided into two distinct periods. The first covers the three decades following 1870.

During this time women's education was decidedly nonvocational. By and large, women appear to have studied the same subjects in high schools as young men, and they performed as well as or better than their male classmates. Labor force participation for those groups of women who attended high schools at this time was relatively low. Women outnumbered men in high schools throughout this period and graduated at a higher rate as well. In many regards the high school (and the public high school in particular) was an institution that served a female clientele and provided young women with an education identical in most important respects with that given to men.

This changed after 1900. The transformation of women's work, and particularly the growth of jobs for women requiring some variety of secondary education, led to a growing market for educated women workers. At the same time, the new vocational orientation of the high schools dictated a higher degree of gender differentiation in courses of study than ever before. As educators set about devising ways to better prepare young men and women for their lives' work, larger numbers of high school students—and women in particular—came to view the high school as a means to getting a better job.

Education and the Division of Labor

Beyond the changing functions of women's education, of course, there is the question of how women's education was related to the division of labor, and to the *overall* pattern of women's work in this period. Education was more than simply an engine of opportunity for middle-class women, after all; it was also a barrier to those who lacked it. At the same time that education prepared some women for relatively well-paying or high-status careers in white-collar or non-manual employment, the failure or inability of other groups of women to extend their schooling made it difficult for them to find work in these new fields. This meant that foreign-born and Afro-American women, for instance, became more concentrated in industrial and domestic employment, despite the growth of opportunities in the more lucrative and attractive nonmanual occupations. As the range of occupations open to women multiplied, the importance of education increased substantially, and as indicated in chapters 2, 3, and 5, it largely was middle-class white women who enjoyed the greatest access to formal schooling at this time. In this regard the changes in women's education and work also were intimately related: female education functioned to reproduce the social division of labor *within* the female work force.[8]

Education, of course, is closely tied to the division of labor in virtually any modern society. Schools help distribute the skills and knowledge necessary to perform the diverse tasks demanded of a highly differentiated social structure. And as Émile Durkheim noted nearly a century ago, perhaps the most obvious division of labor in most societies, modern and traditional alike, revolves around the distinctions made between men's and women's work.[9] This study of women's education and work, accordingly, also deals with the peculiar ways in which schools helped prepare women for *women's* work in the years between the Civil War and the Great Depression.

"Social efficiency" was an important slogan in the Progressive education movement which swept through American high schools after 1900. As the term was used by educators, it was meant to represent an interest in improving the capacity of schools to prepare students for their social roles upon leaving the classroom.[10] Vocational education was one aspect of social efficiency, in that case, as were curricula prepared especially for blacks, immigrants, slow learners, and other groups perceived as needing special preparation for their future positions in society. In this regard social efficiency meant taking the high school away from its traditionally academic function, which was believed by some educators to be elitist and insensitive to the needs and interests of new groups of students then thought to be entering the high schools in larger numbers. Social efficiency, however, also meant changing the high school curriculum to meet the presumed interests and needs of a group that had long comprised a majority of public high school students in the United States: women.

With regard to women, vocationalism and social efficiency predisposed high school educators to respond deliberately to changes in women's work. The movement of middle-class women into the labor force in large numbers in the early twentieth century helped to make women's work a national issue in the years after 1900. The reaction of educators to the perception that unprecedented numbers of women were entering the labor force was to devise curricula intended to help preserve the existing sexual division of labor. They invented courses in home economics and women's industrial trades, partly to hold women students' interest but also to sustain what they believed to be vital female roles in society. Other courses of study developed spontaneously from the growth of new occupations for young women. Valarie Oppenheimer has argued that the rise of such occupations at the turn of the century helped to define new labor markets for women, separate from those for men.[11] As new lines of work became sex typed as female labor (as did clerical work and elementary school teaching), the high school curricula associated with them became sex typed as well.

Women's education responded to the division of labor in yet other ways, of course. High schools in different parts of the country developed curricula in response to different types of labor markets. Concern with commercial education, for instance, was greatest in the urban Northeast, where the largest number of young women were employed as clerical workers. In the South, on the other hand, enrollments were higher in home economics, perhaps because more women were inclined to take such courses in rural settings. Schools did more than distinguish women's work from men's, in that case. They also prepared women for different types of work in geographically distinct labor markets. In this regard women's education was shaped by a regional division of labor dictated by the development of the North American economy.[12] Because women's work varied so dramatically from one part of the country to another in this period, women living in different regions often had remarkably different educational experiences.

In the final chapter I take a closer look at the manner in which women's education developed in different localities. Here I examine the development of women's education and work in a number of particular cities. The object, of course, is to identify a variety of different labor markets in order to determine how female schooling varied from one such setting to another. In most regards enrollment patterns in particular cities appear to have corresponded closely to the general regional patterns of enrollment noted in chapter 4. Women in southern cities enrolled in traditional curricula, while their counterparts in the Northeast and West were more likely to take vocational courses—and commercial education in particular. In this chapter I also examine the social class backgrounds of students enrolled in various courses to determine whether the vocational high school course offered young women opportunities for social mobility in the 1920s. By and large, however, it appears that most working class women did not attend high school at all, even in the vocational courses which could have helped them find better jobs. The high school continued to be a largely middle-class institution in the twenties, and secondary education—at least in most parts of the country— continued to distinguish one group of women workers from another.

The growing connection between women's education and women's work in the opening decades of the twentieth century, in that case, made female schooling especially responsive to the division of labor. As suggested above, schooling helped to reproduce—and perhaps even aggravated—the existing division of labor, both by training women for specifically *female* forms of labor *and* by helping middle-class women to monopolize middle-class jobs by virtue of their relatively high levels of formal schooling.

Summary

Women's education and work were indeed related in the years between 1870 and 1930, but their relationship shifted profoundly as both women's work and the nation's educational institutions changed. The latter nineteenth century was a period of ferment about the *idea* of women's education but also a time when women attended high schools to receive an education generally equivalent to that given young men. When middle-class educated women entered the labor force in large numbers, however, the nature of women's education changed. The sexual division of labor, once limited to the home and to the relatively few other social contexts where men and women worked together (such as factories), now extended to the office and into the schools that prepared its workers. At the same time, women in different parts of the country began turning the high school to a variety of utilitarian purposes, many of them dictated by the character of local labor markets. By 1930 the high school remained a largely middle-class institution, but one that responded remarkably well to the vocational interests of its students. Because of this, and because of the efforts of educators to use schools to reinforce existing sex roles, American secondary schools became guardians of the general sexual division of labor in society. This change has been one of the least appreciated dimensions of the important series of changes affecting American society in the years around the turn of the century.[13] Yet it also may have been a very important development in the history of modern American education.

Chapter One

Women at School:
The Feminization of American High Schools,
1870–1900

A metamorphosis of sorts occurred in women's education during the latter nineteenth century. Prior to the Civil War, female secondary education was a haphazard affair conducted in seminaries and academies which dotted the countryside irregularly, and women were almost totally excluded from higher education. But the three decades following 1870 were an era of expanding horizons for women in education. By 1900 girls outnumbered boys by nearly a third in public high schools, and women accounted for about one in five college students. For the first time in American history women actually may have been better educated than men.

The key institution in this set of changes appears to have been the public high school, which began its evolution from an elite to a mass institution during these years. From early on, most public high schools in the United States were coeducational. This meant that the growth of the high school offered many American women access to a level of education that their mothers generally had not enjoyed. Coeducation also meant that young women in the high school received an education substantially the same as that given young men. This was a critical development in the history of women's higher education in this country. It was from the growing ranks of female high school graduates, after all, that women college students were drawn in this period. But thousands of women attended high schools without continuing on to college, and used their education to take on a range of new social responsibilities then becoming available to women. All told, the rise of the public high school was a momentous occasion in the history of

11

women's education in the United States. The years extending from about 1870 to 1900 may have marked the first general period of gender equality in the history of American secondary education.[1]

The development of coeducational high schools and the growth of female secondary school enrollments in this period was also marked by considerable controversy. Leading male educators and medical doctors assailed the concept of equal secondary (and higher) education for women and men, arguing that women had little need of advanced literary and reasoning skills and that extended study could prove downright harmful to their health and happiness. Most educators rejected these views, however, even though many school systems did take measures to insure the health of female high school students. Supporters of women's education argued that the best test of women's ability to study was the actual experiences of girls in school, and that there was little evidence that secondary or higher education was harmful to female health. By and large, young men and women studied the same subjects, received similar grades, and had generally similar attendance records. In one important American institution, it appears, gender was *not* a critical factor during the nineteenth century. The high school was a vehicle of educational opportunity for women, and thousands of them made use of it.

Visions of Equality

Coeducation was a controversial issue in the nineteenth century because of its close association with the question of social equality for women. A chief objective of early reformers in female education, most of whom were women, was to raise women's education to a level comparable to that of young men. The rationale for doing this varied from one context (and reformer) to another, but most of these women sought to define a new, expanded set of roles for women to play in nineteenth-century society. A major obstacle to achieving that end, of course, was the deplorable state of women's education. So in the first half of the nineteenth century a generation of women educators devoted their lives to the cause of making women's education essentially equivalent (though not necessarily identical) to that of men. The eventual success of the coeducational high school was a tribute to their vision of gender equity in higher education, while at the same time it made their all-female schools (and for that matter, secondary schools run by women) anachronistic.

Women's historians have argued that early female educational reformers espoused a peculiar nineteenth-century variety of "domes-

tic feminism," which advocated new roles for women while upholding the traditional female domestic vocations of wifery and motherhood. These new roles revolved around the process of education and
socialization, and the enhanced importance that child-rearing and
education had assumed in the republican social and political order.[2] If
popular education was essential to the survival of a society predicated on the principle of popular rule, women were seen as the natural
candidates to guarantee each child's proper moral and intellectual
development. This meant, of course, that women themselves had to
be well educated. The problem, as most early women educators saw
it, was that the education available to most women lacked intellectual
and moral substance. It was ornamental, designed to teach girls to be
charming, to dress well and dance, or to play music and embroider.
This sort of schooling, female educational reformers felt, did not prepare women to take on the grave responsibilities of motherhood in
the modern, republican social order. In order to properly raise their
own families, young women needed an education every bit as good
as that given to young men.

This view may have been expressed best in Emma Willard's
treatise on the need for a female seminary, written in 1819 to persuade
the New York state legislature to support such a school. This mani-
festo for improved women's schooling was later published and was
an influential early vision of gender parity, if not outright equality, in
education. At the heart of Willard's argument was an effort to contrast
the existing form of education for young women with prevailing educational standards for "young gentlemen." Schools for the latter,
Willard noted, "are founded by public authority, and are permanent;
they are endowed with funds, and their instructors and overseers, are
invested with authority to make such laws, as they shall deem most
salutary." Schools for girls, she felt, were just the opposite; they were
temporary, poorly endowed, subject to no public authority whatever,
and without the power to require students to maintain proper standards of scholarship or behavior. Is it any wonder, Willard asked, that
society regards women as "pampered wayward babies," when—
unlike boys—they are given so few incentives to serious study? The
solution she proposed for this problem, of course, was the establishment of a permanently endowed school for girls, with standards of
scholarship and deportment substantially similar to those for the best
schools for men.[3]

Willard did not advocate complete equality in education, and
her rationale for women's education was decidedly different from
that for men. Girls, she believed, needed education for motherhood,
not a conventional career. Hence, Willard justified her plea to the state

legislature by appealing to their duty "to form the character of the next generation, by controlling that of the females who are to be their mothers."[4] In short, women needed education principally because it was their responsibility to train and socialize each succeeding generation. Like other women educators of her time, Willard was no revolutionary, and she recognized that any program of women's education that threatened to divert women from their traditional domestic responsibilities was likely to fail. But even if the rationale for women's education was different, theirs was a task that demanded an education substantially equivalent to that given to young men. Women's education was in need of improvement, and the most obvious model to follow was schooling for boys.

Emma Willard was only the first of several important woman educators to make this argument. Others voiced similar concerns throughout the first half of the nineteenth century. Of course, virtually all female educational reformers in this period felt that women's education should be decidedly different from men's. In particular, they believed it required a strong domestic orientation and that it should be supervised by women. Most of them were also champions of the idea that women were especially well suited (and therefore should be trained) to be teachers. Yet they also believed that women needed to value intellectual accomplishment, and intellectual effort, as much as their brothers.[5] Catharine Beecher, perhaps the best-known woman educator of the period, constantly championed the idea that men and women belonged in essentially separate spheres of life. But she also endorsed most of Willard's criticisms of existing practices in female education early in her career and, like Willard, opened an influential school for girls in the 1820s.[6]

Similarly, Mary Lyon was especially concerned with character formation and the moral (and religious) development of her students at Mount Holyoke, yet she also planned to make her school into a college, with a classical curriculum similar to men's colleges, as soon as it was practicable.[7] Women educators everywhere cheered the opening of Oberlin College, with its plan of limited coeducation, and supported other coeducational colleges when they opened later. Such institutions, they felt, were necessary to fit women for the demands of marriage to professional men and rearing cultured, well-educated children.[8] While they did not support the idea of social and political equality for women and men, they strongly believed that women's domestic roles demanded an intellectual preparation substantially equivalent to that provided in men's schools. Women, these reformers believed, were entitled to intellectual fulfillment as much as their brothers, and the new domestic ideology of the nineteenth century, with its heavy emphasis on female duties of nurturing and socialization, gave them a rationale with broad appeal.

Historian Anne Firor Scott has argued that Emma Willard should be considered a feminist regardless of her formal opposition to the women's rights movement of her day, and the same can be said of most other early women educators. Whatever it origins, the commitment of these women to female intellectual equality helped raise standards and perhaps expectations for women's education. Scott has argued that Emma Willard was interested in creating new avenues of social influence for women like herself, despite her allegiance to the ideology of domestic virtue. Willard was an institution builder, who may have seen her role as an educator partly as a way of continuing her own intellectual and emotional development. Similarly, Katherine Kish Sklar has argued that Catharine Beecher spent the better part of her life seeking to define a role whereby women could exercise authority outside of the family and still remain within the boundaries established by Victorian notions of propriety. Much of Beecher's work in this connection may have sprung from her own desire for independence and intellectual growth, even as she publicly ridiculed the leaders of the women's rights movement.

By encouraging women to become teachers for a short time before marriage, however, it was possible to endorse female intellectual accomplishment and to identify a socially critical role for educated women without threatening the patriarchal structure of traditional domestic relations.[9] The combination of all such efforts to improve women's education in the early nineteenth century defined a general movement among educators to achieve educational parity and a general ethic of equity where gender was concerned. Even if it was undertaken within the terms of a conservative comprehension of women's duties, this early campaign to raise the standard of female education left an important legacy to subsequent generations of women. The achievement of higher education for women, whether in high schools or colleges, was living testimony to the vital and demanding role which they were supposed to play in the modern social order.

If Emma Willard and Catharine Beecher were pioneers in advocating higher education for women in the 1820s, by midcentury most educators, whether male or female, appear to have accepted the proposition that women deserved an education beyond the elementary studies offered in the common and grammar schools. In 1854 the Boston School Committee, after long resisting popular pressure to provide public secondary instruction for young women, finally agreed to establish a girls high school. The rationale was substantially the same as Emma Willard's had been more than three decades earlier. "To females belong the most fearfully responsible duties which can be assigned to human beings," the Committee's report stated, and in particular, "to form and give direction to human character." Thus, the report continued, "every reasonable provision should be made" to render women "competent mothers and teachers." Besides which, "no pain should be spared" to see that "woman may become within her sphere, what she seems designed of Heaven to be, the fit companion of high minded and intelligent men."[10] Women's education, it appears, was acceptable as a form of preparation for the domestic "sphere" which women occupied, but women's duties now transcended the drudgery of menial housework. To be proper companions and good mothers, women needed to be intellectually fit. And that meant that they could go to high school (and, by implication, to college). With the ideology of domestic feminism firmly in place by the mid-nineteenth century, the stage was set for the growth of female participation in American secondary education.

Feminization of the High School

Between 1870 and 1900 the public high school became the most popular and prominent form of secondary education in the United States. Replacing the academies and seminaries of the antebellum period, these new institutions were distinctive by virtue of their rapid growth and their connection with the public schools. In the picturesque rhetoric of the day, the high school was the "crown jewel" of local school systems, offering an opportunity for the children from all classes to study the higher branches of learning together. In reality, most of the students in nineteenth-century high schools appear to have come from middle- and upper-class backgrounds. By and large, they were the sons and daughters of established farmers and clerks, merchants and ministers, doctors and lawyers, and other respected members of local communities.[11] But even if the development of the public high school did not afford an opportunity for many working-class children, it did open new doors for middle-class girls.

From the end of the Civil War forward, the overwhelming majority of public high schools in the United States were coeducational. This proved to be a source of controversy in itself (and is dealt with below), but it also meant that teenage girls could be instructed in the higher branches, alongside their brothers, at public expense. Whereas schooling beyond the common or grammar school levels generally had entailed a direct investment for families in earlier periods of American history, one for which the education of daughters promised little hope of material return, in the latter nineteenth century growing numbers of teenagers could attend public high schools for little or nothing. The only real expense entailed in public secondary education, in that case, was the opportunity cost—earnings forgone because of time spent in school. Because relatively few employment opportunities existed for middle-class girls in this period, however, even the opportunity costs of secondary education for young women were low. The development of the coeducational public high school, in that case, undoubtedly made it easier for families to send their daughters to secondary school than before and probably made female secondary education less costly than it was for males. Given this, it is little wonder that the number of young women enrolled in American high schools outnumbered the boys throughout the latter nineteenth century.

What follows is a brief account of the growth of female enrollments in American high schools between 1870 and 1900, both in absolute terms and in relation to the number of male students, and how educators responded to it (a more detailed statistical analysis of enrollment patterns is undertaken in the next chapter). The feminization of the high school was an issue of great concern in the late nineteenth century, one that had important consequences for the history of American education.

As indicated earlier, the high school was a relatively elite institution throughout this period, but it also underwent a rapid process of expansion. And as secondary school enrollments grew, particularly in public high schools, they included larger proportions of young women. According to the federal census of 1870, some 129,404 students were enrolled in public and private secondary schools in the United States. Thirty years later, judging by figures provided by the U.S. Commissioner of Education, the number had climbed to about 650,000, a fivefold increase.[12] At the same time the overall rate of high school enrollment among teenagers in the United States grew from less than 2 percent to more than 5 percent, although there was a great deal of regional variation in overall enrollment rates and enrollment growth in these years. Not surprisingly, most of this growth is attributable to the development of the *public* high school; the proportion of all secondary students attending public schools increased from less than 50 percent to about 85 percent in the same period.

With the expansion of public secondary education came feminization. In 1872, the first year in which the U.S. Commissioner of Education provided comprehensive secondary enrollment data broken into male and female categories, girls numbered about 53 percent of all enrollments for which information on gender was available. In

1900 young women constituted slightly more than 57 percent of all high school enrollments. Although data on male-female differences in enrollment in private and public schools are not available for the 1870s, in 1900 the number of boys and girls enrolled in private high schools was about even, while nearly 59 percent of all the students in public high schools were female.[13] The feminization of secondary school enrollments in this period, it seems, was associated with the development of the public high school.

This process of feminization appears to have started soon after public high schools were opened (or soon after they were opened to girls), and affected schools in all parts of the country. Maris Vinovskis has found that girls were slightly more likely to be enrolled in high school than boys in Newburyport, Massachusetts, in 1860, and suggests that "females were quick to take advantage of these institutions once they were opened to them." Reed Ueda has observed a similar process in his study of Sommerville, a suburb of Boston.[14] In yet other parts of the country, feminization appears to have been linked to shifting employment opportunities for young men. In St. Louis, Superintendent William Torrey Harris suggested it was the Civil War which initially accounted for the preponderance of girls in the city's public high school. While boys had dominated enrollments through the previous decade, he reported in 1872, their numbers had dropped sharply in the early 1860s because of the "demands of productive industry."[15] In effect, the appearance of new employment opportunities had raised the opportunity costs of high school education for the boys. Although the number of boys rose again to a slight majority for a few years after the war, from 1870 onward the high schools in St. Louis enrolled more girls than boys.

Similar trends were evident elsewhere. In Chicago boys also dominated the first several classes of city's public high school, but in the 1860s male enrollments dropped dramatically there too. Girls outnumbered boys in Chicago's high schools for the next fifty years.[16] In these cases and others it is possible that the development of industrial employment was a factor in the feminization of secondary education, but the trend toward larger percentages of women enrolled in high school was evident elsewhere as well. In Baltimore girls outnumbered boys in the public high schools by almost a 2 to 1 margin in the early 1880s, despite the fact that the girls were required to attend separate schools.[17] After conducting his own survey of other city school systems around the country in 1879, Cleveland's school superintendent reported that the "great majority" of high school students were girls in "all or almost all our large cities." Expressing surprise, he wrote, "one cannot help remarking (about) the great change which has taken place within a comparatively short period." Whereas previous generations of women had been denied advanced education altogether, it now appeared possible that the "balance of education" henceforth would favor the girls.[18]

Even if they were pleased with growing enrollments, however, not many schoolmen were happy with feminization of the student body. While few complained that too many girls were in attendance, it was commonplace for superintendents and other school officials to remark that there were far too few boys in city high schools. The observation that boys were leaving the high school, or not enrolling at all, in order to get jobs led to efforts to make the high school curriculum more relevant to the interests and disposition of young men. "There is an idea prevalent in some quarters," a high school principal from Springfield, Illinois, wrote in 1889, "that the higher education unfits a boy for business, and even for the professions."[19] The answer that many educators offered for this dilemma was to make the high school curriculum more practical in orientation. From early on, school administrators proposed that courses in manual arts and commerce (which ironically included typing and stenography) be added to the high school curriculum to help keep the boys in school. "If the schools furnished the young machinist, engineer and architect more thorough instruction in those sciences," the Cleveland superintendent wrote in 1877, "there can be no doubt that they would remain longer in school."[20] In 1875 the Chicago Board of Education established a two-year English course in the city's high schools to serve those "young men who wish early to engage in business or to enter the high professions." In 1883 the president of the board recommended that the city add "manual training" and "business methods" courses to the high schools in order to keep young men in school. In the same year the school superintendent in San Francisco reported that a special business course had been developed for the city's high school to help retain male students. School leaders elsewhere proposed similar curricular innovations.[21] By the 1890s manual training programs had been developed in urban high schools across the country.

Although there were a variety of reasons for the establishment of these courses, among the most prominent was the prospect of minimizing male defections from the high school. Noting that boys constituted only about 25 percent of the high school enrollments in the nation's ten largest cities in 1888, then U.S. Commissioner of Education William Torrey Harris declared the issue "a matter of grave concern." Despite his well-known reservations about manual training and other courses with vocational overtones, Harris suggested that instruction in manual arts may be the only way to redress the gender

imbalance in secondary education.[22] The thought of altering the traditionally classical orientation of the high school curriculum became
attractive to many educators as the relative number of male students
declined. An important element of curricular reform in this period, in
that case, was the objective of keeping the boys in school.

As it turned out, the development of manual training programs
and other courses designed to interest young men did little to reduce
the preponderance of girls in urban high schools. But the appearance
of these vocationally relevant courses of study did mark the beginning of an important change in American secondary education: the
shift to a closer relationship between education and work. Given the
popularity which this new practical orientation in education achieved
after 1900, it is significant that the evolution of high school courses in
vocational subjects was related to concerns about the gender composition of enrollments. In the 1890s, however, the vocational purpose of
high schools was distinctly secondary to their cultural and intellectual
objectives. The high school was still considered in many quarters to
be a popular form of higher education, a "people's college," firmly
associated with the classical orientation of the colleges and universities. And as a number of educational historians have noted, there was
a great deal of resistance from educators to the proposition that secondary schools ought to serve vocational ends at this time.[23]

The other side of the coin, of course, was the question of
whether these courses helped boys get jobs. By and large, young men
did not go to high school to learn a trade; it was much easier and
faster to acquire job-related skills from employers or craft unions or
through specialized schools. Male students, for instance, dominated
the private commercial training schools that flourished in American
cities during this period. And the labor movement (the American
Federation of Labor in particular) was a firm opponent of vocational
training in schools until after the turn of the century.[24] Compared to
existing alternatives the cost of high school—in terms of time and
effort—was high, and the promise of tangible return rather distant.

Vocational education, consequently, does not appear to have
altered the gender imbalance in American high schools at this time.
Even the addition of the manual training course, of dubious vocational value to begin with, did little to change the considerable opportunity cost difference between female and male secondary education. In
1896 the superintendent of schools in Chicago noted that only 29 percent of the city's high school students were boys, even when enrollments for the Manual Training School were included, a fact which he
described as "unfortunate and deplorable."[25] Whatever schoolmen
may have thought about why the high schools were dominated by

women, there was little that they could do to alter the process that resulted in feminization. It was defined, after all, by social and economic forces related to the sexual division of labor in society at large, and there was little indeed that school administrators were prepared to say or do to change that.

There was more to the feminization process, of course, than factors that inhibited male attendance. At the same time that job prospects appeared to divert young men away from secondary education, the structure of female employment may have given some women a positive incentive to attend high schools. As indicated above, the nineteenth-century high school was remarkably detached from vocational purposes, but if it prepared students for any vocation at all, it was teaching. As a number of historians and other social scientists have demonstrated, the closing decades of nineteenth century also was a period of feminization in the nation's teaching force, particularly in urban areas. Between 1870 and 1900 the proportion of teachers in the United States who were women increased from about 66 to 73 percent, and the process of feminization was especially evident in cities. By the turn of the century, slightly more than four out of five teachers in cities with more than 25,000 people were women.

The reasons for this preponderance of female teachers were complex, and linked to prevailing Victorian ideas about the role of women as naturally endowed child-rearers. But the feminization of teaching was also associated with the availability of large numbers of relatively well-educated young women who were willing to teach—and who had few other employment opportunities. Because most middle-class women eschewed manual labor in this period and most professions strictly barred or limited female participation, teaching was virtually the only variety of work generally available to them until the 1890s, when women began to find employment in clerical and other service occupations. The rapid feminization of the teaching force in these years, on the other hand, suggests that many women, whether because of need or simply an interest in working with children, found teaching to be an attractive employment opportunity.[26]

For their part, most nineteenth-century educators appear to have believed that the high school was an excellent preparation for prospective teachers. Noting the beneficial effect of the public high school on the entire school system in 1871, the president of Detroit's Board of Education remarked that the school "affords us a supply of well trained teachers always ready and available to fill the vacancies constantly occurring." A survey of Detroit high school alumni between 1860 and 1882 later revealed that fully 95 percent of those graduates who became teachers were women. Similarly, the New

Haven, Connecticut, superintendent of schools reported in 1881 that some 125 past students in the city's high school presently taught in the public school system and that more than 200 teachers had come from the school in the space of a dozen years—the vast majority of them women. In 1882 the president of the St. Louis Board of Education wrote that "the advanced general education of the teachers of our schools is itself a work, which, in my opinion, justifies the existence of a high school as part of our public school system, irrespective of other questions." A survey of St. Louis high school alumni conducted in 1873 revealed the same pattern seen in Detroit; the overwhelming majority of graduates who became teachers were female (over 90 percent) *and* the biggest single occupation for women high school graduates, numbering over half of more than 700 women surveyed, was teaching in the public schools. Similar reports were issued in other cities.[27]

Of course, the bare fact that many high school girls eventually became teachers does not necessarily mean that most young women attended high schools so that they could teach. As will be seen in the next chapter, the feminization of high school enrollment appears to have been unrelated to the feminization of teaching in most parts of the country at this time. But the eagerness of local school authorities to hire former female high school students as teachers, coupled with the absence of acceptable employment alternatives for middle-class girls, must have served as a positive incentive for many young women to attend high school in some urban areas. There were undoubtedly other reasons for young women to attend high school, as female enrollments were comparatively high even in areas where the teaching force was not highly feminized. But while employment constituted a negative incentive to many young men considering the high school, it probably was an inducement for many girls in similar circumstances. If the high school was generally irrelevant to the jobs to which young men aspired, it was virtually a prerequisite for the one occupation that middle-class women were permitted to dominate numerically in this period.

The Victorian and early industrial sexual division of labor, in that case, dictated a feminized pattern of high school participation, simply because women's work required formal schooling while men's work did not—at least in many of the nation's cities at this time. Even if most women students attended the high school primarily to make themselves better wives and mothers in the future (most female teachers married and stopped teaching after just a few years in this period), the prevailing structure of employment offered them virtually no negative incentives and at least one important positive one.[28] In short, the public high school cost women students little and offered them the prospect of both spiritual and material rewards.

The feminization of the high school was a consequence of social and economic forces that lay largely outside of the schools. However much educators (virtually all of them men) bemoaned the fact that boys were not enrolling in the high school, no policies could be devised to change the fact that young women outnumbered their male classmates in virtually all parts of the country. As William Torrey Harris observed in 1892, the boys were "obliged or prefer to go to work" instead of to high school in this period, while the girls were "left free to pursue the course of liberal culture that the public high school affords." He also noted that if the girls desired "to prepare themselves to become teachers, the high school is right in line to second their efforts."[29] In other words, there were more girls than boys in school because of gender-related differences in students' employment options and interests. But even if Harris and other contemporaries recognized that the cause of feminization in secondary education (and for that matter in teaching as well) was related to structural and ideological forces outside the purview of school policy, it did not forestall the development of genuine alarm about the effects of feminization in certain quarters of the educational establishment.

Male educators eventually worried that women were coming to dominate the schools culturally as well as numerically. In 1903 G. Stanley Hall, a prominent psychologist and president of Clark University, declared at a meeting of the National Education Association that the American high school had become "practically a girls' school." He lamented the preponderance of young women in high school, saying that it resulted in a "feminization of the school spirit, discipline, and personnel," which was "bad for the boys." As a solution Hall suggested developing separate schools and curricula for boys and girls, an issue explored in greater detail in chapter 4.[30] But the very fact of his concern about this matter, and the manner in which he and other men identified the problem, indicates the frustration and alarm some educators felt regarding the feminization of secondary education.

Girls were indeed dominating the high schools in many parts of the country, just as they were coming to dominate the teaching force numerically, and this made school leaders uncomfortable. The solution that Hall and others proposed, however, eliminating or reducing the extent of coeducation in the high school, was hardly original. The notion that boys' and girls' educations should be materially different, after all, was virtually as old as education itself and had inspired the manual training movement. It also had been voiced some thirty years earlier in one of the most controversial nineteenth-century books on women's education. As will be seen below, the feminization of the high school occurred despite the strong opposition of several generations of prominent American men of science and letters. Of course, this too is evidence of the manner in which feminization was related to underlying differences in male and female work roles and not to explicit policy decisions or even debates about the issue. Male critics of the female-dominated high school too often overlooked the fact that the feminization they deplored was a direct consequence of the very sort of gender differentiation they advocated for society in general.

The Coeducation Question

The feminization of the high school, and the deleterious effect that some educators believed girls exerted on boys, was linked, of course, to the issue of coeducation. American secondary schools were unique among those of major Western countries in this period by virtue of the extent to which they enrolled young women and men together. According to several surveys of American high schools, academies, and other institutions of secondary education, coeducational schools outnumbered those designated for either boys or girls by more than a 2 to 1 margin throughout the latter nineteenth century. Moreover, coeducational schools dominated secondary education in all parts of the country and in a variety of different social and economic settings.

This did not mean, however, that coeducation was universally accepted. In certain communities there was considerable opposition to its development as a matter of policy for high schools and colleges. And educators, doctors, and social scientists debated the merits of educating boys and girls together on biological, moral, academic, and vocational grounds throughout this period. Even though most Americans seem to have accepted the idea of coeducation in principle, there was opposition to it as well.

The trouble with coeducation was that it was founded, to one degree or another, on a premise of male-female equality in intellectual and social terms. Some of its opponents feared that serious academic study would harm teenage girls physiologically; others worried that it would leave them ill-prepared to take up their duties as wives and mothers. Still others felt that coeducation represented a danger to the moral development of high school students, particularly the women. At bottom, all critics of coeducation wondered whether some different arrangement for women's education, one attentive to what they believed to be important female frailties and goals in life, was preferable to teaching boys and girls side by side. Men and women played different roles in life, the argument generally went, so they ought to be educated differently as well.

Of course, most supporters of coeducation did not dispute the notion that women's education ought not disrupt the existing sexual division of labor. Many subscribed to the domestic feminist view that a sound liberal, academic education was necessary to fit young women for the duties of modern motherhood. Others, including many male educators, supported coeducation simply because it was an economical or otherwise expedient way of organizing public education. For most domestic feminists, however, the suggestion that women were incapable or otherwise ill-suited for academic study was tied to the idea that female roles were far inferior or subservient to those of men. Thus, the earliest suggestions that coeducational schools ought to be modified brought sharp reactions from educators across the country. In the minds of opponents and supporters alike, the issue of coeducation was intimately connected to the future roles that women would play in American life. This would help to make it a point of continuing controversy.

The principal catalyst in the coeducation debate was a prominent Boston physician named Edward Clarke. A onetime member of the Harvard University medical faculty, Clarke published a slim volume entitled *Sex in Education* in 1873 which argued that extended academic study was downright harmful for young women. As a number of historians have noted, Clarke's ideas were not new, but the fact of his scientific and medical background, along with the clinical orientation of his book, gave his views added force. The book circulated widely, and reportedly went through eleven editions in just six years. The thrust of its argument was aimed at collegiate study for women, and in the conclusion Clarke pointedly criticized colleges that encouraged women to follow a curriculum similar to that in men's schools. But the specific medical and biological arguments in Clarke's book had more relevance to high school–aged girls than it did to those in college. In particular, Clarke maintained that the years between fourteen and eighteen were especially critical for young women, as it was that stage of life in which a woman's reproductive organs took shape. In that time, he wrote, a woman "accomplishes an amount of physiological cell change and growth which nature does not require of a boy in less than twice that number of years." Hence, Clarke felt that young women should not be expected to study as much or work as hard as young men during this critical period of physiological development; and that they should be encouraged to rest and exercise regularly in order to guarantee proper physical development.

In his clinical chapter Clarke described cases of high school girls who suffered from anemia as a consequence of too much recitation or nighttime study, as well as college women who had been the victims of overstrenuous high school and collegiate courses of study. All told, he considered the coeducational high school and college grave threats to the health of American women. And in particular, he warned that overexertion on the part of young women carried the danger of sterility in future life. To Edward Clarke, and those who accepted his medical premises, the issue of coeducation was bound up intimately with the most basic of sex roles. If American women were to be mothers at all, they needed to follow a course of study designed with their peculiar physiological needs in view.[31]

Clarke's book met with both positive and negative reviews, but few readers appear to have been unmoved by it. Opponents of coeducation seized upon his arguments as yet more evidence that the practice of giving girls fundamentally the same education as boys was misguided and perhaps even dangerous. Advocates of coeducation denounced Clarke's views energetically, and a flurry of rebuttals appeared in the years immediately following his book's publication.[32] To a large extent, however, Clarke's ideas merely represented the clearest expression of a persistent undercurrent of opposition to women's education which had existed throughout the nineteenth century.

Prior to the appearance of *Sex in Education*, most opponents of male-female equality in schooling based their arguments on the premise that women had little need of an advanced literary education. Hence, they maintained that high school (and college) training for girls was a waste of valuable resources. Mayor Josiah Quincy of Boston had cited this argument in 1828 when he decreed an end to the city's short-lived High School for Girls. In the eyes of Quincy and his supporters, women's education was less an investment than an item of consumption, a way for middle- and upper-class families to cultivate their daughters for marriage. Quincy and other opponents of the High School for Girls rejected the domestic feminist proposition that higher education was necessary for the new nurturing and socialization roles women played in the nineteenth century. To them a high school was supposed to be an investment in the future prospects of the city's brightest young men. To allow women a high school education was at best a waste of money and at worst a threat to the existing sexual division of labor.[33]

Given the extent of public support for the domestic feminist position at this time, Quincy's was not a popular viewpoint in Boston or elsewhere, and at least one historian has suggested that it may have contributed to his defeat in the following election.[34] But Quincy's views represented an understanding of women's education that was typical of most opponents of coeducation. Women, they maintained, did not require an advanced education simply because their future roles were delimited to the domestic sphere. Even after the principle of female secondary education had been established in most parts of the country, the same argument was used after 1870 against male-female equality in the high school.

Once again, the most vigorous proponents of this position were found in Boston and were led by School Superintendent John Philbrick, although they existed elsewhere as well. Despite evidence of widespread public support for coeducation and the willingness of the city's School Committee to make male and female courses virtual-ly identical, both Philbrick and his successor, Edwin Seaver, opposed the "principle of uniformity" in high school education. In Seaver's view, it was unreasonable to provide the same education to boys, "nine-tenths of [whom] are sure to enter mercantile pursuits", and girls, "one half of [whom] will enter the normal school and become teachers." In short, the sexual division of labor, or in Seaver's words, the "probable future occupations of boys and girls," precluded the possibility of curricular equality in Boston secondary schools.[35]

Philbrick and Seaver were in fact arguing in favor of vocational education for young men and women in high school, giving the boys "bookkeeping and science" and the girls "languages and literature." In this regard they were both stalwart defenders of the prevailing sexual division of labor. Philbrick, for his part, was among the nation's most enthusiastic champions of sewing instruction for girls, and Boston's public school system was often identified by contemporaries as a national leader in the area of sewing instruction in this period.[36] But Philbrick, Seaver and other educators in Boston also were opposed to the principle of girls receiving a rigorous classical education on the same order of difficulty and prestige as that given to young men. And in this connection, the ideas of Edward Clarke were particularly germane.

In 1885 Philbrick published a circular arguing that coeducational high schools were pedagogically unsound because they posed a dan-ger to the health of young women and a threat to the academic vigor of the boys. To make the high school curriculum academically demanding in such circumstances, he maintained, would risk the problems that Clarke had associated with overexertion in teenage girls: anemia and the possibility of sterility. He also reasoned that lim-iting the requirements for study, recitations, and other dimensions of the school's academic life would seriously compromise the potential for achievement in the boys. This argument combined vocational and physiological objections to coeducational secondary schools, main-taining that the high school would cease to be an advantage for young men if it were required to accommodate the girls.[37] By the mid-1880s, both utilitarian and biological arguments were used by opponents of coeducation to argue that young men and women ought to attend different schools.

Added to these arguments against coeducation, of course, was the question of morality. Although many educators and physicians do not appear to have given this issue much attention in the latter nineteenth century, it had been a point of particular interest for ante bellum educators and appears to have been a matter of continuing controversy among religious leaders.[38] The morality question had few implications for women's higher education in sex-segregated contexts, an issue with which Clarke, Philbrick, and others dealt, but rather focused on the moral effect of young men and women attending school together. Essentially, the matter turned on the question of propriety. Coeducation, it was feared, opened the door to potentially promiscuous relations between high school boys and girls, and it established a context where "vulgarity," and "foolish flirting and frivolity" could flourish. Given the important moral component of nineteenth-century schooling, these were serious charges. But the focal point of concern was clearly the future moral development of the young women. A teacher in the Girls' Latin School in Boston warned in 1890 that coeducation would cause girls to "lose their maidenly delicacy and reserve," and could affect the ability of future generations of mothers to properly rear and socialize their children. Opponents of coeducation elsewhere shared this sentiment, particularly in cities where sex-segregated high schools had existed for some time. If women were to insure the moral aptitude of future generations, it was imperative that the education of girls be morally pure.[39]

On the opposite side of the coeducation debate from Clarke, Philbrick, and other opponents of coeducation were the domestic feminists. Among them were women and men who believed strongly in the intellectual ability of women to perform almost any task a man could. And to many of the women who responded to attacks on coeducation, it may have seemed as though its defense was partly a matter of personal vindication. As indicated earlier, the domestic feminists were committed to a vision of separate but generally equal spheres of influence for men and women in American life. They objected to the implication in both the utilitarian and physiological arguments against coeducation that women were incapable of a high standard of intellectual accomplishment. This view suggested, after all, that women were naturally inferior in one critical respect to men, and it threatened to legitimize the subservient position most women occupied in the existing patriarchal social order.

As suggested above, the domestic feminists were not revolution-aries; they did not advocate a fundamental restructuring of the sexual division of labor. Rather, they sought to redefine women's roles in a manner that permitted them to measure their own lives in terms of peculiarly female contributions to social development. Coeducation, in that case, was a key element in the domestic feminist campaign to establish the importance of women's roles and the ability of women to perform them.

As Rosalind Rosenberg has argued, most domestic feminists probably agreed with Clarke's assertion that male and female physi-ology was quite different, and many even may have agreed that women were intellectually and physically weaker than men. But few were willing to concede that women were incapable of higher educa-tion. Accordingly, most of the responses to Clarke emphasized the good health of women who had attended colleges in earlier decades or argued that ill health in women was due to causes other than too much study. Testimonials from female graduates of Antioch, Oberlin, Michigan, Vassar, and other schools were offered as evidence that higher education did not necessarily prove debilitating to young women.[40] Echoing a charge which Catharine Beecher and others had made years earlier, domestic feminist critics of Clarke also argued that the chief cause of illness in American girls was their poor diets and sedentary life styles. In this regard their thinking overlapped with Clarke's considerably, for he also maintained that the regimen of school was too demanding precisely because it allowed too little time for healthy exercise. But rather than urge that coeducational schools be abolished, the domestic feminists argued that exercise simply should be made a more important element in the education of girls.

Writing in 1874, Caroline Day suggested that young women were too irregular in their habits, did not sleep enough, spent too much time indoors, and exercised far too infrequently to enjoy good health. Clarke, she reasoned, had simply assigned the blame for anemia and other ailments in young women to the wrong source. The domestic feminist critics of Clarke believed that higher education in general, and coeducation in particular, was a vital element in the effort of women to live happy, fulfilling lives in an era of widening female roles.[41]

At the same time they denounced Clarke's medical argument against coeducation, many domestic feminists also rejected the utili-tarian view that women's education should differ from men's because of their different roles in life. Anna Brackett, a former normal school principal in St. Louis, probably expressed this view best in one of the few essays in this period to deal with women's education as a whole rather than simply with female higher education. Brackett maintained that special instruction in sewing was a waste of time for girls in the latter nineteenth century, both because most clothing was produced commercially and because she felt sewing instruction was of little pedagogical value. Sewing may have been an appropriate course of study for women in other periods, she argued, but it simply diverted girls away from more important subjects in a modern, urban setting. She felt much the same about courses in domestic science. The most important task a woman has, she reasoned, was to train and educate her children. Learning the mechanical elements of housework was valuable, in that case, but should not displace the time and effort required to develop a sound comprehension of the world and the discipline to change it in some fashion.[42]

In direct contradiction to Clarke, Brackett suggested that it was the absence of a sound, rationally grounded and demanding education that resulted in "insanity and sickness" in some women. Like men, she believed that women required "real work" to make their lives fulfilling. And to play the myriad roles required of middle-class women in the modern age, a solid academic preparation was vital. Men and women, she asserted, were "wonderfully alike" in their quest for a fuller comprehension of the world. To deny girls the opportunity to learn as much as their brothers in a "systematic" fashion was to leave them "dwarfted and crippled," physically an adult but "mentally a child."

At bottom, of course, was the effect of all this on future generations. Brackett suggested that the current "unruly" character of American children was doubtless a consequence of the "narrow and unfinished education which we gave to our girls, now the mothers." Indeed, she argued that women without education "were better childless," for each one threatened to "give her country elements of weakness... future inmates for jails, penitentiaries, and prisons." Like other domestic feminists in this period, Brackett felt that the fullest possible development of women's intellectual powers were essential to the future development of American society.[43] And coeducation represented the best possible guarantee that girls would be systematically and rigorously educated.

As indicated earlier, the domestic feminist conception of women's role in the republican, urban-industrial society of the nineteenth century—and the corresponding importance of women's education—was endorsed by many male educators in this period. And most schoolmen also appear to have shared the domestic feminists' objections to the biological and utilitarian arguments against coeducation. While male educators generally did not react as earnestly to Clarke's book as many women, they nevertheless rejected his condemnation of coeducation as unwarranted and impractical.

One of the earliest commentaries on the coeducation issue was provided by William Torrey Harris in 1871, just a few years after he was appointed superintendent of schools in St. Louis. Noting that St. Louis had only adopted coeducation in its high school after trying it in the elementary and grammar schools, Harris unequivocally endorsed the principle of giving women an education equivalent to that given young men. "It is in accordance with the spirit of our institutions," he argued, "to treat women as self determining beings, and less in want of those external artificial barriers that were built . . . in past times." He also noted, however, that coeducation made possible a more efficient use of school resources, creating larger classes at each grade level and affording greater opportunity for specialization in teaching assignments. And with regard to the morality question, Harris maintained that the presence of girls in class actually improved the behavior of young men. "The rudeness and *abandon* which prevails among boys when separate," he observed, "at once gives place to self restraint in the presence of girls."

Harris also believed that going to school with boys improved the disposition of young women. Rather than corrupting one another, boys and girls in school complemented each other "according to nature's plan," like brothers and sisters, so that a better learning environment resulted. Coeducation, he felt, was the most natural of all possible pedagogical arrangements. Like the family, coeducational schools educated boys and girls together, guaranteeing that both knew and respected the other from direct experience in a common social context. Rather than seeing coeducation as a dangerous or morally damaging policy, Harris—along with many other nineteenth-century schoolmen—believed it to be a healthy and positive element of a morally sound plan of education.[44]

When Clarke's book was published in 1873, Harris wrote a long response rejecting its principal tenets, repeating many of the points he had made two years earlier. Most other schoolmen, it appears, agreed with him, although there was a good deal of variety in their rationales. In 1883 the U.S. Commissioner of Education published the results of a survey of some 340 school districts about local policies regarding coeducation. The overwhelming majority of these, all but 38, maintained entirely coeducational school systems. Respondents were asked to explain why they supported or opposed coeducation as a matter of policy, and their answers were grouped into several categories in the commissioner's Report. The largest number of responses, more than a hundred, featured economy or efficiency as a reason for continued support of coeducation. "To obtain the same excellence in grading and instruction," one superintendent wrote, "would require a much larger teaching force were the sexes separated." Other schoolmen expressed similar sentiments. If age-grading was to be economically feasible, coeducational schools were necessary to provide large enough classes for each age group. This probably was especially true regarding secondary education, where enrollments were generally low and girls constituted a slight majority of students.

Only in large cities, where there were enough young men and women students to support separate high schools, was a policy of sex-segregated secondary education even possible. The second largest category of responses, numbering over eighty, included those who mentioned the positive moral and emotional effect of coeducational schools. "It is mutually beneficial," wrote a superintendent in Little Rock, Arkansas. "It cultivates a respect and esteem in each sex for the other which is necessary in later life." Clearly, this schoolman and others did not believe that coeducation posed a severe moral danger to either the boys or the girls in school. Rather, coeducation was seen as a positive good, one which in the words of another superintendent resulted in a "more harmonious development of both sexes."

Like Harris, a large number of school leaders believed that coeducation was superior to policies of sex segregation on grounds of both pedagogy and economy. Other reasons were offered in support of coeducation as well, of course, including popular preference and local custom. But statements from schoolmen in all parts of the country echoed Harris's outright repudiation of Clarke and other critics of coeducation. In the words of a school superintendent in Oakland, California, it seemed "to be the natural order of things that boys and girls should be educated together." Later surveys undertaken both by the U.S. Office of Education and by local school boards indicate that this level of support for coeducation continued unabated throughout the latter nineteenth century.[45] With regard to public education, coeducation appears to have been the settled policy in most parts of the United States, despite the objections of physicians, religious leaders, and certain influential educators such as John C. Philbrick.

The fact that many male educators supported coeducation as a matter of policy, of course, does not mean that they agreed with all aspects of the domestic feminist ideology. A minority of the respondents to the 1883 survey or later queries about coeducation expressed an outright commitment to male-female equality in education. Perhaps many felt such sentiments were implicit in any endorsement of coeducation. But there is considerable evidence that educators were also at least a little concerned with male-female differences in this period. Although most educators probably disagreed with Clarke's conclusions regarding the inadvisability of coeducation as a matter of policy, they apparently believed that important male-female physiological differences made school more demanding for young women than for boys.

It was commonplace, for instance, for educators in this period to assume that female students required more exercise than males. In 1877 the superintendent of schools in Dayton, Ohio, remarked, "girls need physical training in school more than boys," because the boys got "much more exercise out of school" than the girls. In Kansas City more than a decade later, another educator agreed and argued, "bending over their lessons or music has a tendency to produce contraction of the muscles, round shoulders and narrow chests" in female high school students. "To counteract these injurious habits," he continued, "the only safe remedy is physical training practiced at regular intervals." Other schoolmen concurred. Even if young women were intellectually capable, it was the duty of educators to see that the special needs of female students were met in the high schools.[46]

In some instances the perceived physical limitations of the girls even had a bearing on the design of school buildings. A high school principal in Detroit in 1889 maintained that elevators were necessary in his building because excessive stair climbing was a potential hazard to the health of female students. "Numbers are debarred the privileges of the high school," he declared, "simply because constitutional troubles absolutely prevent this stair climbing." In the same year the president of the Board of Education in Cleveland recommended that grammar and high schools built from that time forward be no taller than two stories. "Especially to the girls," he wrote, "the going up and down stairs represented by from five to ten or an indefinite number of trips daily is a menace to (their) normal functional development."

Despite the fact that they were studying in high school along side young men, teenage girls were seen as especially fragile, and measures were often taken to guarantee their future health.[47] Nineteenth-century schoolmen, after all, also believed Clarke and other physicians when they argued there were important physiological limitations to the ability of young women to pursue an advanced course of study. But most male educators in this period were firm supporters of coeducation, and while they were careful to see that their female students remained healthy, they also remained committed to the idea that the higher branches of learning should be open to women and men alike.

Whatever the precautions taken by educators regarding the frailties of their female students, however, coeducation appears to have enjoyed enormous popular support in this period. If parents were at all anxious about the effect of high school studies on the health of their daughters, it certainly was not evident in enrollment figures. Indeed, when educators discussed the tendency of high school students—

young women in particular—to push themselves too hard, they often commented that overexertion was the result of pressures from parents rather than from the students themselves. Unlike the women's colleges in this period, high schools do not seem to have felt the effect of Clarke's critique of women's higher education.[48] Educators did little to alter the curriculum of studies women pursued; and even efforts to increase the amount of exercise or physical education required of female students were relatively small concessions to the physicians. The fact that many women spent a little extra time each week (generally no more than an hour) exercising did not appreciably distinguish their course of studies from those of their male classmates.

It is possible, of course, that parents exhibited relatively little concern about the health of their daughters simply because most young women in high school (unlike those in college at this time) lived at home. If the high school was indeed a strain on the health of American girls, after all, their families probably would have been the first to notice it. The rapid growth of female secondary school participation between 1870 and 1900 suggests that most people probably did not believe the dire warnings of coeducation's critics.[49] As Harris and many other educators had pointed out repeatedly, the best test of the ability of young women to study as well as boys was the day-to-day experience of young women already enrolled in school. The growth of secondary education, in that case, indicates that the coeducational high school was an unqualified success, at least with regard to the education of young women. Although the criticisms aired by Clarke and Philbrick continued to be heard—and debated—throughout this period, they had little effect on what actually occurred in the development of female secondary education.

For their part, most schoolmen in the United States at this time were consistent supporters of coeducation. As suggested by Harris's remarks in the early 1870s, as well as by later surveys of educators, much of this support may have been derived from the necessity of coeducation for developing modern, age-graded, and subject-differentiated school systems. The only way in which age graded classes and separate instructors for specific subjects were feasible in most parts of the country was by combining boys and girls in the same classes. Most schoolmen also recognized, of course, that without female students (who numbered more than the boys) it simply would have been impossible to maintain high schools in many parts of the country. These must have been sobering realities for those educators inclined to oppose coeducation on medical, moral, or vocational grounds. For without a policy of coeducation, it just was not possible to organize a modern school system with the degree of efficiency believed necessary by most leading educators. Sex-segregated schools simply cost more, all other things being equal, than coeducational ones.

In the end, both efficiency and local custom probably accounted for the success of coeducation in high schools. Of course, most school-men appear also to have agreed with Harris's theory that coeducation was good for discipline as well. Putting girls and boys together, they reasoned, made the boys more manageable and the girls less frivolous. But few were in a position to actually test this and other propositions about coeducation because the vast majority of school systems were coeducational to begin with. As one observer noted in the 1870s, the coeducation debate was more a matter of local custom and personal disposition than a rational or scientific dispute. Like the larger debate over women's equality, the coeducation controversy probably was settled ultimately as a matter of popular sentiment. But it had implications for the relationship of men and women that extended well beyond the physiological issues which Clarke and others succeeded in bringing to public attention. The coeducational high school may have raised the question of women's abilities and male-female equality in a more direct manner than any other American institution in this period. And in this regard it held important implications for the future division of labor in American life.

Equality and the Curriculum

One important consequence of a coeducational policy for high schools was the appearance of an educational context in which boys and girls were taught generally the same things. Even though there is evidence of considerable diversity in high school curricula in these years, there was a high degree of male-female equality in secondary education in the latter nineteenth century. Judging from information taken from one major urban school system, as well as the testimony of numerous contemporary educators, it appears to have been a time of general equity in the performance (as measured in grades) of boys and girls in schools as well. Given all this, the feminization of American high schools may have had even wider implications than those generally recognized by contemporaries. Whatever the effect of high school attendance on the health of young women, or the self-image of young men, it may have given several generations of girls a historically unique sense of their ability to succeed in a context where they often competed with boys. To the generations of women who later became involved to one degree or another in social reform, who organized the nation's first mass women's movement, and who challenged many of the conventions of Victorian society, this sort of experience may have been important indeed.

The oft-cited efficiency argument in favor of coeducation generally was predicated on a system wherein girls and boys attended class together and—consequently—studied the same things. Despite the fact that a diversity of subjects were offered in nineteenth-century high schools, most schools probably offered a rather limited range of courses. Outside of the largest cities, high schools were generally small institutions in this period, with limited faculty resources and space. Thus, the high school curriculum was generally designed simply to transmit a strong sense of what was widely recognized as essential elements of Western culture and principles of modern science. Because the high school had few, if any, explicit vocational aims, moreover, the overwhelming majority of courses were offered in academic subjects. In most parts of the country, in that case, young women who attended coeducational high schools generally studied subjects which in an earlier age were thought only suitable for the instruction of young men: Latin and Greek, algebra and science, and history and literature.[50] In terms suggested by feminist philosopher Jane Roland Martin, the nineteenth-century high school was dominated by a decidedly male curriculum, subjects which for more than a century had stood as essential to the definition of an educated *man*.[51] Yet this apparently was not an impediment to the thousands of young women who enrolled in high schools across this period. The existence of a traditionally male curriculum does not seem to have affected the feminization of secondary schools in the latter nineteenth century.

Evidence taken both from national surveys and local school reports indicate that most female high school students in this period studied generally the same things as their male classmates. The earliest accounts are those taken from individual school districts. In his 1873 response to Clarke, Harris pointed out that the girls in the St. Louis high school took the same courses as the boys. Reports from other coeducational districts suggested that young men and women in high schools elsewhere followed the same course of studies as well. Statistics provided by the superintendent of schools in Cincinnati in 1880 indicated that male and female students in the city's three high schools were evenly represented in most of the courses offered, the only major exceptions being Greek (which was predominantly male) and French (which was more than three-quarters female). Dozens of schoolmen from across the country indicated an explicit commitment to curricular equality in their responses to the U.S. Commissioner of Education's survey on coeducation in 1882. "Both sexes need the same training," declared a schoolman from Ottawa, Illinois. "There is no appreciable difference in the mental capacity of boys and girls during public school life," argued another from Fond du Lac, Wisconsin.[52] In many school districts a commitment to coeducation apparently signaled a conviction that young men and women should be educated in generally the same manner.

Regardless of whether school officials were committed to a principle of equality for women's education, however, the mere fact of coeducation seems to have guaranteed a good deal of curricular equity in public high schools. The earliest national statistics on male-female enrollment rates in various high school subjects did not appear until the late 1880s, but as indicated in Table 1.1, there were few differences in enrollment rates for male and female students in public high schools in 1889. The only subject in which women were underenrolled was Greek, which was generally taken to meet college entrance requirements and attracted a small fraction of the student body. Conversely, the only course in which women were overrepresented was French, which also enrolled a relatively small number of students.

Table 1.1 Enrollments in Various Subjects at Public High Schools in 1889 (in thousands)

Subject	UNITED STATES Male	UNITED STATES Female	NORTH ATLANTIC Male	NORTH ATLANTIC Female	SOUTH CENTRAL Male	SOUTH CENTRAL Female	WEST Male	WEST Female
Latin	28.8	41.6	11.8	15.1	.1	1.7	.85	.99
Greek	4.1	2.1	2.9	1.4	.2	.1	.1	.05
French	4.1	7.8	3.5	5.4	1.1	.2	.02	.1
German	8.7	12.6	3.2	4.5	.5	.3	.1	.2
Algebra	38.7	53.5	13.7	17.6	2.3	3.1	1.7	2.1
Geometry	18.5	24.8	7.4	7.8	.9	1.4	1.0	1.2
Physics	19.2	26.9	7.1	8.9	1.2	1.7	.7	.9
Chemistry	8.4	12.0	3.7	4.6	.3	.55	.5	.5
General History	22.0	33.4	8.4	12.4	1.4	2.2	1.2	1.5

Source: U.S. Commissioner of Education, *Annual Report, 1889* (Washington, DC: Government Printing Office, 1890).

In virtually every other subject the proportion of male and female students was the same, generally between 57 and 60 percent—roughly the same as the overall male-female ratio in high school enrollments. This included, of course, Latin, mathematics, and the physical sciences, subjects traditionally associated with men. If there was an aversion to mathematics and the sciences among young women in the nineteenth century, there was little evidence of it in high school enrollment patterns; women were represented in algebra, geometry, physics, and chemistry in generally the same proportions as in other classes. Even though there was wide variation in the overall enrollment in various subjects, the ratio of girls to boys enrolled remained remarkably consistent across the curriculum.

In many schools, of course, the number of courses to choose from were limited, particularly in smaller communities. But as Edward Krug has noted, larger high schools and academies often gave students a choice of curricula to pursue in this period. Although some classes were generally prescribed, such as Latin and algebra, others could be taken as a part of a particular course of study. These courses ranged from the "classical," which included both Latin and Greek and focused on preparation for college, to the "general" and "English" courses, which required less classical language study and generally did not lead to further education. By the 1870s scientific courses of study (often called "Latin-Scientific") were available in some schools as well.[53] But apart from the tiny college-prepatory courses, no single course of study appears to have been dominated by either men or women. Given the range of options available to boys and girls in American high schools in this period, the degree of uniformity in the male-female ratio of students across the curriculum is striking. Even in circumstances where they had a choice of what they could study, it appears that young women decided to pursue generally the same subjects that their male counterparts did. The result was a high school curriculum largely undifferentiated along lines of gender.

Coeducation, it seems, was critical to realizing curricular equality for girls and boys in nineteenth-century high schools. The statistics in Table 1.1 were taken from public high schools, the overwhelming majority of which were coeducational in this period. In private secondary schools, over half of which were sex-segregated, there was a good deal less equity in the curricula young men and women encountered. In 1890 the U.S. Office of Education's statistics from private secondary schools indicated that boys substantially outnumbered girls in Latin, algebra, and geometry as well as in Greek, despite the fact that the overall male-female enrollment ratio was about even. Only 19 percent of the young women in private high schools for girls studied Latin that year, while more than a third of those enrolled in public high schools did. Girls in female private high schools were also enrolled in lower proportions in scientific subjects than the women students in public schools. In the sex-segregated private schools, young women often pursued a course of studies deemed less demanding and intellectually valuable than that studied by the girls in the public high schools.[54] Much of the difference may have been related to policies of sex segregation.

Even in the public schools, coeducation appears to have been a key element in the determination of curricular equity for girls and boys. In cities where the public high schools were sex-segregated, the girls' and boys' schools usually had different curricula. Not surprisingly, this was the case in Boston, where it was impossible for young women to be trained in classical languages in the public schools through most of the nineteenth century. Even when a girls' Latin School was finally established in 1878, its curriculum did not feature as much study in classical language as the boys' Latin School. Writing in 1894, a teacher from the Girls' High School in Boston argued that secondary education for young women should be organized around the study of literature and history, subjects considered to be less demanding than Latin, Greek, and the sciences. English, he reasoned, was especially appropriate for girls because it appealed to their appreciation for order, and literature because it often evoked emotional responses. He also thought that formal examinations in subjects that required rote memorization (such as classical languages and scientific subjects) were too demanding for women. In short, because women were considered to be frail, emotional, and preoccupied with matters of form, they were to receive an education substantially different from that of young men.[55]

Educators in other sex-segregated school systems agreed. In Baltimore the two high schools for girls featured no classical instruction whatever, while the city's only high school for boys—the elite City College—followed a demanding college prepatory curriculum. Noting "the course of studies in the high schools must be limited," the principal of one of Baltimore's female high schools in 1883 argued that the curriculum should "contain only a sufficient amount of history, literature, biography and physics to insure general culture, with a judicious combination of studies to exercise the critical and reasoning faculties." The presumption, of course, was that women students would not continue their education beyond high school, and the purposes of the school revolved around character-building and moral development rather than scholarship. Accordingly, the curriculum of the female high schools featured literature, modern languages, history, and teacher preparation, while the course of study at the all-male City College was designed specifically to meet entrance requirements for Johns

Hopkins and other universities. Even when the course titles were similar, as in the case of certain English and history classes, the texts used
in the girls' and boys' high schools were different—the girls' books
being those used in several of the city's male grammar schools.

As was the case in Boston, educators in Baltimore were committed to preparing women for a delimited set of domestic roles, even
though they apparently did not think of women's domestic responsibilities in narrow or strictly technical terms.[56] They believed that educated women had an important function to fill in community affairs,
after all, in performing a variety of nurturing functions, whether as
teachers, nurses, organizers of charitable organizations, or even participants in reform movements such as the temperance campaign. But
it was not the same role as men. Educators in these cities, on the other
hand, were equally committed to providing male students with the
highest standards of academic training. These boys were to be the
community's future leaders. The sexual division of labor, in that case,
demanded separate schools to prepare young men and women for
their respective roles in society.

There were a number of other school systems in the United
States with sex-segregated schools in this period, and most appear to
have had different high school curricula for boys and girls. In New
York boys attended City College, which featured a classical curriculum, while the only opportunity for public secondary education for
girls was offered through the city's normal school, established in 1870.
A similar situation existed in Philadelphia, where the elite Central
High School was for boys and young women were required to attend
the separate Girls' High School. In Louisville and Atlanta, segregated
male and female high schools each had their own curricula, with the
boys studying Greek and Latin and the girls history and literature. In
each of these instances, the rationale appears to have been similar to
those offered in Boston and Baltimore.[57]

Given this, it is interesting to note that school systems that practiced sex segregation appear to have been concentrated in certain
regions of the country. Of the thirty-eight towns and cities that reported either complete or partial separation of boys and girls in school in
the U.S. Commissioner of Education's 1882 survey, all but two were in
the Northeast or the South. School systems in these areas were considerably older than those in other parts of the country, and policies of
sex segregation may have dated from an earlier period, when
women's roles were defined in more restrictive terms than those
advocated by the domestic feminists. A superintendent from Massachusetts, for instance, responded to the U.S. Commissioner's 1882
survey by noting that a policy of sex segregation had existed in his

community since the time of the Revolutionary War; another from Georgia wrote that separate schools for boys and girls was the "custom in vogue" when the schools were established. A schoolman from Pennsylvania suggested that the only reason coeducation had not been adopted in his district was because it had never been tried.

In some parts of the country, in that case, much of the opposition to coeducation—and to curricular equity for girls and boys—may have been a function of institutional inertia. This appears to have been the case in the large East Coast cities where separate schools for boys and girls existed through most of this period. In 1891 the superintendent in Baltimore complained about his district's policy of sex segregation, describing it as "an inheritance handed down to us by our predecessors." But he did not succeed in changing it. Educators and local school boards preserved policies of sex segregation inherited from an earlier age, despite evidence of a substantial shift in public opinion regarding women's education and the domestic feminist conception of women's roles.[58]

Other schoolmen claimed that their opposition to coeducation was largely a reflection of existing public opinion, however, suggesting that there was little local support for the principle of curricular equity for boys and girls in high school. Fully 42 percent of those towns and cities where policies of sex segregation were reported were located in former Confederate states (which only included about 8.8 percent of the entire 340 community survey). As Anne Firor Scott and other historians have noted, the sexual division of labor was particularly sharp in the South, where most white women were restricted by a well-defined battery of domestic roles and social conventions. In the South, as in Boston and elsewhere, much of the opposition to coeducation may have been related to the question of propriety; it often simply was not considered proper to permit young men and women to associate to the extent required by coeducational schools.

As a number of feminist scholars have argued, however, the nineteenth-century concern for propriety often functioned to enforce the domestic limitations that Victorian society placed upon female roles. The culture of southern whites, particularly those middle- and upper-class whites who most often sent their offspring to high schools, was deeply patriarchal. In Anne Firor Scott's words, "the acceptable goals for southern women were to please their husbands and to please God, and to this end they were supposed to be beautiful, mildly literate, gracious, hard working, and church going. 'Woman's sphere' as they called it, was well marked out."[59] As a consequence, the ideology of domestic feminism was slow to take hold in southern communities. It is little wonder, in that case, that coeducation was practiced less frequently in the states of the Deep South than elsewhere. A superintendent in Alabama justified his preference for separate schools in 1882 by arguing that it was a "conservative" policy, suggesting that it helped to delineate proper roles for men and women. Another in Mississippi wrote that sex segregation was continued as a matter of policy in his community "in accordance with public sentiment," indicating that there was outright opposition to the notion of giving young men and women an education essentially the same.[60] In some parts of the United States, it appears, policies of sex segregation may have been associated with local preferences for a traditional division of labor between men and women, and not surprisingly, such policies generally resulted in separate curricula for boys and girls local high schools.

The fact that most educational leaders preferred coeducation as matter of policy, of course, by no means indicates that schoolmen generally endorsed a domestic feminist position in this period. But the existence of coeducation in most of the country's school districts also assured a remarkable degree of uniformity in what girls and boys studied in public high schools. If secondary schools featured distinctive male and female curricula in most communities where separate schools for boys and girls were maintained, they were few enough in number to have had little effect on overall enrollment patterns in the various academic courses listed in Table 1.1.

Coeducation brought with it, as many of its critics feared, a new set of standards for women's education, leaving it largely undifferentiated from the education of men. And it also afforded young women an opportunity to compare themselves, both in terms of their academic performance and other aspects of their social and intellectual development, with their male counterparts. The real test of equality in female schooling was whether or not the girls could compete for grades and other distinctions in the traditionally male world of academic scholarship. And it was on these grounds that coeducation received what may have been its most important endorsement.

As the number of young women enrolled in public high schools increased, educators across the country commented on the high level of academic ability demonstrated by female students. Critics of coeducation and the principle of female equality in education, of course, had argued that sustained study would prove debilitating to teenage girls and implied that women simply were not capable of the same degree of intellectual effort that young men were. Their opponents were quick to point out that not only were young women enrolled in high schools in large numbers, but that they also performed well in competition with the boys.

Evidence from large urban school districts in this period appears to bear this observation out. In Cincinnati, for instance, girls outnumbered boys in the top ten ranked graduates from both of the city's two high schools for most of the years between 1870 and 1885. As early as 1871, young women occupied the four highest positions in the graduating class at the Woodward High School, the city's oldest, and six out of the top ten positions, despite the fact that they constituted only about 41 percent of the student body. In 1885 women numbered half of the top ten ranked graduates at the Woodward High School but eight of the top ten (and sixteen of the top twenty) at the Hughes High School. Women also captured a good many academic prizes in these years. In the period between 1857 and 1869, when girls constituted a minority of the students in the Cincinnati high schools, they won the schools' principal prize for excellence in mathematics three out of thirteen times. In the years between 1870 and 1876, however, as female enrollments climbed, girls won the award four times. Shortly afterward, separate prizes were established for girls and boys in the Cincinnati schools. In Denver a special prize for the best historical essay, the Phelps Medal, was established in the mid-1880s. Boys won the first two awards, in 1885 and 1886, and for the next six years it was won by young women. Reports from other districts where boys and girls competed for academic distinctions reflected the same tendencies.

Young women in late nineteenth-century high schools clearly demonstrated their ability to compete with the boys on the field of scholarship. By 1896 a male professor from the University of Texas could remark that the academic accomplishment of female students—and the number of academic honors they won each year—had established beyond a doubt the fact that women could match the best intellectual efforts of men.[61] The opportunity to study alongside young men had given women a chance to demonstrate that they were indeed capable of academic excellence. And such accomplishments probably constituted the most compelling refutation of Clarke's theories imaginable.

Of course, the fact of a relatively small number of women winning academic prizes does not establish the point that women generally performed as well in nineteenth-century high schools as boys did. In most parts of the country, after all, girls constituted the majority of high school students, and they were generally more likely to remain in school long enough to graduate than were male students. It is no surprise, in that case, that women were awarded a good many academic prizes in this period.

To determine whether women students performed as well as the boys in general, on the other hand, it is necessary to examine systematic evidence on academic performance for comparable groups of male and female high school students. Such evidence is generally difficult to locate, since most nineteenth-century school records of grades and other measures of academic accomplishment generally have not been preserved. Fortunately, however, some nineteenth-century schoolmen were inveterate recordkeepers and compilers of statistics. In St. Louis Superintendent William Torrey Harris published lists of high school graduates for twelve years between 1870 and 1885, including each student's name, academic average for the previous four years, and numerical scores for attendance and "deportment."[62] Although this information does not offer the opportunity to compare the performance of girls and boys in specific courses, it does provide a means of systematically examining male-female differences in overall academic performance over a substantial period of time. Additionally, if St. Louis was at all typical of other cities in this period, these data also offer an opportunity to consider the openness of the nineteenth-century high school to the notion of female academic accomplishment.

The results of a year-by-year tabulation of the performance of graduating seniors in the St. Louis High School are given in Table 1.2. Looking at the summary figures for the entire sample of students in the bottom row, it is evident that the overall academic performance of male and female high school graduates was about the same in this period. Interestingly, however, the academic averages of the girls were slightly higher than those of the boys over the entire period (by about two points), despite the fact that female graduates outnumbered males by more than 3 to 1. If there was a process of selection at play that kept the most academically able boys in school where they would compete against a larger, less able body of female students, it is not evident in Table 1.2. Women in St. Louis's public high school performed as well or better than their male classmates through most of the 1870s and 1880s, even though far fewer young women dropped out of high school in these years than young men.

If this record of academic performance is any indication, girls took high school seriously and approached their studies with the same level of energy and interest as the boys. Indeed, judging from the scores given for "deportment" (behavior in class and on the school premises), women were considerably more observant of school rules and the general expectations of their teachers than their male classmates. Even though there were many more female students than males, there was less variation both in the academic and deportment scores for young women than for young men. As a group, it seems, the girls were better behaved and more attentive and responsible than the boys, even though the differences for most male and female students in these regards may have been small indeed.

Table 1.2   Average Grades for High School Seniors by Gender,
St. Louis, 1870–1885

(career means, with standard deviations in parentheses)

	SCHOLARSHIP		ATTENDANCE		DEPORTMENT		NUMBER	
Year	Male	Female	Male	Female	Male	Female	Male	Female
1870	84.8	84.5	97.4	95.9	79.9	88.3	17	49
	(7.0)	(8.1)	(2.9)	(3.5)	(20.1)	(8.8)		
1871	84.4	81.6	93.7	88.7	97.2	98.0	15	41
	(7.0)	(6.5)	(5.1)	(9.5)	(1.9)	(2.1)		
1875	72.6	79.9	96.8	95.6	86.8	94.6	14	42
	(6.0)	(6.3)	(3.8)	(4.2)	(12.5)	(7.4)		
1876	75.6	81.1	98.4	98.3	81.5	93.1	35	58
	(8.3)	(7.6)	(1.4)	(1.8)	(14.6)	(7.6)		
1877	73.8	79.4	93.6	92.0	73.8	93.4	17	40
	(5.3)	(6.1)	(3.7)	(10.3)	(21.7)	(5.4)		
1878	71.6	79.8	93.7	92.6	70.2	92.8	14	44
	(6.2)	(6.0)	(5.2)	(7.2)	(18.8)	(8.7)		
1879	81.1	78.5	95.6	92.4	91.2	92.6	11	54
	(3.4)	(13.2)	(3.4)	(7.1)	(6.2)	(14.1)		
1880	76.5	80.6	95.6	93.3	86.6	96.9	11	79
	(8.6)	(6.1)	(3.0)	(6.1)	(7.7)	(3.5)		
1881	81.6	79.2	97.4	95.8	94.9	96.1	12	51
	(6.5)	(6.7)	(2.9)	(6.0)	(6.8)	(4.1)		
1882	79.3	81.2	98.6	98.3	84.4	95.7	9	72
	(5.7)	(5.2)	(1.9)	(1.7)	(12.3)	(5.8)		
1884	82.5	80.8	92.5	92.0	94.1	97.3	12	52
	(6.0)	(5.2)	(4.9)	(9.9)	(4.7)	(3.1)		
1885	80.4	81.2	92.0	92.3	94.5	97.4	7	49
	(9.2)	(5.4)	(9.0)	(6.7)	(7.1)	(3.6)		
Total	78.9	80.7	95.9	94.2	84.5	94.6	174	591
	(8.2)	(6.3)	(4.3)	(6.9)	(15.8)	(8.7)		

Source: Computed from St. Louis School Reports, 1870–85 (data unavailable
for missing years).

The female attendance record, while slightly worse than that of
the boys, was in fact quite good, especially considering that there
were such large numbers of women students compared to men. If
intellectual effort proved debilitating to teenage girls in this period, it
certainly was not evident in high school attendance records in St.

Louis. Finally, if the traditionally male curriculum of the nineteenth-century high school was in fact alien to young women in St. Louis, it was not apparent in any of the averages reported in Table 1.2. Despite the fact that they studied essentially the same subjects as their male schoolmates, young women in St. Louis performed as well or better than young men in the city's public high school. All of this suggests that equality indeed did exist for young women and men in the nine-teenth century coeducational high school, at least insofar as the cur-riculum and overall measures of performance were concerned. If the sexual division of labor dictated altogether different future roles for boys and girls in this period, in communities like St. Louis the high school may have constituted an important affirmation that—in at least one important respect—young women were at least the equals of their male counterparts.

The strong academic record of women students undoubtedly assuaged many educators' doubts about the wisdom of coeducation, and gave the lie to Clarke and other critics of gender equity in school-ing. As indicated in the data from St. Louis, the women students appear to have been well behaved, hard-working, and bright. Com-menting on his experience teaching young men and women in virtually all of the academic subjects, a high school principal from Utica, New York, remarked in 1886, "In any academic class the boys find their fac-ulties taxed to keep up with the girls."[63] It is little wonder that Harris and other schoolmen often argued that high school girls constituted a good influence on their male classmates; many young women in nine-teenth-century high schools must have seemed almost perfect students.

Of course, today it is not difficult to imagine middle-class girls performing as well or better than boys in school, given more than a century of experience with coeducational secondary and higher edu-cation. But in the nineteenth century, when respected men of science and leaders in education—such as Clarke and Philbrick—emphatical-ly denounced the principle of equality in women's and men's educa-tion, the willingness of women to enroll in high schools in such large numbers and the successes they registered in academic performance were powerful affirmations of the domestic feminist comprehension of intellectual ability. With the rise of the coeducational high school, a new plateau of equity was achieved in women's education. By the end of the nineteenth century, few critics of women's schooling were prepared to argue that young women were less able to study than young men. The coeducational high school—and the growing num-bers of women enrolled in colleges and universities—may have marked an important watershed for the tradition of formalized male supremacy in academic affairs.

Conclusion: An Age of Opportunity

Between 1870 and 1900 women students in high schools came to share in the celebration of an academic culture traditionally reserved for males alone. The central institution in this process appears to have been the coeducational public high school. As the public high school spread to communities across the country, it opened a new field of opportunity for young women. And because opportunity costs were lower for young women than for men, a function of restricted job opportunities for teenage girls, female high school enrollments were higher than those for boys throughout the latter nineteenth century. In a sense, then, women went to school because they had nothing better to do. But once they had enrolled, they exhibited an ability to match and exceed the academic standards set by the boys. More than anything else, the growth of female secondary school enrollment and the apparent success of women students in high schools demonstrated the spuriousness of medical and biological theories of female intellectual inferiority. "The prophecies of Dr. Clarke . . . that coeducation would prove injurious to the health of women," wrote the U.S. Commissioner of Education in 1888, "have not been fulfilled."[64] Moreover, the unwillingness of educational leaders to countenance the high cost of sex-segregated schools in most parts of the country abrogated the possibility of different curricula being widely adopted for young men and women, such as was advocated by John Philbrick and other opponents of coeducation. And judging from their responses to surveys on the issue and pronouncements in school reports, most nineteenth-century schoolmen were impressed by the high moral and academic caliber of female high school students in this period.

All of these developments were part of the feminization of American high schools and part of a larger process which literary historian Ann Douglas has described as the feminization of American culture.[65] Just as authors and clergymen found themselves contending with a largely female clientele in the nineteenth century, so did educators. Schoolmen had to acknowledge the needs of this new constituency if they were to achieve their goal of creating a unified and highly differentiated modern school system. For their part, young women proved to be willing—perhaps even eager—participants in the popularization of secondary education. The result was an unprecedented era of gender equity in American high schools and a new sense of opportunity for young women, developments which contemporaries—both friends and foes of equality alike—clearly recognized. Whether Emma Willard would have been happy that women's secondary education had become generally the same as men's, she doubtless would have been pleased with the general endorsement of female intellectual capability implied by supporters of coeducation. The principle of male-female equality in education, it seemed, had finally been accepted.

Chapter Two

Participation and Purpose in Women's Education: Who Went to School, and Why

At the same time that high schools offered women a new field of achievement in the nineteenth century, there were important limitations that governed the effect of women's secondary education. The first was numbers. Despite its rapid growth, the high school remained squarely middle-class in orientation, and many women were excluded from its benefits by a variety of circumstances. The second factor was the purposes women pursued in school. Few women seem to have been interested in using the equality they enjoyed in high school to prepare for careers or other social roles that would challenge the prevailing sexual division of labor. Consequently, the transformation of women's secondary education did not simultaneously trigger a revolution in gender roles (although female work roles did begin to shift more rapidly in the years after 1900, as will be seen in chapter 3). Confined largely to a rather narrow social strata, female high school enrollment posed little immediate threat to the prevailing Victorian values of mainstream American culture.

Despite the fact that most secondary schools were public institutions in the latter nineteenth century, the high school served a rather elite constituency in many parts of the country. Edward Krug has estimated that a only small fraction of American teenagers attended high school in the 1880s, and an even smaller number graduated.[1] The education afforded by public high schools, consequently, benefited a limited number of women. Others were excluded from the excitement of competing with boys for academic honors and from the other possibilities opened by secondary education. In this chapter I address the question of which groups of women went to school. This is an important issue, after all, in assessing the impact of the changes described in chapter 1.

Equality in education may have entailed such little controversy simply because its potential effects were restricted to certain social groups.

Beyond the matter of inclusion or exclusion, of course, is the question of why young women wanted to attend high school in the first place. Unlike today, comparatively few jobs called for secondary education as a prerequisite in the nineteenth century, and it was even possible to attend a college or professional school without having gone to high school. Relatively few middle-class women worked outside the home anyways. Indeed, the fact that women came to dominate the nation's high schools in a period when their employment options were rather limited presents a difficult historical puzzle.

The answer to this question is elusive, and requires a variety of different strategies and methods of investigation. Unlike the previous chapter, which generally focused on institutional and ideological dimensions of women's education, here I examine social and economic factors associated with female school participation between 1870 and 1900, along with the recollections of nineteenth-century women about their schooling recorded in autobiographies, diaries, letters, and other personal documents. The motivations of these women must be deduced from different types of historical evidence, most of which have been acquired—to one extent or another—from examining behavior (though some of it, such as the recollections left in women's personal documents, are a direct reflection of sentiments too). While this sort of evidence cannot conclusively establish the reasons why a given individual or group exhibited a certain behavior, it *can* associate behavior—in this case, female school participation—with a variety of circumstances that point to motivation.

In this context it is possible to consider the kinds of opportunities women *felt* schools offered them. These are subjective questions, of course, and in the last analysis, it probably is impossible to authoritatively determine just why women did attend school. But it may be possible to identify several potential explanations as being unlikely, and some as being more likely than others. In doing this it is also possible to see some of the limitations inherent in women's secondary education during the nineteenth century. At the very time that growing numbers of women attended school and competed with men there, few seem to have aspired to take this new sense of equality into the male-dominated world of middle-class employment.[2]

Who Went to School

Before determining why young women attended high schools in this period, it is important to identify which groups of women were enrolled in school and which were not. As noted in the previous chapter, the high school was a somewhat exclusive institution through most of the nineteenth century.[3] Identifying the social background of women who did enroll, however, provides evidence for speculating about why female enrollments grew so rapidly. The goals of the nineteenth-century high school, after all, held greater relevance for some groups such as the white middle-class girls who became teachers) than for others. The social composition of female enrollments also may have had a bearing on the willingness of reformers to countenance coeducation and other reforms in women's education. The principle of gender equity may have been acceptable because it was applied mainly to middle-class women who were unlikely to challenge the existing sexual division of labor.

Beyond these questions, the issue of which groups of women attended high schools in this period is important to comprehending changes in women's work after 1900. As will be seen in chapter 3, some groups of women were virtually excluded from employment requiring any degree of advanced education. It is possible, in that case, that secondary schooling also served as a way of distinguishing certain groups of women from those who were not educated, delimiting the employment opportunities of some women at the same time that it may have broadened options for others. As Michael Katz has observed, the most basic question in educational history might be simply "who went to school?"[4] In this case, examining the school participation rates of different groups of women in the decades leading up to 1900 may be crucial to understanding both the role and the purpose of high school in the lives of nineteenth- and early twentieth-century women.

Studying School Attendance: Data and Method

Historians have relied upon census manuscript returns to study the social forces that shaped school attendance in the past. In the discussion to follow, I build upon the research of other scholars to make inferences about patterns of female school participation in the latter nineteenth century. I also examine overall teenage female enrollment rates in cities across the country in 1900, employing a national sample of more than fifteen hundred young women selected from the 1900 manuscript census. With individual level data such as these it is possible to consider a wide range of issues that were simply inaccessible with the aggregate statistics cited in the previous chapter (and the state-level data used later in this chapter). In particular, these individual data can be used to determine the relationship of social class, ethnicity, and a range of other background characteristics to the decisions of women to enroll in school during this period. This kind of information is critical to identifying which groups of women were most likely to attend high school in the closing decades of the nineteenth century. And that is an important step in the process of comprehending why women attended school to begin with.

While census manuscript data offer important advantages in the study of school attendance, they also carry a number of limitations. The most important of these concerns the definition of enrollment. Because census enumerators did not ask what *kind* of school individuals attended, the information on enrollment in these data is limited to a simple affirmation of enrollment in any school at any time in the previous year. Some teenagers who attended grammar schools and colleges, in that case, are probably included in the following analysis. I have tried to minimize the likelihood of this by limiting my discussion to cities, where high school enrollment rates among teenagers were highest and where teenage rates of enrollment in common schools generally were lowest.[5] In many cities at this time, moreover, the courses of study in grammar schools and high schools overlapped considerably, so that a student enrolled in the highest course of the former often studied roughly the same things as those in the first course of the latter. High schools often shared a good deal with the first two years of college as well. Thus, studying teenage enrollment rates in cities, where graded school systems were most highly developed at this time, can provide a general profile of participation levels in what may be broadly described as secondary education, even if some teenage students were not enrolled in high schools.[6]

Manuscript census data have been used by a number of historians to study school enrollment. Most previous studies have focused on the nineteenth century, particularly the antebellum period. For the most part these historians have limited their analyses to particular states and communities, especially those in the Northeast. While few have attempted to perform separate analyses for male and female students, several have included gender as a dependent variable in their treatment of school participation, and their findings cast light on the general profile of female (and male) teenage school participation in the latter nineteenth century. Though there are important differences in the weight that scholars have assigned to various factors in explaining school enrollment, virtually all of these studies have shown that children from lower-class and immigrant backgrounds attended school at lower rates than those from native and middle- or upper-class families.[7] (Results from two other studies are presented in the Appendix.) The structure of school participation for teenagers, in other words, generally mirrored the structure of society itself. As Carl Kaestle and Maris Vinovskis noted, "whatever was learned in school, school leaving taught...youth something about how their world was ordered."[8]

Female School Attendance in 1900

As indicated earlier, other studies of school participation in the past have not devoted much attention to the issue of gender. Even though several historians have included gender variables in their analyses, they have not conducted separate studies of male and female attendance patterns.[9] While a rather substantial body of information exists on overall enrollment rates, in that case, relatively little is known about how *women* attended school in the past.

Table 2.1 presents the results of an analysis of school enrollment performed with a national sample of *female* teenagers taken from the 1900 federal census manuscript returns. The data for this analysis were drawn from the 1900 Public Use Sample, a 1/760 random sample selected from the entire population represented in the national census at the turn of the century. From this large cross section I selected a smaller sample of all teenage women living in cities with populations over twenty thousand.[10] Those living in smaller communities were excluded because of important differences in the enrollment patterns of teenagers in rural and small-town communities and those living in cities. Moreover, a much larger proportion of the young women in urban areas attended high schools than was the case in rural settings. Consequently, the nearly thirteen hundred girls selected for inclusion in this analysis represent a cross section of the population from which high schools drew their clientele. Although the overall enrollment rate reported in Table 2.1 is nearly triple the national high school enrollment rate among teenagers, it may reflect secondary school participation levels in larger cities considerably more accurately.[11]

The method of statistical analysis used in this discussion is multiple classification analysis (MCA), a form of regression that permits the use of categorical independent variables and dichotomous dependent variables, and has been used widely by historians to study school enrollment. MCA compares the variation of means for different subgroups in a given population around a grand mean derived from the entire sample. It produces a table with two measures of association identifying the relationship of each categorical variable to the dependent variable and information on the behavior of each subgroup in the population.

A typical MCA table, for instance, provides a raw mean for each subgroup considered in the analysis, an Eta coefficient to measure the

Table 2.1   Multiple Classification Analysis
—Teenage Women in Cities, 1900

(Public Use Sample)

VARIABLE AND CATEGORY	N	UNADJUSTED MEAN	ETA	ADJUSTED MEAN	BETA
Age			0.27		0.50
13	180	0.80		0.78	
14	196	0.62		0.62	
15	187	0.38		0.38	
16	165	0.30		0.30	
17	171	0.22		0.22	
18	181	0.12		0.12	
19	185	0.06		0.08	
Region			0.01		0.07
Northeast	636	0.34		0.35	
Southeast	109	0.34		0.33	
Northcentral	387	0.37		0.37	
Southcentral	88	0.42		0.34	
West	45	0.58		0.52	
Father's Occupation			0.02		0.16
High White-Collar	202	0.46		0.52	
Low White-Collar	115	0.43		0.43	
Skilled Labor	275	0.37		0.34	
Unskilled Labor	389	0.34		0.30	
Farmer	19	0.21		0.24	
Father Not Present	265	0.28		0.32	
Position in Family			0.05		0.14
Older—small household	119	0.54		0.44	
Younger—small household	47	0.34		0.38	
Older—medium household	349	0.39		0.37	
Middle—medium household	129	0.37		0.39	
Younger—medium household	125	0.32		0.36	
Older—large household	196	0.32		0.31	
Middle—large household	88	0.42		0.41	
Younger—large household	65	0.38		0.41	
Other relatives	69	0.36		0.42	
Unrelated teenagers	78	0.02		0.13	
Race			0.00		0.04
White	1180	0.36		0.37	
Black	85	0.29		0.28	

Table 2.1   (*continued*)

VARIABLE AND CATEGORY	N	UNADJUSTED MEAN	ETA	ADJUSTED MEAN	BETA
Ethnicity (Father's Birthplace)			0.04		0.21
United States	616	0.45		0.45	
Great Britain	96	0.35		0.33	
Scandinavia and Holland	33	0.39		0.38	
Ireland	120	0.29		0.34	
France and Belgium	42	0.26		0.30	
Germany	272	0.25		0.23	
Eastern Europe	62	0.18		0.21	
Italy and Southern Europe	24	0.16		0.12	

Dependent variable: enrollment in school, women age 13 to 19 (N = 1,265; R^2 = .36; grand mean = .36)
Source: Data from U.S. Census, 1900 Public Use Sample

extent of bivariate association between each categorical variable and the dependent variable, an adjusted mean for each subgroup (calculated after the effects of all other factors have been held constant), and a Beta coefficient to determine the independent effect of each categorical factor on the dependent variable (analogous to a standardized regression coefficient). In addition to the summary measures of association usually provided with multivariate analysis, in that case, MCA also provides a wide array of descriptive information on the disposition of each subgroup considered in the analysis. This makes it an especially useful technique for determining which groups of teenagers were most likely to be enrolled in school at a particular point in time.[12]

In setting up the 1900 data for analysis, I have retained several of the variables used by other historians, and I have introduced some of my own. As suggested above, factors common to virtually all school attendance studies include age and variables representing father's occupation and ethnicity. These factors, as it turned out, also were important determinants of female school participation in this period. The use of certain common variables, of course, makes it possible to compare the results of the analysis below with those of other studies of school participation.[13]

One factor included in the analysis below which has not been used in most nineteenth-century studies of school participation is the position-in-family variable. I have adapted this variable from a study by David Angus and Jeffrey Mirel. It is designed to measure the extent to which family size and a child's position in the birth order affected teenage school enrollment.[14] The rationale for considering these factors is related to the family life course. Theoretically, families in the early and middle stages of their life spans are more likely to require the earnings of children, simply because it is at that time that the number of dependents generally is greatest. Families in later stages of their life spans, conversely, usually have fewer dependent children, and correspondingly less demand on resources. The expectation, in that case, is that children born later in the family life course exhibited a higher likelihood of attending school than those born earlier.

Of course, family size is an important consideration in determining which members of a given household are born "early" and "late," and the larger the family the greater the likelihood that older children were required to work.[15] For this reason, I have defined ten categories of position in family, representing three different ranges of household size and two types of nonsibling household members. Designed in this fashion, this factor is intended to capture two dimensions of family life as they may have affected school participation. First, it measures the effect of family size, and thus household consumption requirements, on teenage school enrollment. All things being equal, larger families could afford less schooling than smaller ones. But the variable also considers the relative position of each child in the birth order, to capture the advantages younger children may have enjoyed as a consequence of their older sisters and brothers working. As will be seen below, in some instances these advantages may have been considerable.

Given these elements of analysis, the first question is which of these particular variables were most directly associated with teenage female school enrollment. By and large, the MCA results reported in Table 2.1 are quite similar to those other historians found in their analyses of enrollment patterns in the nineteenth century (see Tables A.5 and A.6 in the Statistical Appendix). The relative magnitudes of the major variables generally are the same as those found by Kaestle and Vinovskis in their study of Massachusetts, with age being far and away the most important factor, followed by ethnicity and father's occupation. The social forces that shaped school enrollment, it seems, had changed little in the closing decades of the nineteenth century.[16]

As in earlier years, the likelihood of a particular girl attending school in 1900 was closely related to her social status. Women whose fathers were native-born and employed as white-collar workers generally enjoyed the highest rates of school participation. Those whose fathers were foreign-born, particularly those from Catholic countries, and were employed as manual laborers exhibited lower enrollment rates. Female school enrollment at the turn of the century continued to be dictated in part by the powerful social realities of class and ethnicity. Regardless of educators' rhetoric about the high school being a "peoples college," it appears that American secondary schools were not patronized equally by all elements of the population. Teenage girls from working-class and immigrant backgrounds were largely excluded from school in this period.

The implications of this, however, are not altogether clear. Looking at the adjusted mean column in Table 2.1, school attendance rates for the daughters of professionals and unskilled workers are widely divergent, but the difference between the rates for daughters of skilled and unskilled workers (often a crucial distinction in status in American life at this time) was not nearly as great. It is possible, of course, that women from working-class backgrounds were more likely to attend school than young men, simply because the opportunity costs for women were lower than they were for men (as suggested in chapter 1). Cost, after all, was presumably a major factor in decisions to attend high school for working-class families. For many such families, sending a teenage daughter to school might not have represented a major reallocation of family resources. Given these considerations, it may be quite reasonable to expect relatively small differences in female school participation related to social class and income.[17]

The presence of sizeable numbers of working-class women attending school, however, may have affected the social context of high schools at this time. Because working-class children constituted such a large group (over 30 percent of the sample in Table 2.1), even with a lower rate of enrollment, the daughters of unskilled workers could comprise a large portion of the female students in school at this time. It is not clear that all of these women attended high school, of course, but if one were to construct a hypothetical high school population with figures derived from the rates provided in the adjusted mean column of Table 2.1, about 45 percent of the female students would come from families with an unskilled father or no father at all. This is a sizeable group, and even if most high schools did not enroll such large numbers of working-class women (this question is addressed again in chapter 5), it suggests that high schools at the turn of the century may not have been quite as exclusive as some historians have suggested, at least for women. A large proportion of all young women enrolled in school in American cities came from working-class backgrounds. Even if all of them did not go to high schools, this indicates that class may not have been a critical determinant of the social composition of urban high schools in the latter nineteenth century.

The most important factor in Table 2.1, of course, was ethnicity, defined here as father's birthplace. Women with American-born fathers had the highest enrollment rates, followed by those with fathers born in Great Britain and Scandinavia or Holland. The groups with lowest participation rates, on the other hand, were women whose fathers were born in eastern or southern Europe, ethnic groups with historically low rates of school participation. These differences in enrollment can be linked to a number of characteristics that distinguished women from backgrounds such as these, particularly religion and language. Higher rates of participation appear to have been linked to Protestant cultures and those where English was the native language or (perhaps) easily acquired. Lower rates, on the other hand, seem to have been associated with Catholic backgrounds or areas where English was not native. In either case, the evidence suggests a cultural explanation for female enrollment rates. Groups that felt most comfortable with the generally Protestant orientation of American public schools—and had the most experience with English as a primary language—sent their daughters to school in greatest numbers. Table 2.1 suggests that factors such as these may have been more important in determining female high school enrollment than income or social class (at least when "class" is defined in occupational terms).

The significance of cultural factors in the development of women's education is even more striking if one considers the ethnic composition of the female student population at this time. Constructing a hypothetical student body once again with rates in the adjusted mean column, some 61 percent of all teenage women in school had American-born fathers. If women whose fathers were born in Great Britain and Scandanavia or Holland are added, the figure rises to 71 percent. Thus a clear majority came from Protestant backgrounds (probably better than three-quarters when women with German backgrounds are included). Women from Catholic families, on the other hand, appear to have comprised less than 20 percent of the women in school. These findings correspond generally with those of other historians who have examined school participation and other elements of social life in nineteenth-century cities. As Olivier Zunz has noted, ethnicity constituted a major point of popular identification in the American industrial cities. Ethnicity, particularly the values associated with certain religious beliefs, appears to have been an important element of school culture at the turn of the century—at least among women.[18]

Insofar as religion is a general indicator of cultural disposition in the nineteenth century, this pattern of participation suggests that there was a high degree of cultural homogeneity in the female population of nineteenth-century secondary schools. In particular, women from Protestant backgrounds, whose values may have proved compatible with the domestic feminist vision of women's education as a preparation for motherhood, probably constituted the overwhelming majority of female students in many high schools. If indeed these background characteristics are a general indicator of such a cultural disposition, they could also explain some of the willingness of educators to endorse coeducation. In order to initiate measures as radical as the changes in women's education, after all, schoolmen needed a good deal of confidence in the values of their female students. The fact that most young women who enrolled in school seem to have shared much of the same cultural heritage—and the values of most schoolmen—may have assuaged many of the anxieties educators and parents felt about the potential dangers of coeducation.[19]

The other important element in Table 2.1 is the position-in-family variable. As noted above, this factor was designed to capture the effect of both family size and the relative position of each child in the birth order on teenager school enrollment. Judging from the results obtained from the 1900 MCA, there is reason to believe that both birth order and family size had an important bearing on female school enrollment in this period, even after the effect of other factors had been controlled.

Examining the adjusted mean column of Table 2.1, several patterns stand out regarding the effect of family size on school attendance. First, the high rates of enrollment for older children in smaller households undoubtedly reflects the school participation rates of only-children (note the much larger number of older children in the two small-household categories), along with the propensity of parents with smaller families to send their children to school anyway. Second, there apparently was little advantage to birth order in middle-sized families, as teenagers at both early and late stages of the family life course (older, middle, and younger) attended school at roughly the same rates. And third, in large families it appears that birth order was indeed an important factor in determining who went to school. In families of six or more children, the oldest teenagers were the least likely to attend school, while teenagers occupying the middle and lower stages of the birth order exhibited relatively high rates of enrollment.

Apart from the influence of ethnicity and class, in that case, individual school participation was sometimes associated with an accident of birth. Daughters born first in large families often had to assume responsibility for their younger sisters and brothers, whether it meant caring for them at home or getting a job to augment the family income, and this sometimes meant that they did not go to school. Younger children, it seems, had an advantage. Because they had fewer younger siblings to care for, and perhaps because household consumption was less, they could attend school in considerably greater numbers than their older sisters. Although this family size-birth order effect concerned only about a quarter of all the women in the sample, its effect constitutes an important caveat to the influence of ethnicity and class on female enrollment patterns in this period. Family size and circumstances of birth, it appears, also determined which girls made it to high school.[20]

Historians have long held that the nineteenth-century high school was a selective institution. To an extent, the foregoing analysis corroborates that observation. While the sample examined for purposes of this analysis undoubtedly included many girls enrolled in grammar schools, private commercial schools, normal schools and even colleges, the general pattern of teenage school participation revealed in Table 2.1 probably held true—at least generally—for high schools as well. By and large, the women who attended high school were overwhelmingly white, native-born, and from middle-class backgrounds (in particular, most were daughters of skilled or white-collar workers). Class seems to have been less important as a determinant of enrollment than cultural disposition (at least insofar as the latter is measured by ethnicity). Still, even in 1900 many urban high schools probably were quite exclusive.

Of course, other factors also affected the propensity of teenage girls to attend school in this period, at least two of which appear to have been family size and position in the birth order. In some families it was younger daughters, those who were in a position to benefit from older siblings' work around the house, who were able to attend school. But these factors were of secondary importance, particularly whan compared to the influence of class and ethnicity. There can be no doubt that secondary school attendance was partly a prerogative of those groups that could afford it. This fact alone probably exerted a somewhat conservative influence on the quality of education in American high schools, regardless of reforms affecting young women.

Added to the question of cost, of course, was the matter of values. The power of the ethnicity variable in the MCA runs suggests that the high school may have exerted a stronger attraction to some groups of women than to others, independently of the effect of income or occupational background. Women from Catholic immigrant backgrounds, for instance, may have enrolled at lower rates because they attached less value to the ideal of educated womanhood than women whose families had lived in the United States longer. The ideas of the domestic feminists, it appears, may have held greater appeal to some groups of women than others, irrespective of class background and other factors. The high school was also a native and a Protestant institution; and its clientele was largely native, Protestant, and middle-class throughout the latter nineteenth century.

In this regard, the general pattern of school enrollment reflected larger social and economic forces and may have made reforms in women's education palatable to the conservative mentality of middling Americans. The women who benefitted from coeducation and the spirit of equity that permeated many high schools in this period did not have to work. They generally were from stable, respectable families and hence were unlikely to turn their educations to radically new purposes. As David Tyack and Elizabeth Hansot have noted, the middle-class, Protestant character of high schools in this period helped to allay the fears of parents and educators that coeducation would result in liaisons with immigrant and lower-class youth.[21] In any case, the middle-class character of enrollments probably was the best insurance against such eventualities occurring (a fact probably not lost on educators). Serving a largely middle-class clientel, young men and women concerned with preserving their status within the existing social structure, the high school served a fundamentally conservative role despite the important changes in women's education which marked this period.

Female School Participation, 1870–1900: An Ecological Analysis

Identifying who was most likely to enroll in high school, of course, does not directly answer the question of *why* women attended high schools in the first place. To address this issue it is necessary to consider a different variety of evidence. One often-used method of identifying the factors associated with a given pattern of behavior is to examine differences in the various contexts within which it occurred. This is known as ecological analysis because it is the characteristics of a given environment, whether social, economic, or biological, that are studied in order to understand the problem at hand. Here, the issue is female secondary school participation in the latter nineteenth century and how it varied from one setting to another. What follows, in that case, is an effort to deduce explanations of female secondary school enrollment through the use of ecological reasoning.[22]

The Data: Regional Patterns of Variation

My treatment of female high school enrollment relies upon state-level data for the period between 1870 and 1900 collected from three sources: the published decennial federal census reports for 1870, 1880, 1890, and

1900; the U.S. Commissioner of Education Reports for 1872, 1878, 1880, 1890, and 1900; and state-level per capita income data for 1880 and 1900 derived from the widely used estimates made by economic historian Richard Easterlin. These data present a number of problems. Because of limitations in the statistics collected from earlier years, much of this discussion deals with the last decade in the nineteenth century. Furthermore, given the high level of aggregation in these data, only the most general relationships can be identified. Still, as will be seen below, even statistics aggregated at the state level can be used to analyze the feminization of American high schools in this period.[23]

Not surprisingly, female high school enrollment rates were closely associated with general patterns of social and economic development in this period. Table 2.2 presents descriptive statistics from these state-level data for the United States as a whole and three important regions across the latter nineteenth century. High school enrollments were highest in the Northeast (defined in this study as the New England and Middle Atlantic census regions). The Northeast was also the region the highest proportion of its population living in urban areas, with the largest number of teachers per child under 10, and the highest proportion of female teachers. Per capita income levels (not shown in Table 2.2) were also relatively high there (higher than the national average), although they were lower than in the West.

Table 2.2   Regional Patterns of Female School Participation and Social and Economic Development, 1870–1900

VARIABLE	UNITED STATES	NORTHEAST	SOUTH	WEST
Agricultural employment, 1870	48.6% (21.6)	29.1% (13.1)	72.7% (8.6)	31.2% (14)
Female high school enrollment rate, 1872 (1)	1.05% (1.1)	1.9% (1.5)	0.4% (0.4)	1.7% (1)
Percent of all teachers female, 1870	55.6% (18.3)	71.4% (7.9)	40.7% (19)	58.9% (18.3)
Percent of high school students female, 1872	58.9% (19.4)	46.9% (5.8)	64.4% (18.7)	69.4% (38.8)
Urbanization rate, 1880	24.9% (21.2)	42.9% (21)	7.8% (6.4)	29.7% (13.7)
Manufacturing employment, 1880	23.4% (18.3)	37.8% (12)	15.8% (27.2)	25.5% (13.3)

Table 2.2 (*continued*)

VARIABLE	UNITED STATES	NORTHEAST	SOUTH	WEST
Female high school enrollment rate, 1880	2.7% (2.2)	3.4% (1.9)	2.1% (1.6)	5.4% (3.7)
Male high school enrollment rate, 1880	2.2% (1.8)	3.8% (1.8)	1.8% (1.5)	2.4% (2.3)
Percent of all teachers female, 1880	55.8% (19.4)	66.6% (23)	41.5% (13.6)	64.5% (6.8)
Agricultural employment, 1890	41.9% (19.6)	21.7% (11.5)	64.2% (9.9)	34.9% (7.2)
Female high school enrollment rate, 1890	3.9% (2.9)	6.2% (2.7)	0.7% (0.5)	3.9% (2.8)
Percent of all high school students female, 1890	58.9% (6.2)	57.27% (4.3)	60.6% (8.4)	60.4% (5.9)
Urbanization rate, 1900	34.8% (24.1)	57.9% (22.5)	12.9% (5.5)	32.9% (14.7)
Manufacturing employment, 1900	23.5% (12.2)	39.8% (8.5)	10.6% (3.5)	26% (4.1)
Female high school enrollment Rate, 1900	10.4% (5.7)	14.1% (4.5)	3.9% (1.3)	14.3% (3.6)
Male high school enrollment rate, 1900	7.9% (4.4)	11.8% (4.3)	3.2% (0.9)	9.4% (2.3)
Percent of all high school students female, 1900	59.1% (2.2)	57.7% (1.8)	60.1% (1.9)	59.4% (0.7)

unweighted means for regional groups of states;
standard deviations in parentheses—U.S. figures are averages of state level data.

Sources: figures on enrollment rates and teachers are taken from annual reports of the U.S. Commissioner of Education for the years reported. General population and occupational figures taken from decennial U.S. Census population volumes, 1870–1900.

(1) Enrollment rates are calculated by dividing the teenage female population of each state, as reported in the U.S. Census, into the overall high school enrollment reported by the U.S. Commissioner of Education.

In the South, on the other hand, high school enrollments were lowest of any major region (the South is defined in this study as the states of the Confederacy). The nation's least educationally developed region throughout this period, the South featured the lowest per capita income, the worst teacher-child ratio, and the least feminized teaching force in the country. Unlike the other major regions, the southern economy continued to be dominated by agriculture well into the twentieth century, and the region underwent relatively little urbanization.

In the West (defined in this study as Nevada, Colorado, and the three West Coast states), female high school enrollments were relatively high, while male enrollment rates were lower than in the Northeast. The West was characterized by a balanced pattern of economic development throughout this period, with about a quarter of its labor force engaged in manufacturing and a third in agriculture. By 1900 nearly a third of the region's population lived in urban areas, and the level of income there was the highest in the country—though it may have been negated somewhat by a high cost of living as well. The Western states also possessed rather highly developed educational systems, as evidenced by the relatively high teacher-child ratios and high level of feminization in the teaching force for the region as a whole.[24]

In general, the patterns of feminization in high school enrollments identified in Table 2.2 correspond to the account of feminization in high schools given in the previous chapter. There was little variation across regions, despite the important social and economic differences that distinguished one part of the country from another. Only in 1872 did boys register a majority of the high school students in any part of the country (the Northeast—and even this is suspect because of inconsistent reporting of gender data at that time), and by 1890 virtually all regional differences in this regard had disappeared. The feminization of the high school, it appears, was nearly a universal phenomenon by the end of the nineteenth century and does not appear to have been associated with any general process of social and economic development. Just *why* this ocurred, however, is not clear from examining the regional statistics presented in Table 2.2. To better address the question it is necessary to employ a variety of more powerful techniques of statistical analysis.

Feminization and Graduation: A Correlation Analysis

If the feminization of American high schools cannot be associated with a particular region of the country and does not appear to have been the consequence of forces evident at the regional level, just what *was* associated with this process? Taking the percent of all high school students in a given state that are female to be an index of the feminization of American high schools, it is possible to use bivariate correlations to determine which social and economic characteristics of the states the feminization process was associated with. While this method cannot establish what in fact *caused* the number of female students to exceed males in high schools at this time, it can pinpoint sources of variation in the degree of feminization which may help to explain its development.

Table 2.3 presents the elements of a correlation analysis of the feminization of high school enrollments as defined above. The variables listed on the left of the table are important social, economic, and educational characteristics of each state. These have been selected to represent various aspects of the social structure and economy that could be associated with the feminization of high school enrollments. Urbanization, of course, is a general measure of each state's social and economic development, but both "trade" employment and the percentage of all teachers female are employment characteristics that could reflect the local demand for educated women. It is possible, in other words, that these factors contributed to an atmosphere that encouraged women to attend high schools in large numbers by offering the prospect of employment. The other variables in Table 2.3 are each state's high school feminization rate for 1872 and 1890. The coefficients represent the zero-order correlation of these latter variables with the state social, economic, and educational characteristics for 1870 and 1890 respectively. Thus, the coefficients on the left represent the association of feminization with various factors in the early 1870s, and those on the right their association in 1890.[25]

Table 2.3   Feminization of High School Enrollments
—A Correlation Analysis

SOCIAL, ECONOMIC, AND EDUCATIONAL FACTORS	PERCENT OF HIGH SCHOOL ENROLLMENT FEMALE IN 1872[1]	PERCENT OF HIGH SCHOOL ENROLLMENT FEMALE IN 1890[2]
Urbanization	-0.239	-0.259
"Trade" employment	-0.160	-0.264
Percent of all teachers female	-0.207	-0.089
Female high school enrollment rate	0.112	-0.021
Male high school enrollment rate	-0.377	-0.271
South	0.247	0.169
Northeast	-0.358	-0.154

1. N = 36; critical value: +/- 0.329.
2. N = 40; critical value: +/- 0.312.

Perhaps the most obvious feature of Table 2.3 is the low correlation between any of the factors on the left side of the table with the two feminization variables. As noted above, there was relatively little variation from state to state in the feminization of enrollments. Some variation *was* evident along regional lines in 1870, and the feminization of high school enrollments was negatively associated with the Northeast at that point in time—a pattern evident in Table 2.2 as well. But by 1890 much of this regional variation appears to have disappeared, although the signs on the two regional dummy variables in the analysis remained the same for both years.

Given this regional pattern of association, it is not surprising to find that the feminization of high school enrollments was negatively associated with urbanization, employment in "trade" occupations (which included clerical and most other service employment, and excluded domestic employment), and the feminization of teaching. Each of these features of states in the late nineteenth century was most evident in the Northeast, where the feminization of high school enrollments had proceeded the least. However slight the state-to-state variation in this factor may have been, the general pattern of association evident in Table 2.3 is consistent with the regional differences reported earlier.

This pattern of variation is *not* consistent, on the other hand, with the hypothesis that feminization occurred because women were drawn into high school in order to get jobs as teachers or as clerical workers—or even because women went to school in the urban Northeast, where school systems were most advanced and high schools most plentiful. Rather, feminization was most pronounced in those areas of the country which were not highly urbanized, where employment in "trade" was relatively low, and where feminization of the teaching force had not occurred as yet. In short, the feminization of high schools was not caused by the growth of female employment in this period, not even the feminization of teaching. Whatever else women went to school for in the late nineteenth century, this analysis indicates that the preponderance of women in American high schools at that time probably was not a function of changes in women's work.[26]

While the various employment variables in Table 2.3 were insignificant, the most important factor was a measure of education. The remaining two variables in the table are those associated with the general level of high school enrollments in each state. Unlike the feminization variable, these are absolute rates—the percentage of all boys and girls age fifteen to nineteen (all school-aged boys and girls in 1870) in high school. Of course, feminization itself was a function of both these rates, as there was a higher enrollment rate among girls than among boys throughout this period. The question, however, is which overall enrollment rate was *more* strongly associated with feminization? The low coefficients on the female high school enrollment rate variables in both columns suggests that feminization was generally *not* associated with high levels of female high school participation. The strongest association in both columns, on the other hand, was between feminization and *male* high school enrollments. The sign on the male enrollment variable in both 1870 and 1890 was negative, as expected, but the relative strength of this variable's association with feminization indicates that the process of feminization in American high schools was the consequence of male—as well as female—behavior. Simply put, female enrollments were higher than male enrollments almost everywhere, but the gap was greatest in those parts of the country where relatively few boys enrolled in high school.

Nineteenth-century educators had long lamented what they felt was a tendency of boys to leave school too early—earlier than girls, for instance—in order to pursue other opportunities or earn a living. The problem of feminization as they saw it was not a matter of there being too many girls; rather, it was a question of there being too few boys. The analysis in Table 2.3 corroborates this view to an extent, but it raises a number of new questions as well.

Given the relationships identified above and what most scholars know about the development of American education in this period, it is not hard to guess which factors were associated with high levels of male enrollment in high schools. The 1890 male enrollment variables in Table 2.3 were strongly and positively related to urbanization (0.63), employment in "trade" occupations (0.58) and the feminization of teaching (0.77), which in turn was highly associated with the overall development of each state's school system. It was in the areas of the country where these factors were most evident, of course, that employment opportunities for boys probably would have been greatest. Yet both male enrollments and *relative* male enrollment (compared to female enrollment) was greatest in those areas of the country where employment in manufacturing or trade was highest. It was in those parts of the country where such opportunities were *least* evident that male high school enrollments were lowest, and where the feminization of high schools was most evident. Rather than dropping out of high school where job opportunities were most plentiful, in that case, high school boys remained in school longer in the urban Northeast and elsewhere where white-collar and "service" employment was greatest. They dropped out fastest (or did not enroll) in those areas where there were fewer opportunities for such work, perhaps because they could see little point in studying at length for a small number of commensurate positions.

In short, the general profile of male school participation in 1890 "matches" the general demand for educated labor suggested by urbanization and white collar employment patterns.[27] Female high school enrollment in 1890, on the other hand, was also associated with urbanization (0.48) and trade (0.47), but not as strongly. As indicated above, female high school enrollments did not drop as low as male enrollments in those parts of the country where urbanization and employment opportunities were not in evidence. It was in these circumstances that the variation in feminization, and male high school participation, was the greatest. Given the high association between male enrollment levels and urbanization and white-collar employment variables, however, the most important question may not be "why did boys leave high school," but "why did girls stay in?"

If the feminization of American high school enrollments was not related to urbanization and employment variables, neither was the graduation rate of women high school students in 1890. Table 2.4 presents correlation coefficients measuring the bivariate association between male and female graduation rates and various social, economic, and educational characteristics of states in 1890. While the male graduation rate was moderately (and significantly, at the 0.05 level) related to nearly every factor in the table, female graduation rates were not. The results of this analysis, in that case, correspond with the findings of the analysis of feminization above. With the exception of a moderate and positive but insignificant relationship with employment in "trade" occupations, female graduation rates were unrelated to the occupational and economic variables in the table.

Table 2.4   Correlates of Male and Female High School
Graduation Rates, 1890

SOCIAL, ECONOMIC, AND EDUCATIONAL VARIABLES	FEMALE HIGH SCHOOL GRADUATION RATE	MALE HIGH SCHOOL GRADUATION RATE
Urbanization	0.071	0.398
"Trade" employment	0.255	0.370
Percent of all teachers female	0.123	0.475
Per capita income	0.192	0.427
Female high school enrollment rate	0.198	0.511
Male high school enrollment rate	0.133	0.463
South	-0.071	-0.302
Northeast	0.123	0.331

N = 39 critical value: +/- 0.316.

Especially striking is the absence of any relationship between female high school graduation rates and the feminization of teaching. Contemporary schoolmen often commented on how female high school graduates were such an important source of new teachers for them. Apparently, the prospect of a teaching career (if women's short teaching tenures could indeed be referred to as careers) was not a strong incentive for women to remain in school in areas where the teaching force was highly feminized. Put another way, women in the latter nineteenth century appear to have remained in school long enough to graduate whether there were prospects of employment afterward or not.

This behavior was decidedly different from that of young men, who seem to have stayed in school longest in those parts of the country where a high school diploma could be of greatest value. As suggested in Table 2.4, male graduation rates were highest in the urban Northeast, where young men with high school diplomas could find white-collar jobs, or where they could go to college. This latter possibility may account for the positive and significant relationship between male graduation rates and per capita income. Graduation rates for young women, on the other hand, were unrelated to per capita income. They were even unrelated to the overall rate of female high school enrollment. Women everywhere, it seems, graduated from high schools at comparably high levels. Again, the question here seems to be one of *why* women would want to attend and graduate from secondary school in such comparatively large numbers in circumstances where their brothers clearly did not.

Both the analysis of feminization and the discussion of male and female graduation rates herein suggest that the development of women's secondary education in the latter nineteenth century (or at least prior to 1890) was largely unrelated to changes in women's work. Young women enrolled in high school, and graduated, at rates higher than boys everywhere, but the difference was greatest in those parts of the country where the boys had the least to gain from getting a secondary school education. The correlation between the percentage of high school graduates who were female in a state and the graduation rate of males was -0.39, and with male enrollment rates it was -0.31. The correlation with female graduation rate was only 0.23, and with female enrollment rates it was only -0.17. There was clearly a good deal more variation in male secondary graduation and enrollment rates across the United States in this period than there was in female rates—or at least more variation along the regional lines that reflected state-to-state differences in social and economic conditions.

Women went to school in proportionately greater numbers

where employment opportunities and urbanization were least evident. For these women, at least, secondary education probably did
not obtain meaning in career terms, at least not for careers outside of
becoming a good wife and mother. For them, and doubtless many
other young women as well, the high school may have been a part of
a larger preparation for life, an enlarged sphere of women's activities
that entailed advanced education as a means to more effective motherhood and nuptial compatibility. These women were not getting an
education for employment; they simply may have been trying to learn
all they could before taking on the awesome responsibilities of motherhood in the modern world. While the foregoing does not directly
indicate *why* women went to school in this period, it does point to
what they did *not* go to accomplish—and what their male classmates
appear to have been more interested in—that is, to get a job.

Female High School Attendance, 1890–1900

If there was little variation in the feminization of enrollments or the
graduation rates of female high school students from one part of the
country to another in this period, the opposite was true of overall
female enrollment rates. As indicated in Table 2.3, there were enormous differences in the development of school systems from one
region to the next, and corresponding variation in the extent of
teenage female school participation. Consequently, even if feminization and female graduation rates were generally unrelated to important social and economic contextual characteristics at this time, enrollment levels were associated with a wide range of such factors.
Moreover, since both feminization and female graduation rates were
unrelated to female high school enrollment levels (indeed, feminization may have been partly a function of male enrollments), it is possible that young women in this period did in fact attend high schools in
response to a number of particular social and economic conditions,
even if such conditions were unrelated to the *relative* enrollment rate
of young women (feminization) and the rate at which they graduated.

For this reason it is important to examine the absolute growth of
female high school enrollments in the latter nineteenth century to
round out this discussion of contextual factors associated with female
school participation. Indeed, given the difficulties in interpreting the
information in Tables 2.3 and 2.4, overall enrollment rates are probably the most direct and meaningful quantitative indicator of how
young women and their families felt about high school during this
period. Examination of female high school enrollments, in that case, is
an essential element in determining why young women attended

high schools in the closing decade of the nineteenth century.[28]

The method I use to analyze enrollments is multiple regression, which identifies the independent association of different factors with a given phenomenon, assuming that the factors in question are themselves generally unrelated.[29] The first step in conducting a multivariate analysis is to consider salient factors to be included in the discussion and ways in which they can be identified for purposes of statistical analysis. In this case, it is a matter of weighing contextual factors that may have been associated with overall female secondary enrollment levels. It is possible, for instance, that female employment in "trade" (particularly clerical) occupations or teaching may have been associated with high school enrollment rates for girls, even if they were not associated with the proportion of all students that were women or with female graduation rates. Other studies have suggested that teenage female enrollment rates were indeed associated with white-collar employment in certain contexts during this period. Among the independent variables considered in this analysis, in that case, is the proportion of each state's teachers who were female, a measure of the opportunities for women to find employment as teachers. Overall employment in "trade" occupations, which included clerical and sales employment for women, has been included as an independent variable as well.[30]

These variables, together with the other factors in the analysis, provide a measure of the institutional and economic and cultural context that may have affected the growth of female secondary school participation in these years. They have been selected to capture the effects of interstate differences in the development of school systems, overall income levels and degrees of social development, and the general employment prospects of educated women. The separation of these different *types* of factors is essential to identifying just which aspects of the social and economic context of a state were associated with high rates of female high school enrollment.

The results of a multivariate analysis of these variables are presented in Tables 2.5 and 2.6. Because of the generally low level of economic and educational development in the South in this period, eleven states of the deep South have been excluded from this discussion. While this restricts the analysis to a narrower range of contexts, it also reduces the extent of variation in certain key variables—thus avoiding possible distortions in the analysis caused by the inclusion of southern states (for the results of a parallel analysis using a full thirty-nine–state national sample, see the Statistical Appendix). Table 2.5 is a correlation matrix, which shows the manner in which the various factors described above are interrelated. Except for the two 1900 enrollment variables, all other elements of the analysis represent different characteristics of states in 1890.

Table 2.5   Correlation Matrix—28 States, Excluding the South

	(1)	(2)	(3)	(4)	(5)	(6)	(7)
1900 Female high school enrollment (1)	***						
1900 Male high school enrollment (2)	0.91	***					
"Trade" employment (3)	0.20	0.12	***				
Urbanization (4)	0.14	0.24	0.69	***			
Income (log) (5)	0.49	0.48	0.67	0.52	***		
Percent of all teachers female (6)	0.63	0.73	0.22	0.45	0.41	***	
Teacher-student ratio (7)	0.45	0.51	-0.18	0.01	-0.14	0.46	***
1890 Female high school enrollment	0.82	0.87	-0.08	0.17	0.26	0.72	0.51
Northeast	0.19	0.38	0.20	0.59	0.21	0.61	0.34

Critical value = +/- .37.

As expected, female high school enrollment rates for 1900 were highly associated with enrollment rates in 1890. Both enrollment variables were strongly associated with the feminization of teaching in 1890. And female enrollment in 1900 was also strongly associated with the general level of income ten years earlier. Predictably, both measures of enrollment were positively associated with the general level of development in state school systems (expressed in the teacher-student ratio). And the two general measures of social and economic development (urbanization and per capita income) were both positively associated with "trade" employment. As is often the case when using aggregate data defined at this level, variables measuring different dimensions of social and economic development (including education) are highly associated. In general, however, excluding the states of the Deep South reduces the degree of interassociation among these variables, making it somewhat easier to distinguish the relationship of each one to the growth of female high school enrollments in the last decade of the nineteenth century.[31]

Table 2.6 presents the results of a regression with female enrollments in 1900 as the dependent variable. Enrollments in 1890 have been included as an independent variable, in order to control for the level of enrollment in each state ten years earlier. The coefficients on the remaining elements of the equation, in that case, can be interpreted as representing their association with the *growth* of female enrollments in the last decade of the century.

Table 2.6   Regression Analysis of Female School Enrollment
—28 States, Excluding the South

INDEPENDENT VARIABLES	B	STANDARD ERROR	PROBABILITY	PARTIAL R²
1890 Enrollment	1.3700	0.2395	0.00001	0.6090
Urbanization	-0.0873	0.0283	0.00561	0.3119
Income (log)	0.0782	0.0398	0.06304	0.1550
"Trade" employment	0.5782	0.2097	0.01182	0.2657
Teacher-student ratio	0.7582	0.4404	0.09983	0.1237
Percent of all teachers female	-0.0273	0.0634	0.67078	0.0088

Dependent Variable: female high school enrollment rates, 1900; N = 28; adjusted R^2 = .82

Constant = -0.1789; standard error of estimate 0.0193

Although there are signs of interaction between key variables in Table 2.6, a number of observations are possible. Surprisingly, the two most important factors in the regression, once the effect of prior enrollment levels was controlled, were urbanization and "trade" employment—two variables that were weakly associated with 1900 enrollment levels in the correlation matrix. The sign on the urbanization variable is negative, indicating that the growth of enrollments was slower in highly urbanized states than elsewhere, perhaps because of the large immigrant and working-class populations that characterized those parts of the country. All other factors fell to insignificance, even average per capita income and teacher-student ratio. These aspects of a state's social and economic environment were less highly associated with state-to-state differences in the growth of female secondary school enrollments than other factors.

The most striking result in this analysis, however, was the performance of the employment variables. The weakest element was the 1890 level of feminization in each state's teaching force, a finding that corroborates the earlier suggestion that the prospect of employment as a teacher probably was not an important incentive for many young women to attend high school in this period. But the promise of other types of employment may have boosted enrollments in some parts of the country. The strength of the "trade" employment variable suggests that rising high school attendance among young women in the 1890s was related to the development of clerical work (and other forms of labor subsumed under the general "trade" category) as a peculiarly female branch of labor. This probably was *not* true of earlier decades, as female employment in clerical jobs was marginal prior to the 1890s.[32] But by the closing decade of the century, it seems, the changing profile of women's work exerted some influence on the growth of women's secondary education.

The regression results reported in Table 2.6 qualify the findings presented earlier regarding feminization of enrollments and female graduation rates. While there is little evidence of an employment effect on female secondary school participation before 1890, by the end of the nineteenth century, some young women may have enrolled in high schools in response to employment prospects in the rapidly growing field of clerical work. At least this seems to have been the case in certain parts of the country outside the South. As many contemporaries had claimed, the growth of women's education was indeed associated with important changes in women's work. But, as will be seen in chapter 4, the full impact of this change would not become evident in American high schools until after the turn of the century.

As noted above, the results of this analysis must be interpreted carefully. Even though there apparently was a substantial association between one type of employment context for women and the growth of enrollments, it is unlikely that such a relationship affected women in all parts of the country. The effect of the "trade" employment variable, after all, only accounted at most for a fourth of the variance in 1900 enrollment levels, and this was after eleven southern states were excluded from the analysis altogether. These results do not suggest that changes in women's work were the most important factor in the growth of female secondary education. Rather, the analysis reported in Table 2.6 indicates that the existence of certain types of employment opportunities may have contributed to the growth of secondary enrollments in this period. The effect of this factor was probably strongest in the urban Northeast and the West, where clerical employment opportunities for women were greatest. Of course, male enrollment levels were high in those parts of the country as well. This regional pattern of development probably accounts for the low association of employment variables and feminization. In certain contexts, however, it appears that female enrollments were indeed related to women's work.

All things considered, in that case, female high school attendance was largely unrelated to the question of work in the latter nineteenth century. Some girls may have gone to school to become a clerical worker, or to enhance their employability as a sales clerk or telephone operator, but many did not. And it is this larger group of women who probably did not see the high school as a form of vocational education which is most important to understanding the growth of female secondary enrollments in this period. If the association of high school enrollments with new forms of women's work struck contemporaries with such force, it was because it was new and unusual. For most women the high school seems to have remained a distinctively nonvocational type of education throughout the latter nineteenth century.

Why, then, did American women attend high schools in such large numbers between 1870 and 1900? Unlike their male cohorts, most do not appear to have enrolled in order to aid their working careers. Teaching, the most important occupation for educated women throughout this period, was not independently associated with any of the various measures of female enrollment employed in this ecological analysis. And although there is evidence of a relationship between the existence of other employment opportunities for women and the growth of enrollments, most young women probably remained unaffected by such trends. While some women attended high schools in this period to prepare themselves for some form of work, the majority apparently did not.

These findings, of course, are negative: they point to explanations apparently *not* associated with the rapid growth of female secondary schooling at this time. While findings such as these are important, they do not settle the issue at hand. Determining just which factors *were* associated with the rise of women's secondary education is a much more difficult task than identifying which ones were not, and probably is not possible with data of the sort utilized in the foregoing discussion. Ultimately, the why question is one of motivation, and for that, it is necessary to find evidence of what young women and their parents *thought* about schooling in this period. And that requires an altogether different discussion.

The Personal Record

If young women did not go to high school to get a job, why did they go? What drew them into these bastions of formal learning, and what impelled them to work so hard at their studies? Attending high school, after all, represented something of a departure from traditional female roles, particularly from the circumspect domesticity that had preoccupied earlier generations of American women. What were the motives that drew women into school at this time, and how does one discover them?

The question of what people thought about something, or the reason why they exhibited a given behavior (the question of motivation), has always been a particularly vexing problem for historians. Like detectives, historians must deduce motives from the evidence at hand; rarely do they have an opportunity to ask someone to explain their behavior.[33] Sometimes the questions have already been asked, of course, as in the case of the survey of superintendents on coeducation discussed earlier. In this instance, unfortunately, the evidence does not include the handy results of a poll asking young women why they went to high school. There is no direct way of knowing just what motivated middle-class girls in this period to attend school rather than stay at home, get a job, or do something else with their lives.

There are other ways, however, of discovering how young women felt about schooling and about many other aspects of their lives. It is possible to determine how these women thought by reading their diaries, letters, school papers and other personal documents that have been preserved for the past hundred years or so. Women's historians have made extensive use of these sources to comprehend the way in which women viewed themselves and their world in the nineteenth century.[34] For purposes of this study I have examined the diaries, letters, and other personal papers of some two dozen nineteenth-century girls in order to fathom the meaning which they assigned to education, and to high school in particular.[35]

My method in this part of the study is necessarily different from that employed in the statistical analyses above. Like an anthropologist, my goal here is to derive an explanation of female school participation by examining the manner in which education fit into the larger pattern of young women's lives in this period. I have tried to address this issue below by determining what schooling *meant* to teenage women in the latter nineteenth century. In this regard, my approach to this body of evidence is ethnographic in orientation, principally because the object is to discern the meaning of a given pattern of behavior. Therefore, in grasping the significance young women attached to school, it is important to begin with the themes they themselves emphasized. This entails reading their personal documents without anticipating the importance of one issue or another: to let these girls speak freely, in a sense, and for themselves. To assess the role schooling played in the lives of these women, moreover, I have tried—as much as is possible—to weigh everything they wrote, and to view the world in the way they saw it. In short, the best place to start this discussion is with the actual words these women used to describe their perceptions.[36] In doing this I hope to allow their collective vision of schooling to emerge.

As will be seen below, young women in the nineteenth century rarely addressed their educational goals or their general plans for life in their diaries and correspondence. They did, however, comment on a wide variety of issues which were of importance to them. By examining what these women both did and did not discuss in these personal statements, it is possible to refine the inferences about why they went to school made with the statistical data above. While the diaries and letters written by these women generally did not directly address the question of why they went to high school, this evidence can be used to answer questions that the statistical data cannot—such as what women thought about their schooling and the manner in which some of them felt it affected their status. Such sentiments can constitute important clues in determining what motivated women to attend secondary schools.

The School as a Social Milieu

Sociologists have long noted that schools serve both formal and informal functions in modern societies. At the same time that children learn to read, write, and add, they also encounter a distinctive social milieu that teaches them important lessons about acceptable behavior in civil society. Some of this is the byproduct of conscious efforts on the part of educators to impart civic virtue. But other parts of it, perhaps the largest portion, is created by the students themselves, as they relate to one another and begin to form associations that will carry them beyond their immediate families and into the larger world. This culture of peers is especially important for adolescents (a term that probably described many high school students in this period), as they are most immediately concerned with the transition to adulthood, and with learning all the cultural and social conventions that accompany adult status. In modern society this transitional period of learning through one's peers has come to be viewed as a critical step in the life course. For teenagers, in that case, the informal functions of the high school are often more important than its more formal objective of imparting academic knowledge and skills. For purposes of this discussion, it is useful to distinguish between the formal and informal functions of high school in order to better discern the importance which adolescent women assigned to their school experiences in the closing decades of the nineteenth century.[37]

Not surprisingly, the formal, academic side of high school life was not a major theme in most young women's personal documents at this time. For the most part, these women focused their attention on the informal side of schooling, that large element of institutional life that sociologists say contributes to the general process of social-ization. Socialization is as old as society itself, of course, and the themes that emerge from a reading of these personal papers revolve around issues that perennially have concerned young women about to enter the adult world. They wrote about their friends and family, about household responsibilities, about clothes and fashion, and—inevitably—about romance, whether real or prospective. Rarely did consideration of these matters entail discussion of school, except as a setting for a conversation, an observation about a friend or rival, or some incident worthy of preservation or reflection. For some girls, especially those who lived in smaller communities or who circulated in tightly knit groups of friends, the school was just another context in which they saw the same people they saw elsewhere. The social set-ting provided by the high school for these women was generally unexceptional. For others, however, it offered an alluring exposure to a larger field of potential friends and social contacts.

As in most secondary schools today, high school in the latter nineteenth-century society apparently entailed a good deal more than classroom exercises and home study. Students typically expressed more enthusiasm for the nonacademic side of school life than the daily regimen of schoolwork. Moreover, high schools in this period provided a rich array of extra curricular activities for interests such as these to find fulfillment. Many schools, for instance, sponsored after-school clubs for a wide range of purposes, from literary exercises to staging evening socials. In 1884 the superintendent of schools in Springfield, Illinois, noted the existence of a "Society for General Improvement," organized by the high school girls and directed by one of the women teachers. Meeting each month, the group heard reports on a variety of issues, including health, etiquette, and women's work. Similar groups were organized in other school dis-tricts.[38] Sometimes they met during school hours and were rather informal in organization. Writing about her duties in 1885, a woman high school teacher in Dayton, Ohio noted that in addition to teaching classes in history and physiology, "an hour each week was spent with the girls seated in my room in reading from and talking about the Vic-torian authors." Another female teacher from the same school report-ed that she reserved a block of time before recitations on Wednesdays for "newspaper work," a time when the girls in her class could report on and discuss anything they found of interest in recent newspaper articles. "Conversation on the topics is encouraged," she wrote, "questions freely asked, and, as far as possible answered by the girls" (though she added, "Partisan politics, crime and scandal, are, of course, forbidden topics."). Such activities were usually designed to promote social responsibility in students but provided a context in which they could develop other nonacademic interests.[39]

Given the sort of openness to dialogue and the expression of personal interests embodied in activities such as these, the nineteenth-century high school no doubt provided a fertile ground for the development of friendships among students and teachers. It is little wonder, in that case, that it was this social dimension of school life that was featured most prominently in the diaries, letters, and other personal documents of schoolgirls.

The diaries and letters of high school girls at this time are dotted with references to the many different social activities they participated in. Noting the difficulties of her studies at the high school in Ann Arbor, Michigan, in 1871, Alice Devin wrote a former teacher that her social life at the school kept her in good spirits. "Last week it consisted in going to the senior social and a lecture," Devin noted, adding that she "spent a pleasant evening at the former and an *exquisite* one at the latter," due largely to a "very entertaining" escort (emphasis in the original)[40] Eleven years later, Lois Wells reported having a "splendid" time staying at another girl's home to celebrate New Year's Eve. Such overnight excursions appear to have been fairly commonplace among nineteenth-century high school girls, a distant precursor of the mid-twentieth-century pajama party, and generally were given more attention in diaries and letters than the academic side of school life. Wells also became active in a local branch of the Women Christian Temperance Union, another popular extracurricular activity for high school women during this period.[41]

Sometimes these interests proved distracting. In the mid-1890s Nellie Clark, a student at the Central High School in Detroit, devoted more effort to composing a "toast" for her senior "class day" than she did for any of her academic courses. "My mind is so filled with other matters," she wrote in her diary, "that it is difficult to keep it on my lesson, when I study." When she was finally ready to graduate several months later, Clark expressed sadness. "It makes me sick," she wrote, "to think that in a great measure it means new friends. I could wish that the old associations need not be broken." For many young women, the social life of the school constituted a critical part of the enjoyment they derived from attending high school. And in an age when high school attendance was not in any way mandatory (indeed, it was downright unusual in many parts of the country), this may have been a major factor in the decision of many women to enroll in high school to begin with.[42]

For most of the women whose papers I read, the high school comprised a rather self-contained social world. Not surprisingly, this miniature society gave some girls the opportunity to sharpen their fashion consciousness, much as high schools do today. In one letter Alice Devin noted that her female classmates "dress a great deal for school," an observation corroborated by a number of schoolmen in the latter nineteenth century. Of course, there was always the presence of boys in coeducational schools, which undoubtedly made many young women especially self-conscious about their appearance and demeanor. "I think as a general thing here that the gentlemen are more handsome than the ladies," Devin wrote upon arriving in Ann Arbor in 1870, "indeed, I am afraid that if I am not careful my head will be quite turned seeing so many."[43]

For the most part, however, high school girls in this period drew their most intimate friends from their female classmates and teachers. It was with these members of the school community, after all, that young women spent most of their time. "For five years we sat in the same seat at school," reminisced one woman about a close friend, "and Sarah and I were more fond of each other than of the other girls, perhaps because our families were intimate." It was not uncommon for such friendships forged in high school to extend well beyond graduation, as women remained in touch long after marriage, or after they had moved considerable distances from one another. Another woman recalled being a "lonely homesick girl" standing "forlorn in a boarding school parlor in Buffalo" when she first met Gayley Browne, a lifelong friend and correspondent. "She lovingly and silently put her arm around me," the woman wrote, and "our arms have been around each other ever since, even when the ocean was between us."[44]

Such sentiments may have been a part of what historian Carol Smith-Rosenberg has described as a nineteenth-century "female world of love and ritual," wherein women formed special networks of intimacy to compensate for the rigid formality that often prevailed in Victorian male-female relationships. Smith-Rosenberg has argued that cultivating relationships with female classmates often formed an important step in the lives of women in the nineteenth century, for it marked an extension of the female network they had grown up with in their families and communities. Although most of Smith-Rosenberg's research dealt with women in all-female schools, her illumination of the importance young women attached to these friendships is helpful to understanding the growth of female school participation in the age of the coeducational high school. Many young women may have attended secondary schools largely because of the friends they made there, along with the excitement of daily interaction with dozens of other middle-class peers of both sexes. As some scholars have suggested is the case today, for many of these young people the main attraction of the high school may have resided in the nonacademic aspects of school life.[45]

School Work and Women's Role

School was not all fun and games, of course. The foregoing raises the question of women's academic performance at this time. If high school girls were preoccupied with the informal dimensions of schooling, what of the formal or academic side of education? Put differently, if they were largely concerned with making friends, why did young women do so well in school? And if there were so few employment opportunities for women at this time, and teaching was not a compelling reason to attend high school for most women, why did they take school so seriously? Questions such as these defy ready explanation, and there is little direct evidence in the diaries and other personal papers to shed light on such issues. In carefully weighing what women did write about, however, it is possible to imagine a number of possible explanations.

One reason why teenage girls did well in school may have been the fact that in most high schools at this time there was considerable institutional pressure to succeed. The high school typically was an academically elite institution, notwithstanding democratic rhetoric about its social purposes, and students whose grades fell below a certain level often were expelled summarily. There was very little of what has come to be known recently as "social promotion" in nineteenth-century high schools.[46] Complaining about the strictness of her teachers (and the difficulty of preparing for approaching exams), Alice Devin reported that if a student's average "for the first four weeks in a class falls below 80 you are cautioned, and you are granted the privilege of making it up."[47]

Compulsion aside, however, there is a good deal of evidence that high school girls approached their academic responsibilities resolutely. Exams often were the object of trepidation in the letters and diaries that I read, even among good students. "That horrible examination is over," Vera Barton wrote to a friend at the end of a term in 1893, "and I passed in everything." The fact that her average was nearly 90 percent does not seem to have made her any less anxious about the ordeal. Similarly, Jeannette Gilder agonized over having to learn Latin, until she finally simply forced herself to memorize it. After that, she reported delight at the added knowledge of English she acquired from studying classical languages, declaring that she "loved Latin." Other girls reported similar experiences. Doing well in school was a challenge they accepted on its own terms, even if it was not particularly enjoyable at first. For many middle-class girls in this period, it may not have been acceptable to perform inadequately at anything they were expected to do. And even if young women were not preparing for a career in the conventional sense that their male classmates were, parents and teachers alike appear to have expected them to succeed at school.[48]

If nineteenth-century girls did well in school because of the expectations of adults, their teachers—and women teachers in particular—may have played an important role in motivating them to succeed. Many of the women whose diaries and letters I examined expressed a strong devotion to their female teachers. "I have at last received what I have been wanting ever since I came," Agnes Hankered excitedly wrote her parents from St. Mary's Academy in Monroe, Michigan in 1891, "a compliment from my music teacher." She also reported similar encouragement from her elocution teacher. Both of the teachers in question were women.[49] Other girls frequently inquired about particular teachers in their letters or reported news about their comings and goings to former classmates. Often over the course of a girl's high school career, close and even intimate relationships would develop with one or more of the school's women teachers. "I have such a feeling toward those who have been my teachers," wrote Nellie Clark just before she graduated, "as I can hardly describe. They have been more to me than all the books that I have studied." As was typical in other diaries and letters written by girls during this period, the only teachers mentioned by name in Clark's diary were women.[50]

For their part, women teachers seem to have taken great pleasure from their relationships with female students. Both of the teachers from Dayton whose extra curricular activities are described above declared that their time spent with the girls outside the normal academic routine constituted the most rewarding aspect of their jobs. Nellie Clark's favorite teacher, a Mrs. Bishop, urged her to go on to college in 1894, and confessed that she too was sad at graduation because "she didn't want the girls to leave her." Sentiments such as these could hardly have been lost on the young women who spent the better part of each week in class with these women during the school year.[51]

The reciprocal relationship of admiration and caring that many women high school teachers and their female students shared in this period must have been a powerful incentive for young women to perform well in school—and to aspire to become teachers themselves. No doubt, it also constituted yet another reason for those girls who started high school to remain enrolled until graduation. If women took high school more seriously than boys in this period, it may have been partly because they identified more strongly with their teachers than most boys could find possible. For many high school girls at this time, relationships with particular female teachers constituted a vital part of their lives. It was in these relationships that the school's social milieu and academic life intersected.

Apart from references to their friends and the various social activities they were involved in, however, few women appear to have commented on school in their diaries and other personal papers. Of course, in trying to understand the significance someone assigns to schooling (or anything else for that matter) it is often as important to consider what they have *not* said as it is to weigh the implications of their stated values.

By and large, for example, middle-class, school-aged women in the nineteenth century do not appear to have thought about their schooling in vocational terms. And most did not see themselves as radically altering the roles women played in society. While many of these women may have planned to use their secondary schooling to teach or obtain some other variety of employment for a time after graduation, such plans rarely found their way into the diaries, letters, and other personal documents I examined. In fact, there was little mention of work—or for that matter, life after school—at all. Even when taking classes with clear vocational implications, high school girls rarely pondered their future working careers very seriously in this period. "I practice at the typewriter now," Agnes Hankered wrote to her parents in 1891, "so you need not be surprised to receive a letter written on it in the near future." She went on to note that she even had been approached to do some typing for pay. But for the time being, she was simply content to learn about the typewriter and to perfect her skills. Declaring that she did not know whether the person intent on hiring her was in a hurry or not, she remarked, "It will not make a difference what she expects—I hardly think she'll get it very soon."[52]

Pecuniary considerations, it appears, generally ranked below educational ones in the eyes of many nineteenth-century high school girls. And schooling was valued for the preparation it afforded for life in general, more than as training for a particular line of work. "Since I have been to this school I have enjoyed study more than ever before," wrote Frances Quick from the Framingham Normal School in Mas-

sachusetts, "the really beautiful part of study has been brought
out—learning for its own sake and to impart it to others." Of course,
Frances Quick's reference to "imparting" knowledge may have been a
reference to teaching, but it may also have been an allusion to the
domestic feminist vision of every woman's natural role in socializing
her own children.[53] The most likely explanation is that it was both,
but teaching—like virtually every other type of work white middle-
class girls aspired to—generally was only a short interlude prior to
what most nineteenth-century women considered to be their primary
purpose in life: raising families of their own. Given this, it is little
wonder that vocational goals were discussed so infrequently in the
diaries and correspondence of these school girls. Whatever value the
academic side of high school promised young women, it would be of
greatest use not in the marketplace for educated labor but in rearing
their own children to be virtuous, intelligent and discriminating
members of the modern social order.[54]

Even when young women discussed the likely future roles of
American women in this period, they made few references to work
outside the home. Like the prominent women educators and schoolmen discussed in the previous chapter (not to mention participants in
the women's rights movement and domestic feminists everywhere),
many high school girls recognized that they lived in a period when
female roles were rapidly evolving. Perhaps the most commonplace
context for considering the implications of this process of change was
in essays and addresses that young women wrote for school. Although
these documents were not personal statements in the same sense as
diaries and letters (as they were often written for a public audience),
they did offer an occasion for young women to address issues broader
than those discussed in more personal documents, which generally
were reserved for matters of private or intimate communication.

Female students' essays and addresses, in that case, often reflected the ways in which high school girls thought about themselves and
their social role in a period when nearly everyone agreed that women
were practically at the center of social change. "Women of the present
day possess an agency which the ancient republics never knew,"
wrote Mary Bracken, a student at the Washington Female Seminary,
in an essay characteristic of this period. "The temple of science, so
long hidden from the eye of woman, is thrown open—its innermost
sanctuary is unveiled, and she is invited to enter." Bracken's radical
vision did not extend to new social roles for women, however.
Instead, she argued that since it was the influence of Christian religion that accounted for the advance of women's education, women
should primarily concern themselves with being devout and satisfy-

ing themselves with the nurturing and socializing roles with which they were traditionally associated.[55]

Likewise, in 1877 Roberta Hawn, a student at the Saginaw High School in Michigan, denounced the efforts of "philosophers" and "modern scholars" (all of them men) to denigrate women's education, a circumstance which she said women felt to be "vastly humiliating." Much of the problem, though, lay with women themselves according to Hawn. "Mental insipidity, which is only too prevalent among certain feminine ranks," she argued, was a consequence of young women being preoccupied with appearances and not with their intellectual and moral development. But her critique was delimited as well. Hawn rejected the argument that education unfitted women for domestic duties, noting that "the standard of womanly virtue" was not "measurably lowered" as a consequence of women's educational advances and the fact of some women entering "the learned professions." Even if education offered individual women the opportunity to consider careers, the final measure of its efficacy was the extent to which women retained those qualities of discrimination, gentleness and "conservative power" which defined their nurturing roles.[56]

In 1897 Rose Casassa, a student at the city normal school in San Francisco, wrote a particularly revealing essay entitled "Woman and Education." The aim of women's education, she declared, was "power," but she did not use the term power in its conventional political meaning. Instead, she argued that the goal of education was to show women "how much of might there is in intelligence, how much of strength in gentleness, how much of true joy in the pure affection and devotion to high purposes." In short, the purpose of women's education was to establish their moral power. "So long as life-begetting, life sustaining and life developing powers hold mightier sway over woman's soul than over man's," Casassa wrote in a rhetorical flourish, "so long will woman's heel crush the serpent's head and woman's arms bear salvation to the world." Whatever career advantages higher education might hold out to women, the principal benefit to be gained from attending high school (or college for that matter) was the ability to perform the socialization and nurturing roles that women had always played, though perhaps on a larger scale than in earlier times.[57]

Rather than allowing women to assume new roles, women's education in the nineteenth century was often seen by women themselves as better enabling them to perform their traditional functions. The ideology of domestic feminism, it appears, continued to dominate the thinking of women in high schools throughout this period. And the principal vocation for which most young women prepared themselves was motherhood.

If high school girls made few references to vocational purposes in school themselves in this period, so did their parents. Examining letters written to daughters at school also reveals infrequent mention of what in fact these educated women would do after graduation. Most parents, it appears, did not see the education of their daughters in vocational terms. Rather, schooling was seen as a type of spiritual investment, something that young women enjoyed and would help them to lead happier, more fulfilling lives, but not an investment that would later bring a material return. "I want you my dear child to have the advantage of school and music lesson," wrote Josiah Little-field to his daughter Ellen in 1887, "it is a delight to me to have you love and to get such things as will make you truly happy." Littlefield went on to advise his daughter against becoming preoccupied with the "foolishness of fashion" or coveting material possessions. Although Ellen eventually enrolled in the University of Michigan and worked for a time as a teacher, her father never discussed her school-ing in vocational terms in his surviving correspondence with her.[58]

In a similar spirit, in 1889 Edwin Phelps lamented the fact that his daughters seldom wrote him when he was away on business. "(I) sup-pose they have so much running and company they have no time to think of their poor father," he wrote, "off here working that they may have a good education and every comfort." Schooling, he felt, was something to be enjoyed, a luxury rather than a necessary step in his daughters' maturation. Yet he also felt that the expense of educating his girls would help them to lead better lives. "The time may come," he continued, "when they will understand how much they owe their par-ents and will do all they can to cheer our declining years." Phelps did not intend to get material support from his daughters as much as he wanted to draw solace from their own happiness and their loyalty to the family. In this regard providing education for one's daughters was assurance that they would lead happier, more fulfilling lives, making their parents' lives more complete at the same time.[59]

If the socially prescribed vocation for young women in this peri-od was motherhood, few middle-class parents wanted their daugh-ters to take careers that might interfere with that end. Schooling, in that case, was one means of parents seeing that their daughters had happy childhoods, while assuring themselves that their girls eventu-ally would be good mothers. It was both a matter of consumption (it was fun for most girls) and investment, though not the kind of invest-ment that guaranteed a material return. Rather, parents of high school girls in this period simply may have gotten peace of mind, feeling that they were contributing to the well-being of their daughters and to future generations. By and large, they appear to have accepted the ideology of domestic feminism, particularly the argument that educated women made better wives and mothers.

Why then did white middle-class American women attend high school in the latter nineteenth century? Perhaps the most direct answer to that question, judging from the diaries, letters, and other personal documents I examined for this study, is that they genuinely enjoyed it. For many girls the high school presented an alluring cycle of social functions and an opportunity to mingle with dozens of young women and men from generally the same backgrounds. In Sommerville, Reed Ueda found that young women were considerably more involved in extra curricular activities than boys.[60] High school was a place where close friendships were forged, where inspiring teachers were encountered, and possibly where a future spouse was to be found. It presented an opportunity to escape the narrow definition of domesticity, which had constrained the lives of previous generations of women, but in a manner that posed little threat to the Victorian sensibilities of middle-class parents.

Of course, there was always the question of learning, not for material advancement or professional career, but for intellectual growth and pleasure. At the same time that the high school offered access to skills and knowledge that might have allowed women to aspire to new social roles, the ideology of domestic feminism focused their attention on the improvement of existing ones. Consequently, most young women who attended high school in this period seem to have studied simply to improve themselves. "Schoolwork is as usual today," Nellie Clark wrote in her diary, "I like it better each day and I think that I learn so much that is valuable for everyday life and thought."[61] Like other female high school students in this period, Clark never discussed her plans for work after her education was finished. Neither the students themselves nor their parents appear to have been concerned about what high school girls would do after graduation. In an age when only 10 or 15 percent of all teenage women attended high schools nationally, and few women aspired to anything more than raising their own families, secondary education for women had few vocational purposes.

Domestic feminist ideology, of course, held that educated women made better wives and mothers, a proposition many young women and parents appear to have accepted. High schools did not create a revolutionary new outlook in young women. But if the girls themselves had not wanted to attend high school, whatever their reasons, it is doubtful that enrollments would have grown as rapidly as they did. In the last analysis, young women in the nineteenth century may have gone to high school because it offered them an opportunity to step outside the narrow domestic setting they knew in their parents' households and their immediate neighborhoods. Most of them had entered the stage of life that Erik Erikson has called "identity versus role confusion," in which they were "primarily concerned with what they appear to be in the eyes of others," and looking ahead to adulthood.[62] For these women, most of whom could not realistically consider working as teenagers, the school provided an opportunity to creat their own identity in a context broader than that afforded by their families. To many of them, the high school was indeed a "people's college," a window to the more cosmopolitan world of scholarship, peer groups, and social responsibility. Given this, it is possible that the high school represented something of a new step in the maturation of middle-class women, as David Allmendinger and other historians have suggested. It was a setting where young women could view a wider field of experiences before setting about on their adult lives, allowing them a broader range of options than those afforded by their immediate families.[63]

All things considered, it is little wonder that female enrollments grew between 1870 and 1900, independently of changes in women's work or other aspects of social and economic development. Given what young women themselves had to say about the matter, it appears that going to high school was part and parcel of the general broadening of women's lives that occurred at this time. Regardless of the generally conservative outlook many women cultivated in school, the very fact that they attended was significant. The growing tendency of women to pursue higher education—in all its various forms—would eventually lead to yet other changes in their lives.

Conclusion: Stepping into a Larger World

Young women attended American high schools in the nineteenth century for a variety of reasons. For most of them, however, it was not to get a job. In some large cities many may have aspired to jobs as teachers, and in certain parts of the country, some may have wanted to find employment as secretaries and typists, especially after 1890. But the foregoing discussion of both statistical and documentary evidence suggests that the expansion of female secondary school participation probably would have occurred even if these job opportunities had not existed. Most native, middle-class girls, it seems, attended high school in order to better prepare themselves for matrimony and the rapidly growing demands of nurturing a family in the modern industrial social order. In this regard, the liberating potential of gender equity in secondary schooling probably did not realize its full potential. But this does not seem to have affected the high school's popularity. (Indeed, it may account for it!) Judging from the accounts left in diaries and letters, many (maybe most) women genuinely enjoyed high school as well. It was an institution that mediated the transition to adult roles and may have given them a new sense of control over their futures. They appear to have viewed the high school as an opportunity to learn, to cultivate their social skills, meet new friends, and to embark upon the long developmental journey that would take them away from their immediate families. In this regard, the high school constituted an important stage in these women's lives, but it also produced few fundamental changes. Perhaps because the vocational potential of female secondary education was not yet apparent, most nineteenth-century women could not see a realistic or attractive alternative to the domestic roles they grew up with.

Education and women's work (in terms of paid labor), it seems, were only remotely associated in the closing decades of the nineteenth century. In this regard, a variety of constraints worked to delimit the liberating power of female schooling, whether by excluding certain groups of women or influencing the vision of those who enrolled. It would take a dramatic set of changes in women's work, and a correspondingly rapid change in the curricular orientation of high schools, to bring these disparate aspects of women's lives together.

Chapter Three

Women at Work:
Female Labor Force Participation and Education,
1890–1930

In the years around 1900, the pace of change in women's lives seems to have quickened. Schooling was only one area of new opportunity that became available to them at this time, and it was hardly the most important. A profound transformation reshaped women's work as well, particularly for young white middle-class women—the very group that attended the nation's high schools in such large numbers. The number of women working in the wage economy increased dramatically between 1890 and 1930, and the types of work they performed also changed. These years witnessed a rapid expansion of clerical employment for women, along with the rise of new female professions and new opportunities for women as saleswomen, as telephone operators, and in a host of other service occupations. Many of these jobs required schooling, even if only to alphabetize records or to speak properly, and together, they dramatically changed the quality of women's work.

In the four decades following 1890 the number of women working at white-collar jobs grew from 15 to 40 percent of the female labor force. Of course, changes in the extent and character of female labor force participation varied significantly from one region of the country to the next. And the shift from manual to white-collar work affected different groups of working women differently. But the cumulative effect of all these events was the emergence of a more highly skilled and better educated female labor force.[1]

Like developments in women's education in earlier decades, these changes were not revolutionary, but they did present a variety

91

of new opportunities for women. Despite their rapid pace, and a widening sphere of activity for women in social and political affairs, changes in female employment had limited effect on women's traditional roles. Most working women at the turn of the century were quite young by today's standards; for many of them a working career began in their middle to late teens and lasted only four to six years. Work typically was an interlude between school and marriage, undertaken to augment family income or to offer a wider field of experience before meeting a prospective marriage partner. Consequently, the expansion of female employment did not mean that most women enjoyed a higher degree of financial independence in this period. For many women work was merely a prelude to their long-term career, that of wife and mother. Yet these changes in employment did represent a wider range of options for women and offered an alternative to traditional female roles to those who sought it—whatever the reason.

The impact of changes in women's work was delimited by yet other factors in this period, however. Because so many of the new jobs available to women required at least some secondary education, women who did not possess requisite training were largely excluded from these new fields of employment. Generally, the start of a young woman's working career meant that she was through with school. Few women (or men for that matter) appear to have continued school while working. The decision to leave school, in that case, may have determined the type of work a young woman could aspire to. The point at which women from different social and economic groups left school in order to work varied a great deal. Indeed, the fact that certain groups of women were largely excluded from secondary education, and hence, the opportunity to compete for the newly emerging female white-collar jobs, resulted in a sharp division of labor between women from different backgrounds.

Forces of opportunity and constraint, in that case, both operated in women's work during this period of rapid change. In this chapter I examine changing patterns of female labor force participation and consider their relationship to patterns of variation in school enrollment at this time. Much of the discussion which follows, accordingly, is statistical, and concerns the age structure of female labor force participation. Of particular interest is the transition from school to work. I use aggregate data on school-leaving and labor force entry to identify conditions under which women left school in order to work. In this fashion it is possible to see how changes in work and education were connected, and how they benefited certain groups of women and not others.

In the end it appears that white native-born (and largely middle-class) women benefited most from the growth of female employment in this period, the same group that exhibited the highest rates of school participation. Most of the growth in female labor force participation was the consequence of women working in new and rapidly growing occupations, particularly the battery of jobs generally classified as clerical work. A number of recent studies, most of them by historians of women, have made it possible to identify the relationship between women's education and these new positions at the turn of the century. While it is not clear that most of these jobs required an especially high level of proficiency in writing or other academic skills, employers appear to have preferred women with at least some high school–level education to hire for such positions. In general these jobs offered better working conditions and higher pay than most other kinds of work women could find in this period and consequently proved quite attractive to young middle-class women wondering what they should do after leaving high school. The development of female secondary education, in that case, helped prepare some women for a new set of working experiences, which many of them found to be quite appealing—at least for a time. The movement of large numbers of women into clerical work and other nonmanual occupations probably comprised the most important *direct* effect that education had on women's work in this period.[2]

The Changing Shape of Women's Work, 1890–1930

As indicated above, the forty years following 1890 witnessed considerable growth in labor force participation among American women. Although at no single point in time did most women work outside of their homes, the overall proportion of women working grew nearly 33 percent. Table 3.1 presents data on female labor force participation rates in 1900 and 1920. At the start of the third decade of the twentieth century, nearly one in four women were at work. This alone is important, of course, but if the age structure of the female labor force is considered, the increase is even more impressive. Because most working women were quite young and left the labor force after a relatively short time, many more women had acquired work experience than were employed at any one time. By the 1920s roughly half the nation's female population age 20 and older had worked for a wage at some point in their lives, most of them between the ages of fifteen and twenty-five. In a sharp departure from the ideal of domesticity promoted in the nineteenth-century cult of "true" womanhood, American women were leaving the home in order to work—even if only for a while—in larger numbers each decade.[3]

Table 3.1   Female Nonagricultural Labor Force Participation Rates,
                  Age 16 and Over, for 1900 and 1920

	1900	1920
Female labor force participation rate	20.6%	24.0%
Proportion of entire labor force female	17.7%	20.2%

Source: Joseph Hill, *Women in Gainful Occupations* (Washington, DC: Government Printing Office, 1929) pp. 52 and 232.

Changes in women's work, however, entailed more than simple growth. Among the period's most striking developments was the rapid expansion of clerical and professional jobs for women. Data on the distribution of women in various occupational categories are presented in Table 3.2. Women employed in professional and clerical occupations increased from 13 percent to over 35 percent of the nonagricultural female labor force between 1890 and 1930. On the other hand, women working in the chief manual labor categories, manufacturing and domestic employment, dropped from 83 percent to 54 percent of the female nonfarm workforce at the same time. Overall, in that case, there was a shift from manual to white-collar labor in women's work. But this change was directly related to the growth in female labor force participation. Changes in the distribution of women between different occupational categories did not occur because women were leaving factory and domestic service jobs to work in offices and schools. As Elyce Rotella and other historians of this process have noted, the growth of female white-collar employment in this period was the consequence of greater numbers of women moving into the labor force, not the result of working women shifting jobs. The number of women employed in manufacturing also increased, even though the proportion of all working women employed in manufacturing jobs declined precipitously. Most of the overall growth in female labor force participation, in that case, was the result of new groups of women entering the work force to take white-collar jobs. The nature of women's paid employment was changing at the turn of the century, and women who in an earlier decade might not have entered the labor force at all went to work in response to the development of an entirely new world of female employment. Between the nineteenth century and the twentieth, the popular image of the working girl shifted from a factory or shop setting to an office.[4]

Table 3.2   Occupational Distribution of Female Workers in 1890,
1910, and 1930

OCCUPATIONAL CATEGORY	1890	1910	1930
Agriculture	17.3%	22.4%	8.5%
Manufacturing	26.2%	22.5%	17.5%
Domestic Service	42.6%	31.3%	29.6%
Trade	5.8%	5.9%	9.0%
Professional	7.9%	9.1%	14.2%
Clerical*	–	7.3%	18.5%

*Clerical was included under "Trade" in 1890.

Source: U. S. Census, *Thirteenth Census of the United States Taken in the Year 1910*, vol 4, Occupation Statistics (Washington, DC, 1914) Table 15; *idem, Fifteenth Census of the United States, 1930*, vol 5, General Report on Occupations (Washington, DC: Government Printing Office, 1933) pp. 40–49.

A variety of factors accounted for the movement of women into clerical work. Probably the most important simply was the rapid growth of clerical positions, caused by the expansion of large-scale business enterprises (from steel and railway companies to mail order catalogues) and governmental agencies in this period. With the growth of big business and the advent of government regulation in many spheres of life, recordkeeping and correspondence became critical dimensions of American enterprise. Consequently, demand for competent and personable clerical workers increased dramatically in the opening decades of the twentieth century. As Margery Davies has suggested, the *feminization* of clerical work was largely the result of large numbers of literate women being available at the very time that these jobs began to appear. Technical advances helped as well, particularly the invention of the typewriter, which seemingly reduced many clerical jobs to a narrow range of technical skills deemed appropriately feminine (typing, for instance, was often compared to piano playing). Both supply and demand factors, in that case, accounted for the movement of women into clerical jobs in the opening decades of the twentieth century.

With the appearance of large numbers of women in clerical positions, and the nearly absolute feminization of several categories of clerical work by 1920, a new division of labor became manifest in American businesses. Long a recognized starting point for young men interested in management careers, clerical jobs became routinized and carefully regulated, offering little opportunity for promotion. Just the same, the prestige of working in an office—where hours were relatively short, pay was comparatively high, and one could rub shoulders with managers—proved appealing to many women. While clerical work became less inviting to men, in that case, it remained an attractive job prospect for many young women throughout the opening decades of the twentieth century.[5]

While the movement of women into white-collar jobs represented a major expansion of the kinds of work available to women in this period, it did little to change the sharp sexual division of labor in American public life. Women found themselves restricted to certain types of clerical jobs (clerks, typists, and secretaries), while others were often reserved for men (such as bookkeeping). Similarly, the overwhelming majority of women teachers worked in elementary schools, while half of all secondary teachers and the majority of educational administrators were men. The concentration of women in each of these positions generally exceeded 80 percent throughout this period. As a number of scholars have noted, it appears that these occupations became "typed" as women's work fairly early in their development and, consequently, drew many more women than men. And once they became identified as largely female occupations, these positions generally were accorded lower prestige—and assigned less remuneration—than other jobs within the same fields (such as bookkeeping or high school teaching). Even though the appearance of white-collar jobs was an important new development in female labor force participation, in that case, it did little to augment the social and economic status of working women—other than opening a *relatively* well-paying and comfortable new line of women's work.[6]

Other changes also marked the development of women's work in this period. As indicated earlier, most working women were quite young. Table 3.3 presents aggregate data on the labor force participation rates of women in different age groups for 1890 and 1930. In both years women age 16 to 24 registered the highest rates of labor force participation. Most women's working careers were relatively short. Accordingly, female labor force participation throughout this period peaked in the 16-to-24 age range, and dropped as women in older age categories left the labor force. Examining the two columns in Table 3.3, however, important differences between the age structure of female labor force participation in 1890 and 1930 are evident. In 1930, for instance, girls under fifteen were employed at much lower rates than in 1890. This was probably a reflection of improved teenage school-going rates in most parts of the country. Between 1890 and 1930 the proportion of all adolescents aged 15 to 19 enrolled in school increased from less than 40 percent to almost 60 percent.[7]

Table 3.3   Female Nonagricultural Labor Force Participation Rate by Age for 1890 and 1930

AGE GROUP	1890	1930
10–15	5.57%	1.13%
16—24	27.04%	35.15%
25–44	11.86%	23.92%
Over 45	7.64%	14.12%

Sources: U.S. Census, Occupations at the Twelfth Census (Washington, DC: Government Printing Office, 1904) Table 38; *idem, Fifteenth Census of the United States, 1930,* General Report on Occupations, pp. 118–137.

On the other hand, a greater proportion of all high school–aged women in 1930 entered the labor force than in 1890. As shown below, this may have been associated with the shift to female employment in white-collar occupations, which generally required at least some secondary education. By the end of this period the highest rates of labor force participation were registered by women in their late teens and early twenties. Over a third of all high school and college-age women (those 16 to 24) in 1930 were at work, an indication that employment had become an important aspect of women's lives as they made the difficult transition from adolescence to adulthood.

Changes in women's work during this time did not only affect younger women, of course. The most striking difference between the two columns in Table 3.3 concerns the labor force participation rates of women age 25 and over. Between 1890 and 1930 the proportion of women age 25 to 44 at work more than doubled. At the same time, the labor force participation rate of women over 45 increased by 85 percent. As a result the median age for working women was considerably higher in 1930 than it had been in 1890. Judging from the figures given in Table 3.3, this seems to have been only partly a consequence of changing patterns of school participation for younger women. Older women appear to have remained in the labor force for longer periods of time as well. While women were entering a variety of new occupations, in that case, they also were working at progressively older ages.

By the fourth decade of the twentieth century, the female labor force was characterized by a wider diversity of job categories and was more demographically representative of the whole female population than it had been in the latter nineteenth century. If patterns of labor force participation are in any way a reliable indicator of attitudes, the ideology of domesticity was clearly in retreat.[8]

Given these general trends, there can be little doubt that women's work underwent an important transformation in the opening decades of the twentieth century. Moreover, it is easy to see a number of points where the rise of female labor force participation was linked to women's education. As noted earlier, for instance, the general decline in employment for girls under 15 between 1890 and 1930 reflected the growth of school participation. And the growth of white-collar employment, the principal source of expansion in women's work, caused employers to seek workers with at least a little secondary education or its equivalent. As other historians have noted, the changing skill requirements for women's work corresponded well with the general expansion of teenage enrollment levels across the period in question.[9]

School-Leaving and Labor Force Participation: Regional Differences

The effect of changes in women's work and education varied from one part of the country to another—largely because of the rather sharp regional division of labor that characterized the American economy at this time. Women in different parts of the country in this period generally performed different types of work. Regional patterns of economic development accounted for these differences, and at the turn of the century, there was wide variation on this score from one part of the country to another. Tables 3.4 and 3.5 present data on the regional occupational distributions of American women in 1890 and 1930. The opportunities that new fields of employment represented varied significantly from one area to another.[10]

No one region, of course, monopolized any particular line of employment, but each part of the country was characterized by a distinctive mix of occupational opportunities for women. In the Northeast, for instance, more women in this period were employed in manufacturing than any other line of work. Women in New England and the Middle Atlantic states worked in countless factories and shops, and often in their own homes, spinning cloth, sewing garments, rolling cigars, or assembling artificial flowers. This pattern of female employment was consistent with the region's overall employment profile. Just as the Northeast was the center of American manufacturing generally, it was also the center of manufacturing employment for women in this period.[11]

Table 3.4   Industrial Distribution of Female Workers by Region for 1890

REGION	AGRI-CULTURE	MANU-FACTURING	DOMESTIC	TRADE	PROFES-SIONAL
North Atlantic	1.5%	42.6%	40.3%	8.1%	7.5%
South Central	48.9%	8.1%	37.3%	1.6%	4.1%
West	5.6%	24.3%	48.4%	7.6%	14.1%
U.S. Total	17.4%	26.24%	42.6%	5.8%	7.9%

Source: U.S. Census, *Compendium 1890*, Part 3 (Washington, DC: Government Printing Office, 1897) Table 75.

Table 3.5   Industrial Distribution of Female Workers by Region for 1930

REGION	AGRI-CULTURE	MANU-FACTURING	DOMESTIC	TRADE	PROFESS-IONAL	CLERI-CAL
Middle Atlantic	0.6%	23.5%	26.6%	8.8%	13.4%	23.9%
East South Central	35.4%	9.9%	31.0%	5.2%	9.5%	7.5%
Pacific	2.5%	10.4%	28.6%	14.1%	18.7%	22.3%
U.S. Total	8.5%	17.5%	29.6%	9.0%	14.2%	18.5%

Source: U.S. Census, *Fifteenth Census of the United States, 1930*, General Report on Occupations, p. 61.

In the South, on the other hand, most nonagriculturally employed women in 1890 were working as domestic servants. Fewer than 10 percent of the female labor force was employed in manufacturing. The South, of course, was dominated by an agricultural economy throughout this period, and economic development occurred slowly there. The availability of large numbers of women from poor families, most of them black, made domestic service employment especially important—at least in quantitative terms—in southern cities at this time.[12]

In the western states there was a considerably more balanced pattern of female labor force participation. While domestic service employment was also the largest single category of female employment in the West in 1890, a quarter of all working women were employed in manufacturing. Perhaps the most striking feature of female employment in the West, however, was the relatively large number of women working in white-collar jobs. The proportion of women workers employed in professional occupations in the West was nearly twice the national average in 1890, and in 1930 a higher proportion of women worked in white-collar (clerical and professional) jobs there than in any other region.[13]

Because of regional differences in economic development, in that case, women in these parts of the country found themselves situated in different kinds of labor markets. These differences were related to teenage school enrollment patterns and appear to have been associated with regional variation in the ages at which women started work. The result of these relationships was clearly defined regional patterns in the age structures of female enrollment and labor force participation. Figures 3.1, 3.2, and 3.3 present age profiles for women in school and at work in each of these regions in 1910. Regional occupational structures, it appears, were associated with distinctive patterns of school-leaving and labor force entry.

In the Northeast (Figure 3.1), for example, school enrollment rates dropped sharply between the ages of 12 and 18, as young women left school in large numbers. At the same time, female labor force participation rates climbed sharply for teenage women in the Northeast, particularly between the ages of 14 and 18. This was probably due to the highly developed industrial economy of the region, which required large numbers of unskilled or semiskilled women to work in factories. Indeed, the age profile of working women in the Northeast closely matches that of women employed in manufacturing throughout this period. Public school systems were highly developed in this part of the country, of course, and compulsory attendance laws undoubtedly prevented many teenagers from starting work even sooner. The existence of these laws, and school systems concerned with their enforcement, may account for the acceleration in labor force entry evident after age 14 in Figure 3.1. Even so, by age 18 female school participation in the Northeast was lower than in any other major region of the country, and labor force participation was higher. Because of the importance of manufacturing employment in the Northeast, I have decided to describe this pattern as an *industrial* profile of school-leaving and labor force entry.[14]

In the South, not suprisingly, there was an entirely different pattern of school participation and labor force entry among young women. As indicated in Figure 3.2, women left school at a somewhat slower pace there between the ages of 12 and 18 than they did in the Northeast. Even though a considerably smaller proportion of southern women were enrolled in school at age 12 than in other regions, a

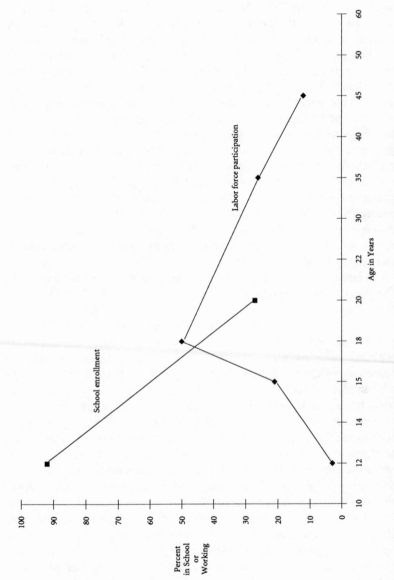

Figure 3.1 Age Structure of Women's Schooling and Work for the Middle Atlantic States in 1920

proportionally greater number of eighteen-year-olds were enrolled in school there than in the urban-industrial Northeast. This does not mean, of course, that these young women were attending high schools. As indicated in chapter 2, secondary school enrollments in the South were quite low in this period. Rather, it appears that many children in southern states attended common schools, particularly in rural settings, well beyond the age range customarily associated with school-leaving elsewhere. At the same time, however, young women in the South also exhibited unusually high rates of labor force participation. This probably was due in part to the seasonal quality of employment in the region's agricultural economy. As I have noted elsewhere, southern school terms were notoriously short in this period, particularly in rural areas, and well-suited to local demand for extra hands during peak periods of work (such as during the summer and fall). Many young women in the South, in that case, appear to have attended school and worked at the same time. This probably occurred less often in the cities than in the countryside, but even in southern cities school terms were often shorter than in other parts of the country, and it was possible to combine work and school more easily than elsewhere.

The ability of young women in the South to combine work and school may have hinged on the *type* of work available there. As noted above, most southern women worked in the countryside, where a seasonal production cycle allowed for alternating periods of work and school in any given year. Similar patterns of work may have existed in southern cities as well. Domestic service, the largest category of women's work in southern cities throughout this period, was especially well-adapted to the needs of school-aged women who needed to work. It was possible, for instance, for a girl to work for a period as a domestic after school, or to switch from school to work and back again on a seasonal basis, simply because school terms were often short and the demand for domestic servants was high. For all of these reasons, the South presents unique regional profile of school-leaving and labor force entry in this period. Because, as John G. Richardson has argued, even urban school systems in the South were established with a rural perspective, it seems appropriate to label the overall pattern of teenage school participation and labor force entry in the southern states at this time an *agricultural* model of teenage female behavior.[15]

In the far western states it appears that yet another pattern of school-leaving and labor force participation existed in this period. As indicated in Figure 3.3, the overall rate of school enrollment among teenage women in the West was quite high, with about 40 percent enrolled at age 18. Unlike the South, much of this teenage enrollment

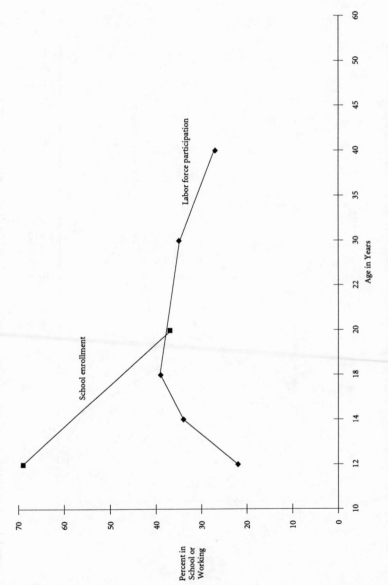

Figure 3.2   Age Structure of Women's Schooling and Work for the East South Central States in 1920

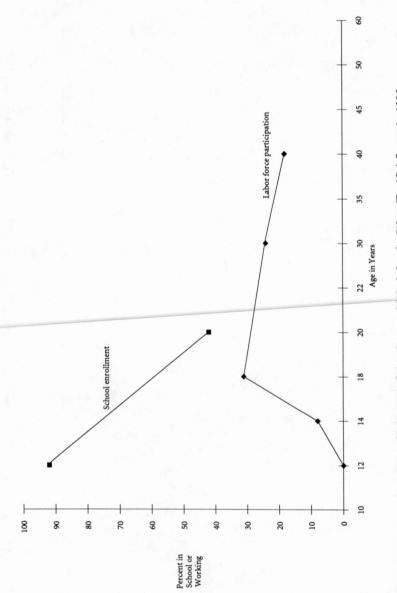

Figure 3.3 Age Structure of Women's Schooling and Work for the West (Pacific) States in 1920

was in high schools, as secondary enrollment rates in the Pacific states were the highest in the country. Western school systems featured a much larger number of secondary schools in this period than school systems in the South. But there were other factors that may have helped to generate high demand for secondary education in the West. High schools may have been popular there because of the region's relatively high levels of income, and to its comparatively limited job opportunities for young women in manufacturing and domestic service. A very high percentage of teenage women attended school, it seems, because they did not need to work, and had relatively few opportunities to earn a wage before finishing school anyway.

As might be expected in a region with high rates of teenage school enrollment, labor force participation rates among women in the West were lower than in the Northeast or the South. Young women appear to have entered the labor force most rapidly in their later teens, as was the case in the Northeast—though not at quite the same pace. The most interesting aspect of the age distribution for working women in Figure 3.3, however, is the relatively slow decline of labor force participation between ages 18 and 30. This suggests that women remained in the labor force longer in the West than in the other economically developed regions of the country; and it might also indicate that the peak age of female labor force participation was somewhat older there than elsewhere (although it is difficult to see this in these figures because of the broad age categories provided by the published census returns).

One explanation of this pattern may lay in the region's occupational distribution. With large numbers of women employed in white-collar occupations, and a larger proportion of women in professional positions than any other part of the country, it is little wonder that the West had a slightly older profile female labor force participation than the Northeast at this time. To prepare for these jobs, after all, young women needed training, which meant that they could not enter the labor market as quickly as their counterparts working in manufacturing or in domestic service. While it is not clear whether the high level of white-collar employment in the western states *caused* the higher rate of teenage school enrollment there, or vice versa, it does appear that the two phenomenon were related. Put simply, it probably was not possible to have one without the other. For this reason, I have decided to describe the overall pattern of teenage female school enrollment and labor force participation in the West at this time as a *white-collar* model of women's schooling and work.[16]

It is impossible, of course, to devise general models for the explanation of regional differences in school enrollment and labor force participation that capture the full complexity of these phenomena. For this reason, the terms I have used above to label these regions are best seen as heuristic devices for characterizing each area in the opening decades of the twentieth century. It is important to remember that women were employed in every major occupational category in each region of the country. The differences that distinguished one region from another in regard to enrollments or labor force participation patterns were often quite subtle. Yet they were also important. As indicated in Table 3.5, by 1930 more than 40 percent of all working women in the western states were employed in white-collar work. In the Northeast, on the other hand, the proportion of women working in manufacturing was more than twice as high as in either the South or West. And in the South two-thirds of all working women were employed in either agriculture or domestic service, two occupational categories that were in sharp decline elsewhere. Thus, even though there were common trends across all three areas, each region was characterized by a particular pattern of female employment in this period.[17]

Regional patterns of female employment, of course, were related to differences in the age structure of labor force participation. And these differences, in turn, appear to have found reflection in regional patterns of teenage female school enrollment. In the industrial Northeast young women left school in large numbers between the ages of 12 and 18. In the South they appear to have combined work and education, or simply worked, through much of adolescence. And in the West many teenage women seem to have postponed work until they finished school and could get a nonmanual job. Looking at these regional patterns, women's work and education do indeed appear to have been connected in the opening decades of the twentieth century. But before it is possible to make firm generalizations about the relationship between these phenomena, it is necessary to take a closer look at what working women were doing in this period and ways in which specific occupations were related to female education.

Occupations and Education

As indicated earlier, women's work underwent a transformation of sorts between 1890 and 1930. The most critical changes revolved around the emerging white-collar and professional occupations for women, the two most important being clerical work and teaching. Clerical work was a relatively new occupational category for women; teaching was an established female profession by the turn of the century but had only recently become a major category of female employment in many areas, largely because of the rapid growth of school systems across the country. Women also moved into a range of other nonmanual occupations in this period. They worked as sales persons in big department stores, social workers in settlement houses, and as academics in colleges and universities, as well as in nursing, as telephone operators, and at a number of other jobs that came to be identified with women in this period. Of course, thousands of women continued to be employed in manufacturing and domestic service. But most of the *growth* in female employment was associated with the movement of women into these new female occupations.[18]

Many of these new jobs clearly called for a relatively high level of formal education. Teaching, for instance, often required at least a high school diploma by the turn of the century, and women who worked as bookkeepers or stenographers had to know—at a minimum—the basic elements of arithmetic and spelling. Social workers and college teachers generally required university training. Other nonmanual jobs appear to have demanded a greater degree of schooling than work in a factory or as a domestic, but for many of these positions academic skills may have been largely irrelevant to routine job performance. It is not clear, for instance, why saleswomen needed high school backgrounds, or whether telephone operators required anything more than rudimentary academic skills (though they clearly needed to speak properly). The general growth of "nonmanual" work for women in this period, accordingly, raises the question of how education was related to major changes in female employment, and how schooling figured in the day-to-day lives of women in these positions. Was access to these jobs limited to certain groups of women, such as those who had attended high school? Was a relatively high level of schooling required for these jobs by employers, and if so, why? And how did the appearance of these new jobs for women affect the general division of labor within the female labor force? Did the rise of white-collar (or "pink-collar") work for women mean that education and other background characteristics distinguished distinct classes of women workers from one another in this period? In order to address these and related questions, it is necessary to examine the relationship of education and particular female occupations in greater detail.[19]

One way to begin examining the relationship between education and women's work is to simply compare the age structures of various occupational categories. The ages at which women entered and left different jobs varied substantially in this period. Figure 3.4 depicts the age distributions of women working in different occupational groups in 1920. The main reason for comparing the age distributions of women in various occupations, of course, is to note differences that may have been related to education. Jobs with large numbers of younger women (teenagers) probably did not require much education and seem to have drawn women who had dropped out of school in order to work. Jobs with older women workers, on the other hand, *may* have required at least some high school education. Of course, it is possible that the average age in any women's occupation was also determined by how long the women in such positions remained in the labor force, a factor that may or may not have been related to education. In any case, examining the age structure of various female occupations in this period can help to illuminate the process by which greater numbers of women entered the labor force. It also provides yet more information on ways in which education may have been related to changes in women's work.[20]

Examining the distributions in Figure 3.4, it is clear that there were important differences in the ages at which women entered various occupations in this period. The largest number of teenage women were employed in manufacturing. Many of these women clearly took jobs in factories as an alternative to attending school in this period. Educational requirements for this type of employment were relatively low. And the availability of paid employment for teenage women raised the opportunity costs of attending school in many areas. For parents who were willing to see their daughters work in factories, schooling often was a problematic issue. It was one thing to send one's daughters to high school when they had little else to do, but it was quite a different situation when teenage girls could get work in a factory. This pattern of early labor force participation, and dropping out of school, corresponds closely to the general profile of school-leaving and labor force entry identified with the Northeast earlier.

School participation, in other words, was especially difficult for young women who lived in industrial areas. In communities with high industrial employment, teenage women were less likely to attend school simply because it was relatively easy to find a job. Families in these areas, moreover, often needed the additional income provided by sending young women out to work. For many women who grew up in the shadow of the factory at this time, schooling was either a luxury beyond their means or irrelevant to their goals. As indicated in Figure 3.4, most women employed in manufacturing left the labor force at relatively early ages, most of them to marry and rear families. For many women from working-class backgrounds, the high school was seen as unnecessary for either work or their future roles as mothers and homemakers.[21]

Factory work, of course, was not the only employment option for women in their teens. Trade and domestic service employment also

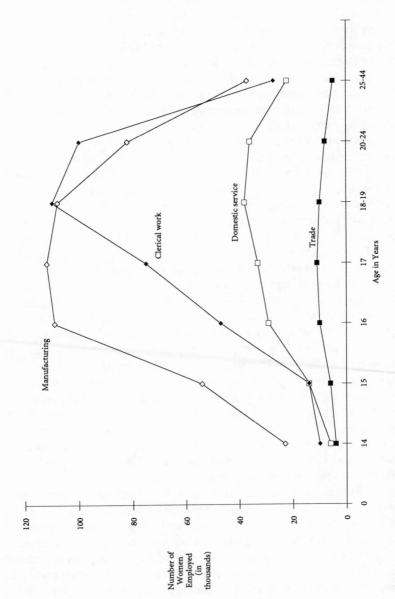

Figure 3.4   Age Structure of Women's Work by Occupation for 1920

peaked in the 15-to-19 age range, suggesting that these jobs too required little formal training. Far fewer women were employed in these types of work, however, than in manufacturing. Labor force participation declined less precipitously in these occupations in later age groups than was the case in manufacturing, however, perhaps because they also attracted women at later stages of life or because women in these jobs continued to work for longer periods than their counterparts employed in factories. Historians who have studied these two groups of women have argued that they were indeed somewhat older than women employed in manufacturing, partly because employers in both retail sales and domestic service often valued the experience that older workers represented. For many women who worked as servants, however, work was often a matter of bare survival. This appears to have been true especially of domestic servants in the South, where black women often worked well beyond the age at which most other women left the labor force altogether. And as David Katzman has demonstrated, it was not uncommon for older women to work as domestic servants in other parts of the country in this period as well.[22]

For women employed in the "trade" category, on the other hand, a somewhat different pattern of employment seems to have prevailed. Even though many older women were employed in stores, the majority of women in these jobs were quite young, and most do not appear to have remained in the labor force as long as their counterparts in domestic service. Rather, as Susan Porter Benson has pointed out, employment in stores attracted young women from a variety of backgrounds, including many who had attended high school. For this reason "trade" employment was nearly as high for women in the 20-to-24 age group as it was for teenagers in 1920. For many women a job in a retail setting, and particularly in the large department stores then appearing in American cities, represented a step up from work in a factory or as a domestic servant. Because of this, female employment in the various "trade" occupations had a somewhat older age distribution than women in manufacturing.[23]

The most striking pattern of labor force participation for women past their teens, however, was in the rapidly growing fields of white-collar employment. If manual labor drew large numbers of younger women, a rather different pattern of labor force participation appears to have existed for women working as clerical and professionals in this period. Fully one-third of all women in clerical employment, the most age specific category of women's work at the time, were in the 20-to-24 age group alone. And the percentage of all professional women in this age group was nearly as high. Significantly, the age period of most rapid entry into both of these fields of work was around age 20. Over twice as many female clerical workers were in the 20-to-24 age group as were in the 15-to-19 group (even though it may not be evident in Figure 3.4), and women in their early twenties out numbered teenagers in the professions by better than 5 to 1. In short, women entering clerical and professional jobs in this period appear to have entered the labor force at different points in their lives than women who worked in other occupational categories.

The reasons for this are not difficult to discern. As shown below, for most of these jobs at least a little secondary education was required, and for many it was necessary to have a high school diploma. Unlike their contemporaries who took manufacturing jobs, women interested in finding work in an office or in teaching generally did not leave school before age 15 or 16. Consequently, they often entered the labor force considerably later than women seeking employment in occupations calling for manual labor. With the growth of female employment in the clerical and professional fields, in that case, the overall age distribution of female labor force participation shifted away from women's teenage years.[24]

An even better view of these differences can be seen in Table 3.6, which shows the industrial distribution of women in a more carefully defined range of age groups in 1930. In the youngest of these cohorts, women age 14 to 16, manufacturing and domestic service employment occupied the largest number of working women. At age 16 nearly three out of four working women were engaged in manual labor. Yet by age 18 or 19, the proportion of women engaged in manufacturing had dropped substantially, and the number employed in clerical jobs increased dramatically. In the 20-to-24 age group nearly half of all working women in 1930 were employed as clericals or professionals, and the number engaged in manufacturing had declined to less than a fifth. Of course more women in this age cohort were leaving manufacturing employment than entered it in this period, so that the number of women in manufacturing declined absolutely as well as proportionally as women entered their twenties. Yet even trade and domestic service, which both drew women aged 20 to 24 in this period, failed to grow as rapidly as white-collar employment for women, and thus employed smaller shares of the 20 to 24 age group than they did the 18 and 19 age cohorts. Younger women workers, particularly those under age 18, were heavily concentrated in occupations calling for manual labor. And working women in their twenties congregated in occupations requiring at least some formal training: professional and clerical employment. By 1930 women workers appear to have been distinguished by age nearly as much as by the different types of work they performed.

Table 3.6   Nonagricultural Female Labor Force Industrial Distribution
by Age for 1930

AGE	MANU- FACTURING	TRANSPOR- TATION AND COMMUNI- CATIONS	TRADE	PROFESS- IONAL	DOMESTIC	CLERI- CAL
14	40.3%	0.5%	5.3%	.8%	49.4%	3.4%
16	41.2%	3.2%	9.5%	1.2%	32.6%	12.2%
18–19	25.2%	4.7%	9.7%	8.5%	23.4%	28.6%
20–24	17.7%	3.9%	8.1%	18.8%	21.5%	29.7%
25–29	16.0%	3.3%	8.3%	19.6%	26.7%	25.9%
30–34	17.2%	2.9%	10.0%	17.6%	31.1%	21.1%
35–39	18.2%	2.9%	11.5%	15.9%	36.3%	15.5%
40–44	18.5%	1.6%	12.3%	15.3%	39.3%	12.5%
45–59	17.8%	1.3%	12.3%	14.6%	43.9%	9.7%
50–54	17.1%	1.1%	11.6%	14.9%	47.4%	7.6%

Source: U.S. Census, *Fifteenth Census of the United States, 1930,* General Report
on Occupations, pp. 116–117.

As suggested earlier, of course, a ready explanation of
interindustrial age differences in female labor force participation
involves the levels of schooling required for different occupations.
There is considerable evidence that the educational requirements for
employment in different lines of women's work varied widely in this
period. Manufacturing employment, for instance, generally demanded little more than a willingness to endure ten- or twelve-hour days
and exhausting physical labor, although women could acquire skills
that might improve their employability and pay. These skills were
most often learned on the job, however, and women seeking factory
jobs had little need of the skills imparted by schools.[25] Hence, teenage
women who had dropped out of school could generally find employment in a factory setting, given its availability. The same was true of
domestic employment, even though large numbers of older women
worked as domestic servants as well. As noted in the next chapter,
programs designed by educators to prepare young women for jobs in
industry and domestic service generally floundered in this period,
simply because most teenagers interested in such positions recognized that schooling was not necessary to find work. Employers often
were no more likely to hire a girl who had been to school for these
jobs than one who had no schooling whatever (indeed, many employ-

ers may have preferred girls without education for manual jobs because of the higher expectations regarding pay and working conditions schooling often engendered). For women interested in finding work in a factory, high school was at best irrelevant and at worst a waste of precious time.[26]

For women in other occupational categories, however, schooling was considerably more important. As suggested above, employment in stores as clerks and saleswomen demanded little formal education, but employers often preferred women with some high school training for positions that dealt extensively with the public. Susan Porter Benson has argued that this was especially true after 1900, when retail employers began to realize the importance of women salesworkers in ensuring good customer relations and boosting sales. Saleswomen had to be pleasant and courteous and generally had to have at least some knowledge of business arithmetic and the merchandise they were selling in order to conduct transactions. In most stores, however, formal education was valued more as an indicator of desirable attitudes and disposition than particular academic skills. Employers looked for proper speech and presence of mind more than abiltiy at arithmetic or other particular skills, since most felt that generally competent women could learn the latter on the job. Women with education, it was felt, were simply more likely to exhibit these qualities. In any case, young women with at least some high school probably held an advantage in competing for jobs as store clerks and saleswomen.

Education appears to have become gradually more important for women working in stores in this period. After the turn of the century, large department stores in some cities instituted training programs to offset educational deficiencies in their sales forces, focusing on general education as well as techniques of dealing with the public. Later, public school systems in the nation's largest cities established high school courses for women in salesmanship. While employment in trade required little formal education at the start of this period, by the 1920s many employers clearly preferred women with high school training—and even college—for positions as saleswomen. This accounted in part for the relatively large number of women age 20 to 29 employed in "trade" occupations in this period. Retail employment was a peculiar form of service occupation for women. It typically required more education and paid higher wages than manufacturing, and yet called for considerably less training than clerical or professional jobs. As time passed, however, schooling became an increasingly important consideration for women seeking work in the retail industry.[27]

At the top of the female occupational hierarchy in this period, of course, was clerical and professional employment, and it was these jobs that required the most formal education. Employers typically emphasized the need for academic preparation in such positions, and commentators were in nearly universal agreement on the need for better training for female clerks, secretaries, teachers, and nurses. From early on, educators recognized the challenges these new female occupations posed. In 1885 the principal of the Hughes High School in Cincinnatti remarked on the large number of girls who had expressed an interest in learning to type when he acquired a typewriter for the school. He suggested that the school board consider installing a special course to train young women for clerical work, particularly since it appeared that there was a surplus of female applicants for teaching jobs. In 1887 a schoolman from Kansas City, Missouri, noted that "the avenues for (women) to become independent and self supporting are widening rather than narrowing." Calling upon his fellow educators to address the changing needs of female secondary students more carefully, he argued, "Women are now filling important positions as teachers, clerks, bookkeepers, stenographers, etc., with fidelity and skill."[28] By the early twentieth century, as clerical and other white-collar jobs for women became even more important, the matter of educating women for these positions recieved yet greater attention.

Almost all clerical jobs required women to be literate, and many demanded special skills such as typing or stenography which could only be acquired in schools or on the job. For many employers, however, the latter option was not very attractive. "The merchant of today has neither the time nor the inclination to be a schoolmaster in his own office," declared one turn-of-the-century business school brochure. "He demands employees that are thoroughly prepared for their duties, and he has learned that young women are often as satisfactory as young men." As clerical work became more routine, and as the number of clerical workers increased dramatically, employers turned to the schools to find suitably trained personnel. In her study of clerical workers in Pittsburgh at this time, Ileen DeVault has suggested that women generally needed between one and three years of schooling beyond the grammar school level in order to compete for these jobs. Other historians agree. Clerical workers had to know how to spell and often were called upon to help keep books and to manage accounts, duties that required facility with numbers as well. Consequently, at least some high school training (or its equivalent in a commercial school) was a prerequisite for most clerical jobs in this period, though the educational requirements of various positions varied significantly. As DeVault notes, by the latter nineteenth century, "proponents of office work for women proclaimed that stenography had become 'the other thing' educated women could do beyond teaching school."[29]

It is an open question, of course, whether high school training was really necessary to perform many clerical jobs in this period. After all, there was considerable routinization in clerical work, and many clerical workers did little more than type or maintain file records. There is evidence, moreover, that many employers may have used educational requirements to select certain kinds of women for employment in offices. A recent study by historian Christine Anderson has suggested that questions of personality and ethnic background were often critical factors in determining which women were hired for clerical positions in the 1920s. This appears to have been especially true when employers could chose from a number of sufficiently educated job applicants. Perhaps in areas where high school–educated women were plentiful (and for jobs for which academic considerations may have been secondary) academic performance was less a consideration for many employers than whether a particular women would "fit" into a certain office culture, the latter typically defined by the men who worked there. Consequently, some employers hired only younger women, others refused to hire Jewish or Catholic women, while others merely looked for "attractive" or "pretty" job applicants.

Education, in that case, was only one of a battery of characteristics employers considered when hiring clerical workers, many of which may not have been related to job performance. Of course the ability of employers to exercise such discretion was limited by the needs of each particular firm or agency and by the pool of qualified applicants. Some clerical jobs required more specific or highly developed skills than others. And virtually all employers wanted secretaries and other women clericals who were personable and possessed a workable knowledge of English. For these reasons, education remained an important consideration, even if other factors sometimes determined whether or not a particular woman was hired. The manner in which these factors may have typically operated together was expressed in the words of one personnel director at the time, who confessed that his firm hired women who were "intelligent high school graduates of a family, not Jewish." High school attendance requirements helped employers exclude large numbers of women from work in their offices, and they developed additional criteria of exclusion to keep out still other women they judged to be undesirable.[30]

Schooling, in that case, was an important prerequisite for clerical employment. As suggested above, the technical requirements of many clerical jobs dictated the level of education needed to fill them. A survey of employers in Chicago during the early 1920s found that women hired as stenographers generally were required to have a high school diploma or its equivalent in training. Because they handled correspondence, stenographers needed highly developed literary skills and a relatively high level of formal schooling, and they often commanded relatively high salaries. Anderson has noted that women who worked as private secretaries to businessmen were called upon to perform a wide range of tasks, many of which required a rather high level of formal education.

Over time, a clear hierarchy of skills developed within the clerical field, with some jobs requiring more schooling and experience than others. In a study published in 1924, W. W. Charters and Ivalee Whitlee concluded that secretaries typically performed some 130 different duties for their employers over the course of a business year. While Charters and Whitlee intended to demonstrate ways in which the work of secretaries could be simplified, their study revealed the high degree of personal initiative and managerial skill required for the job. For these reasons private or executive secretaries enjoyed the highest status (and pay) among women clerical workers and often were expected to have the highest levels of formal education and training. For other clerical positions, however, employers appear to have preferred younger, less-educated women. Younger women were considered more tractable and were cheaper to hire for such routine jobs as clerk, typist, and office machine operator than those with high school diplomas. While some education was necessary for any type of office work, for many of these jobs schooling seems to have served something of the same purpose it did in retail sales: a way of guaranteeing personable employees with at least a modicum of academic skills.

The seemingly arbitrary educational requirements for some clerical jobs, however, appear to have deterred few potential applicants for these positions. The mere availability of comparatively high-paying clerical jobs was a powerful incentive to many women to prepare for them, and as indicated in the following chapter, commercial courses proliferated in schools during this period. As larger numbers of young women became interested in the growing field of office employment, educational background became an important criteria for employment, and consequently, the age distribution of clerical workers was considerably older than for women employed in manufacturing.[31]

The relationship between education and work for teachers was rather different than it was for other women at this time. Formal schooling beyond the grammar school level was a virtual necessity for most teachers. Because their job dealt with the direct transmission of academic skills, teachers were generally required to attend either a high school or a normal school, depending on the rules or expectations of their local school district. A national survey of American teachers conducted in 1910 by Lotus Coffman found that about two out of three women teachers possessed at least a high school diploma or its equivalent. Coffman's sample, moreover, was biased toward rural districts, which generally had lower educational requirements for teachers than urban school systems. As indicated in chapter 1, city school districts often relied heavily on their own high schools to provide teachers for their burgeoning elementary and grammar schools. Because of high rates of female high school enrollment and the fact that teaching was generally considered a desireable job by many women in this period, there was often a surplus of high school educated women applying for city teaching jobs. Pay scales in the urban schools were higher than in rural areas as well, and they often attracted better educated and more experienced teachers.

Teachers, in that case, represented the best educated of the major female occupational groups in this period. Numbering some 639,241 by 1920 (about half the number of women clerical workers), with three-quarters or more of them possessing at least a high school education, teachers skewed the age distribution of women professional workers away from the pattern of early labor force participation characteristic of manual employment at this time. Women who wanted to become teachers had to go to school in this period, and this meant that they were typically older than their contemporaries who worked in factories and shops. As was the case with clerical workers, the somewhat older age distribution of teachers probably was a reflection of educational requirements for the job.[32]

There were other jobs for which women were educated in this period, of course. College women often worked in settlement houses as early social workers, and a small but growing number of women studied to become doctors, lawyers, and professional academics in these years. The field of nursing, long dominated by women, was professionalized in this period, and schools were established to train women to become nurses as well (although it was possible to become a nurse without attending such schools well into the twentieth century). All told, education was a key factor in the development of women's work in the early twentieth century. Without attending school beyond the elementary or grammar levels, it was virtually impossible for women to gain access to the rapidly expanding white-collar and technical occupations opening up to them in this period.[33]

In general, pay scales for different types of women's work seem to have corresponded fairly closely to the educational levels required to perform them. Although women teachers were often paid less than their male counterparts, they typically earned more than other work-

ing women—at least during those months of the year they were
employed. In urban school districts women often received as much as
five or six hundred dollars for eight months of work, a pay rate of
twelve to fifteen dollars a week. This was nearly twice as much as
women were paid for working in factories or as domestics. Clerical
workers were the next highest paid group of women in this period,
generally earning between eight and twelve dollars a week. The highest paid female clerical workers appear to have been private (or executive) secretaries, who sometimes commanded salaries of fifteen dollars a week or more with experience. Stenographers typically were
paid more than clerk-typists, though experience appears to have been
an important factor in these jobs as well. The women who worked in
stores seem to have earned slightly more than those in factories,
though usually less than clerical workers.[34]

Generally speaking, in that case, a loosely defined but distinctive hierarchy appears to have existed within the female labor force.
The jobs that required the most education—and traditional academic
skills—commanded the highest pay and greatest prestige. They often
featured better working conditions and more stable employment
prospects than manual labor jobs, which were subject to periodic
(often seasonal) fluctuations in employment levels. All things considered, white-collar work was preferable to manual labor for women in
this period. It is little wonder that women in white-collar jobs appear
to have stayed in the labor force longer than those who worked in factories. And the advantages of white-collar work made the decision to
forego teenage employment in order to attend school a rational choice
of employment options. White-collar jobs may have attracted older
women, in part, simply because such positions represented a more
desireable set of working conditions.[35]

Education, it appears, was closely linked to women's work in
the opening decades of the twentieth century. The growth of female
white-collar employment, chiefly comprising jobs in offices and
schools, created a vast new field of employment for young women
with at least some high school education. Women who were forced to
leave school before high school, whether because of inclination or circumstances beyond their control, were generally required to take jobs
calling for manual labor. In general, both working conditions and pay
scales in these jobs were worse than they were in the new fields of
white-collar employment.

For women who possessed the requisite educational background,
on the other hand, jobs in offices and schools often offered an appealing
alternative to the restrictive domestic roles they had grown up with. As
Ileen DeVault has suggested, female white-collar workers in this period

often considered themselves in far better circumstances than their counterparts in manufacturing or domestic service employment. While still near the bottom of the overall occupational distribution, they were clearly near the top of the *female* occupational distribution. A job requiring education, and associated with the high status of work performed in offices and schools, became a badge of honor that many young women wore proudly in this period. Schooling, in that case, came to distinguish two quite different worlds of women's work at the start of the twentieth century. The different age distributions linked to manual and white-collar work identified above were associated with yet other characteristics of women workers at this time. Along with education went social status, after all, and the rise of female occupational groups with different educational requirements pointed to a sharpening division of labor within the nation's female work force.[36]

Ethnicity, Education, and Women's Work

The opening decades of the twentieth century were marked by a growing distinction between the types of work performed by different groups of women. As suggested above, education served as a critical dividing line separating one group of women workers from another. Perhaps the most important distinction among working women in this period was the one made between manual and white-collar labor. In general, white-collar occupations paid better than manual jobs for women, offered better working conditions, and were afforded greater prestige within the community at large. Working in an office or a school was generally seen as preferable to working in a factory or someone else's home as a domestic. The hours were usually shorter, and managers were often somewhat less autocratic in offices and schools. And because employers often made social and cultural background characteristics an important criteria for employment in these jobs, there was the added prestige of association with an occupation widely seen as being somewhat socially exclusive.[37]

With time, female employment in white-collar jobs became dominated by white, native-born women. Given the fact that it was largely this very group that populated the nation's high schools in this period, this development may have been an inevitable consequence of the educational requirements for most white-collar jobs. But it helped account for a sharp division of labor in women's work that separated white native-born women from their black and immigrant counterparts. As white-collar employment became more important in the twentieth century, this ethnic—and class—division of labor intensified.

Not surprisingly, the ethnic division of labor in this period was reflected in the ages of labor force participation for women from different ethnic backgrounds. As will be seen below, those groups of women that were most likely to be employed in white-collar jobs tended to be older than their counterparts who worked largely in manual occupations. Indeed, these ethnic age of employment patterns appear to have matched female occupational age distributions rather closely. Age, ethnicity, and field of employment—along with education—seems to have separated one group of working women from another at this time in the United States. The implications of this development for understanding ways in which class, ethnicity, and other aspects of social status may have affected the behavior of women are only beginning to be explored by historians. Before considering the social and cultural consequences of these changes, however, it is important to determine more precisely just how they occurred.

To begin this discussion it is important to consider the relationship between ethnicity and class at this time. Much of the analysis to follow revolves around evidence about ethnicity. Another important dimension of this process of change, however, was its association with social class, or economic status. As will be seen below, the vast majority of immigrant and black women in this period were from unskilled working-class backgrounds, and these women generally took jobs that entailed manual labor. Many white native-born women, on the other hand, were the daughters of white-collar workers, professionals, or skilled manual workers, men who generally could afford to send their daughters to school. Given these differences, much of the ethnic variation in female labor force participation described below was probably due to income variation associated with differences in social class and family income. By and large, this aspect of the relationship between education and work is analyzed here only insofar as the major ethnic groups can be characterized in class terms.[38] Most of this discussion, in that case, is limited to considering evidence on ethnic differences in female labor force participation, based largely on census data. The issue of social class is considered more closely in chapter 5, which draws upon an alternative body of evidence.[39]

Women from all major ethnic groups worked in every occupation, of course, but different groups of women tended to congregate in particular job categories. For purposes of this discussion, I have used the very broad definitions of ethnic background provided by the census, realizing that there was a great deal of variation among *particular* ethnic groups (comparing, say, Russian Jews and Italian Catholics) within these categories.[40] Tables 3.7 and 3.8 reveal the occu-

Table 3.7   Nonagricultural Occupational Distribution for Working
Women from Different Ethnic Groups for 1890

ETHNIC GROUP	MANUFACTURING	DOMESTIC	TRADE	PROFESSIONAL
Native	33.7%	39.0%	8.8%	18.4%
Second-generation immigrant	48.3%	31.4%	11.3%	9.0%
Foreign-born	30.6%	62.1%	4.7%	2.7%
Black	5.0%	92.9%	0.4%	1.6%

Source: U.S. Census, *Compendium, 1890* Part 3, Table 78.

Table 3.8   Nonagricultural Occupational Distribution for Working
Women from Different Ethnic Backgrounds for 1920

ETHNIC GROUP	MANU-FACTURING	DOMESTIC	TRADE	PROFESS-IONAL	CLERICAL
Native	23.0%	19.4%	10.5%	19.5%	23.3%
Second-generation immigrant	30.8%	16.5%	10.4%	12.2%	26.4%
Foreign-born	38.4%	37.1%	8.3%	6.5%	8.5%
Black	9.9%	74.6%	1.1%	3.7%	0.8%

Source: U.S. Census, *Fourteenth Census of the United States,* vol 4, (Washington,
DC: Government Printing Office, 1923) p. 340.

pational distribution of women in four major classifications of ethnic
background in 1890 and 1920: native women of native parentage,
native of immigrant parentage, foreign-born or immigrant, and black.
These distributions reflect the extent to which women from these
groups were concentrated in particular occupational categories. In
1890, for instance, over a third of all native working women and nearly half of all second-generation immigrant women were employed in
manufacturing. Almost two-thirds of all foreign-born women, on the
other hand, worked as domestic servants, as did better than 90 percent of all black working women. In all four groups the vast majority
of women were engaged in manual labor. Just one out of four native
white women and one out of five second-generation immigrant
women were employed in trade or professional jobs. The prevailing
feature of the occupational distribution of all four groups in 1890, in

that case, was the predominance of unskilled manual labor.

By the third decade of the twentieth century, however, the occupational distributions of all these groups had shifted. As indicated earlier, important changes in the types of work women performed occurred in this period, particularly the growth of clerical and professional employment. The proportion of women doing domestic work in each group declined, and the number engaged in trade, the professions, and clerical employment grew substantially. But these changes did not affect all four groups in the same way. The greatest decline in domestic service employment, for instance, occurred among white native-born women, including women both from immigrant and native families. The fall in domestic employment among immigrant women was not as great as it was for natives, and of course black women continued to be highly over-represented in domestic service throughout the period. Black and foreign-born women, in that case, became more concentrated in domestic service employment than any other group.[41]

The same was true of employment in manufacturing. While the proportion of white native-born women from both native and immigrant backgrounds employed in manufacturing declined precipitously between 1890 and 1920, the proportion of foreign-born and black women employed in manufacturing *increased*. Thus, in 1920 the vast majority of black and foreign-born working women continued to be employed in occupations demanding manual labor, while the proportion of native-born women employed in manufacturing and domestic service dropped to less than half. In the opening decades of the twentieth century, it appears, a growing division of labor altered the ethnic character of women's work in the United States. And the most ethnically homogenous group of women workers (at least on a national scale) may have been those employed in the emerging white-collar occupations.

The rapid growth of clerical and professional employment in this period clearly benefited white native-born women more than immigrant or black women. In 1920 nearly one out of four native working women were employed as clericals, while only one in twelve immigrant women workers were, and fewer than one in a hundred black working women. In 1930 (not shown in either table), over 90 percent of all women employed as clericals in the United States were native-born; in 1910 the figure was 92 percent. White native-born women continued to dominate the emerging field of office employment throughout the opening decades of the twentieth century. The same seems to have been true of professional employment. Although the proportion of immigrant and black women working in professional jobs more than tripled between 1890 and 1930, by the latter date women from these two groups continued to be under-represented

among female professionals. In 1890 white native-born women constituted 88 percent of all women professionals. In 1930 fully 89 percent
were from this group alone. If clerical and professional women are
lumped together in a single occupational category, nine out of ten of
them were native-born and white throughout this period.[42]

The sudden appearance of large numbers of white native-born
women in the labor force was directly linked the growth of white-collar jobs. As indicated earlier, the most rapidly expanding occupations
for women in this period were clerical and professional employment,
along with jobs connected with trade and commerce. White native-
born women comprised the vast majority of women entering these
fields. The occupations in which foreign-born and black women were
concentrated, manufacturing and domestic service, declined in
importance. Accordingly, immigrant and black women constituted a
progressively smaller share of the female labor force, even though the
number of women employed in manual labor also increased in absolute terms. Female employment in manufacturing and domestic service simply did not expand as rapidly as white-collar job opportunities for women. One of the most important features of the period
between 1890 and 1930, in that case, was the entry of thousands of
young, relatively well-educated native-born women into the labor
force, particularly into the expanding fields of retail and office work
and professional employment.

The movement of native women into the labor force helped to
establish a clear ethnic differentiation in women's work. Jobs that
required the most skill, particularly skills acquired in school, or which
required direct communication with the public, such as secretaries or
sales girls, were taken mainly by native women. And as indicated in
chapter 2, white native-born women, regardless of their parentage,
were generally better educated than women from other backgrounds.
The existence of a large pool of relatively well-educated and culturally acceptable women could have been a key factor in the massive shift
to female clerical and professional employment in this period. At the
same time that female employment in white-collar jobs was expanding, of course, teenage school enrollment rates were rising, particularly in the highly urbanized Northeast. As Margery Davies and other
historians have suggested, education may indeed have been important to the development of the female labor force in the United States,
particularly the movement of women into the burgeoning white-collar field of employment.[43]

Educational and occupational differences that distinguished
these major ethnic groupings were also reflected in the age pattern of
labor force participation for women from different backgrounds. Fig-

ure 3.5 features the age distribution of working women from these groups in 1920. Nearly half of the white native-born female workforce was employed in white-collar occupations at that time, and the vast majority of female clerical and professional workers were native-born. This would account for the relatively stable labor force participation rates for white women of native parentage between the ages of 18 and 24 in Figure 3.5. While many white native-born women entered the labor market in their teens, others did so later, presumably after a period of schooling which enabled them to get white-collar jobs. Thus, rates of white native-born female employment remained relatively high (near their peak) through the early twenties age range, a pattern decidedly different from that of immigrant women.[44]

Immigrant women, on the other hand, poured into the labor force in their teens. At the peak of foreign-born female labor force participation, over 50 percent of all immigrant women age 10 to 18 were employed. This pattern of labor force entry, of course, corresponded with the relatively low rates of teenage school participation among immigrant women in this period. The high immigrant female employment rate in Figure 3.5 also corresponds with the image of the immigrant family painted by both contemporary commentators and more recent studies. In 1920 immigrant workers in the United States were almost twice as likely to be employed in manufacturing as natives. And most immigrant workers were unskilled, particularly the "new" immigrants from southern and eastern Europe. In 1907 the Dillingham Commission, a federally sponsored survey of the immigrant population, reported that fully 85 percent of the immigrants entering the country at that time were unskilled. Most of these workers commanded dismally low wages. Many immigrant families, in that case, saw women's work as a means of supplementing family income, and they sent their daughters to work in factories, mills, shops, and other people's homes in great numbers.[45] As suggested earlier, the low school enrollment rate registered by immigrant teenagers at the close of the nineteenth century was linked to this pattern of labor force participation.

The other major ethnic group in Figure 3.5, black women, fell between rates of labor force entry for natives and immigrants in the early twentieth century. Black women entered the labor force at a relatively early age. This was probably due in part to the fact that many black women at this time were employed in agriculture, which featured relatively high rates of labor force participation among younger women. Greater numbers of black girls under age 13 were employed than in any other group, probably because many black women continued to be employed in agriculture during this period.

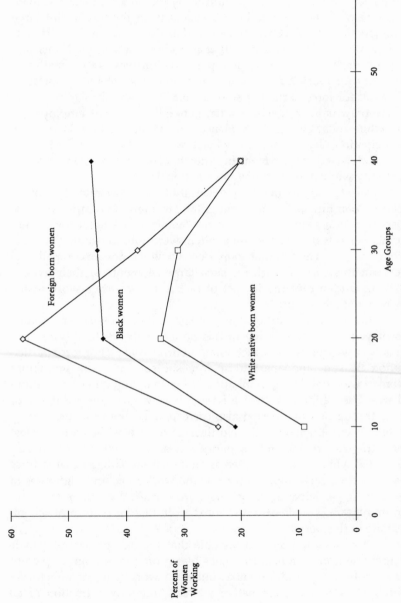

Figure 3.5 Ethnic Differences in the Age Structure of Women's Work for 1920

On the other hand, black women also exhibited the highest rates of labor force participation among older women as well. This too may have been associated with agricultural work, which engaged women at all ages in the countryside—particularly in the South. But large numbers of older black women worked as domestics in this period as well. As Elizabeth Pleck and other historians have argued, this pattern of black female labor force participation was both a matter of necessity for black families and a function of a greater openness to female labor force participation in the black community. Unlike white native-born women, black women generally were not employed in the white-collar occupations. Hence, the pattern of high labor force participation rates among older black women does not reflect a pattern of deferred employment in order to acquire education, as it did for many white native-born women at this time.

Despite the fact that they generally had higher rates of teenage school enrollment than immigrant women (perhaps because discrimination kept them out of the factories that employed immigrant teenagers), black women often were employed in the most menial of jobs. The fact that so many black women were compelled to perform this sort of work for such large segments of their lives is striking evidence of the impact of racism on women's work in the early twentieth century.[46]

As indicated earlier, the largest single cohort of women employed in manufacturing in this period were 18- to 19-year-olds. This was also the age at which foreign-born female labor force participation peaked, and apart from domestic service, more immigrant women were employed in manufacturing than any other occupational area. The rapid rate at which foreign-born women entered the labor force throughout this period also corresponded with the age pattern of female employment in the Northeast, which was the nation's most industrialized region in this period. In short, foreign-born women exhibited what can be identified as an industrial pattern of labor force participation; early, rapid entry into the work force and high rates of labor force participation for younger women. And as suggested earlier, immigrant women also displayed an industrial pattern of school-leaving in this period.

Of course, it was also possible that the age pattern of female employment in manufacturing jobs was a unique immigrant pattern of school-leaving and job entry, but most women in manufacturing jobs in this period were native whites. And only a fraction of all domestic workers were black women, even though the age pattern of female employment in domestic service was flatter than that of any other occupational group. It appears that the type of jobs that women held dictated differences in the age pattern of labor force participation along ethnic lines. Most immigrant women were from working-class families, and their work was often an important source of additional family income. Many of them appear to have found jobs in industry largely because they lacked the schooling or attendant cultural orientation to qualify for more stable and lucrative positions in stores and offices. A majority probably left school to go to work, and later left the labor force to get married and begin the task of raising a family.[47]

White native-born women exhibited an altogether different pattern of labor force participation at this time. They generally did not enter the labor force as early as immigrant women, nor did they enter it as rapidly or in as great proportions. By 1930 the peak ages of white native-born female labor force participation were 20 to 24, not 18 and 19. And while nearly 40 percent of all white native-born working women were engaged in manual labor in 1920, an almost equal number were employed in offices or as professionals of some sort. This accounts in part for the peculiar age distribution of white native-born women workers in this period. For this reason, the native pattern of female labor force participation in this period can be characterized as white-collar.

These findings, of course, only indirectly reflect the class backgrounds of different groups of women. A number of recent studies, however, have examined the social origins of clerical workers more closely. In her study of students in a clerical course of study in Pittsburgh at this time, Ileen DeVault found that the largest group of young women planning to pursue clerical jobs were the daughters of skilled workers, from families of middling status. She has argued that these women viewed clerical work as a means of affirming or preserving their middle-class status in a period when the traditionally privileged position of skilled craftsmen was under attack in many American industries. These women did not work because of economic necessity. Rather, they took jobs as clerical workers, teachers, and telephone operators (as well as in other emerging white-collar occupations) in order to widen their horizons in ways that were consistent with the expectations of their parents and communities.[48]

Other studies of women clerical workers in this period have confirmed this picture. As will be seen later, many of these women came from families that could afford to see them through school, or at least enough schooling to guarantee them an office job. And contemporary accounts suggest that working women from native backgrounds were less likely to contribute their pay to their families than were immigrants, keeping it instead for their own consumption and savings. Native women in office and professional jobs often saw their work as a conduit into a stable and secure middle-class future.[49]

Work began early in life for many black women, on the other hand, and continued well beyond the age when most other working women had left the labor force to rear families or seek fulfillment in domestic life. Black women had the highest overall rate of labor force participation of all the principal groups of women in this period, and the vast majority of them were employed in domestic service. The age structure of black female employment reflected this, with high rates of participation among middle-aged and even older women. There can be little doubt that black women, mothers and daughters alike, took on these tasks to help support their families in the face of continuing economic and social insecurity. These jobs required little schooling, but black women approached them with determination and strength acquired from generations of struggle against the immense obstacles they were required to negotiate in their lives.[50]

Given the foregoing, it appears that class and ethnicity were important factors in determining which jobs young women were likely to get at the turn of the century. As indicated in the previous chapter, young women from immigrant, working-class backgrounds were considerably less likely to be enrolled in school than those from native, middle-class households. And schooling was often a critical element in determining who would be hired in the emerging white-collar jobs—and who would not. As professional and clerical employment became more important fields of women's work in the early twentieth century, a striking ethnic and class-based division of labor appeared within the female labor force. Education, it seems, was both a vehicle of opportunity for some groups of women, and a mechanism of exclusion to others. In this respect, the rise of secondary education for women at this time—generally restricted to native whites—served to sharpen distinctions between different groups of women as larger numbers of them sought to improve their lives materially in the labor force.[51]

Conclusion: Opportunities and Constraints in Female Employment

Changes in women's work represented an important range of new opportunities for young women in American life. The very fact of nonmenial employment being available on a large scale, of course, made it possible for many women to work in this period, especially those from groups that had shunned menial labor in the past. Particularly, for middle-class, white, native-born women, it meant a role (however inconsequential) in business, government, and other spheres of life, and an opportunity to exercize somewhat greater earning power than earlier generations of women. While these changes did not pose a fundamental challenge to traditional female roles, they did allow these women to broaden their experience and, for some, offered an alternative to the domestic roles played by most women. The expansion of female employment, in that case, was an important step in widening the range of life choices available to American women at the turn of the century—even if most ultimately chose marriage and domesticity over work.

Constraints were evident in women's employment patterns as well, however. I have identified the broad contours of an ethnic division of labor in women's work, which took shape across the opening decades of the twentieth century. Changes in female employment that posed new opportunities for some women also highlighted constraints that relegated some groups of women to the most menial forms of labor. Schooling, it appears, may have played a major role in defining these various occupational roles. Ethnic differences in female labor force participation, after all, seem to have paralleled differences in teenage school participation in this period. These differences also corresponded to regional variation in the age patterns and industrial distribution of female labor force participation, and regional differences in female school participation as well. Ethnic and regional distinctions in the types of work women performed, moreover, appear to have changed little in this period. The ethnic and regional division of labor, at least insofar as women's work was concerned, remained intact between 1890 and 1930. Generally rising rates of teenage school participation, however, may have been related to the growth of clerical labor, which occurred in all parts of the country—albeit more in some areas than others.

The basic continuities identified herein, of course, are rather tentative. Yet they clearly describe certain broad relationships in the development of women's work and education. They are general trends that can be identified along the lines of regional and ethnic categories used to organize data in the census. Unfortunately, aggregate census data do not permit a closer examination of ethnic or industrial differences in female labor force participation, such as examining the behavior of specific ethnic groups or women from various class backgrounds. A more deliberate comparative analysis of the relationship between women's school participation and employment patterns in particular communities is undertaken in chapter 5. Before turning to that discussion, however, it is important to examine the changes in women's education that occurred in this period. The revolution in women's work, it seems, affected more than overall patterns of female school participation. It was also associated with a dramatic set of changes in high school curricula. At the same time that larger numbers of young women decided to enter the wage labor force, even if only temporarily, the nation's schools found themselves faced with the prospect of preparing thousands of women for work both in the home and out.

Chapter Four

Vocationalism Ascendant: Women and the High School Curriculum, 1890–1930

The dramatic changes in women's work that occurred after 1900 raised important questions about women's education, particularly in light of the rapid growth of new jobs requiring relatively high levels of education. As it turned out, this also was a time of equally profound change in women's schooling. The four decades following 1890 witnessed the emergence of a variety of new programs for women in high schools, along with important changes in the way most educators viewed women's education. These developments were part and parcel of a series of changes that altered all of American education in the opening years of the twentieth century, many of which were intended to help schools better prepare students for the world of work.

A vocational education movement swept through American high schools in the opening decades of the twentieth century. This reform impulse has been studied extensively, although most histories have focused on programs designed for young men. Schools also featured programs to help women prepare for working careers, however, particularly in light of the new importance attached to women's education in the labor market. Indeed, the new forms of women's work that appeared at this time inspired a dramatic revision of secondary school curricula for women. In this regard, women's schooling reflected one of the principal educational themes of the period: the growing responsiveness of schools to the labor market. But because of the peculiar quality of women's work and the fact that women generally were employed in different jobs than men, the advent of vocationalism occasioned a remarkable transformation in women's secondary schooling. For better or worse, the opening decades of the twentieth century witnessed the appearance of a distinctively *female* curriculum in American high schools.[1]

In this chapter I consider ways in which vocational purposes shaped curricular policy for women in secondary schools, along with other aspects of the educational experiences of female high school students. Once again, the forces of opportunity and constraint were both in evidence. Although young women and men generally had studied the same subjects in the nineteenth century, particular features of the high school curriculum were designed especially for women in the years after 1900. A new sex-typed curriculum appeared in American high schools, revolving around such subjects as home economics and commercial education. This represented a dramatic change from curricular policies in earlier years, when most public high schools made few distinctions between subjects studied by boys and girls. The twentieth-century female curriculum was considerably more restrictive, even though it offered many young women the opportunity to focus on subjects that they could use in the labor market (such as typing and stenography).

The evolution of these aspects of curricular policy was an important dimension of the relationship between women's education and women's work in the opening decades of the twentieth century. At the very time when new opportunities appeared for women in employment, curricular policies regarding women's secondary education became more restrictive. As will be seen below, courses in home economics and other "female" subjects were introduced partly because of fears that young women were losing domestic skills and values. On the other hand, courses in stenography and other "business" subjects were offered to meet the demand for skilled women to fill positions in the burgeoning clerical sector. In either case, ideas about women's education came to be dominated by changes in women's work, and the result was a more narrowly defined curriculum.

Beyond the question of curricular reform, of course, is the matter of whether or not young women were responsive to these changes. Just because new programs were developed for them, after all, does not mean that teenage women *wanted* to study a distinctively female curriculum. This is not an easy question to answer. Few historians of American education have sought to determine the manner in which changes in educational policy have been related to the preferences of students or their parents. As is the case with many historical questions of popular tastes or ideas, there is little evidence that speaks directly to the question of what students thought about their courses.

There *is* evidence on which courses women took in this period, however, and by comparing enrollment levels in various programs in different parts of the country, it is possible to make inferences about the popularity of particular courses. Once again, I use behavioral evidence to make inferences about popular preferences.

New Purposes in Women's Education

As indicated in chapter 1, the nineteenth-century high school had few explicitly vocational purposes. The overwhelming majority of students in the 1870s and 1880s had enrolled in courses that were academic in orientation. Manual arts high schools, though increasingly important in large industrial cities, generally were relatively few in number. As suggested in chapter 2, most young women in high school during the years before 1900 appear to have had few vocational goals in mind while going through school. Many seem to have enjoyed school both for the intellectual stimulation they gained there and for the alluring peer culture that the high school afforded them. For women at least, American secondary education in the nineteenth century was largely devoid of vocational intent.

All of this appears to have changed remarkably in the opening decades of the twentieth century. As vocationalism began to affect American secondary education in the 1880s and 1890s, there were few programs designed to prepare young women for work. With the growth of female labor force participation in subsequent decades, however, and the movement of women into new types of jobs, educators expressed a growing concern about whether secondary schools were doing enough to equip women for their future roles. New courses were prepared for women students, designed to correspond to the types of work they would perform as adults. The thrust of these curricular innovations varied, from domestic science or home economics to female industrial education, but all of them shared a single objective: to better enable high school women to fulfill specifically *female* work roles in society at large.

These changes in women's education were part of a larger vocational revolution that transformed American secondary education during these years. The world of work began to exert a telling influence on the high school curriculum at the end of the nineteenth century, though it affected young men first. The manual education movement, which had been inspired partly by concern over boys dropping out of school in the 1880s and 1890s, eventually gave way to a broader movement to enable schools to train boys for industrial jobs. This shift was partly inspired by anxieties about international industrial competition but also reflected a more general Progressive impulse to make schooling increasingly responsive to observable social and economic needs. Educators used the term "social efficiency" to describe their objective of making the school address the needs of students more closely, and making public education an agency of social reform. In secondary education, this meant using high schools to better prepare students—male and female—for their future roles as citizens and workers. By the second decade of the twentieth century, in that case, vocationalism had become a dominant theme in American secondary education. Whether labeled manual, industrial, technical, or commercial, the high school curriculum increasingly was geared toward the tasks that individuals faced when their school careers were finished. This purpose was a common thread running through most discussions of curricular policy in the years following 1890. Education for a growing number of the nation's young people in this period was decidedly vocational.[2]

Women's education may stand as one of the best examples of this, simply because most vocational programs were designed (or turned out) to be gender-specific. The advent of vocationalism, even those aspects that affected only boys, had a profound impact on women's schooling. Major changes in women's education during this period, most notably the development of instruction in home economics, were largely inspired by the vocational education movement. The development of commercial education, which affected the high school careers of tens of thousands of girls (particularly in northeastern industrial cities), was a direct response to changes in the nature of women's work. And a number of programs were developed in this period for female manual workers, ranging from courses in dressmaking in cities like New York and Boston to instruction in agriculture for black women in the South. The very idea of preparing women for work, of course, was difficult for many educators to accept. But the fact that larger numbers of young women were entering the labor force, particularly educated women, made the question of women's vocational education impossible to ignore. Everywhere educators decried the growing tendency of women to leave school to work, yet they also established programs to make women better workers once they left the schools.

The arrival of vocationalism affected aspects of school life other than the curriculum as well. Coeducation, long a celebrated feature of precollegiate education in the United States, gave way to a studied sexual differentiation in secondary schools, guided by educators' images of the roles men and women were supposed to play in society generally. Although the principle of coeducation was rarely renounced in practice, there is considerable evidence that boys and girls met in the same classrooms a good deal less after 1910 than they had earlier. The tradition of gender equality which had been a feature of American secondary schools in the nineteenth century seems to have given way to a new creed of gender segregation promulgated largely on vocational grounds.

In light of these points, changes in women's work seem to have been a driving force shaping educational policy for women. The principal innovation in women's education during the years following 1900 was home economics, or domestic science education as it was sometimes called, but other changes in the high school curriculum affected women as well. In the sections that follow three major elements of the emerging secondary curriculum with particular relevance for women in this period are discussed: home economics, commercial education, and industrial education for women. This is followed by consideration of ways in which these different programs complemented one another and an examination of the urban contexts in which they developed most fully.

The Home Economics Movement

Home economics was probably the most important feature of the new high school curriculum developed for women at the start of the twentieth century. Generally speaking, home economics was intended to be the female counterpart to industrial education, which was generally thought of as a male vocational feature of the high school curriculum.[3] This lineage was both the source of home economics' link to vocationalism, an association that helped such programs get support from federal vocational education legislation in this period, and a source of considerable confusion about its purposes. While most educators agreed that homemaking was indeed a vocation (and one for which women were divinely suited) some insisted that it was also much more than that. To its most enthusiastic promoters, home economics was a cornerstone of Western civilization, simply because of the importance of the family in the performance of basic services and transmission of essential values. In this regard, home economics represented a genuine reform movement, one of the many Progressive reforms of this period aimed at eradicating the overcrowding, poverty, disease, and potential for social turbulence associated with rapid industrialization and urbanization.

The idea of educating women for their domestic responsibilities was not a new one at the turn of the century. Domestic feminist advocates of women's education had long recommended courses of study focused on domestic affairs. In the mid-nineteenth century Catharine Beecher published a popular textbook on domestic science which apparently was used in a number of schools. Other women educators urged study in domestic science throughout the closing decades of the nineteenth century. In identifying the home as a focal point of formal study, domestic feminists hoped to highlight the importance of women's household roles. The domestic feminist argument that women occupied a separate but equal sphere of influence in social progress, after all, suggested that household and family problems were just as worthy of academic attention as the affairs of men.

Despite efforts at instituting domestic science courses at several of the important women's academies in the nineteenth century, however, this idea does not seem to have had a big impact on female secondary education prior to 1900. There is little evidence of many women having taken such courses in the principally coeducational public high school, which enrolled the largest numbers of women after the Civil War. Until the advent of home economics, in that case, the notion of making the home and family a focal point of advanced study was a somewhat radical proposition. The nineteenth-century high school was primarily a traditional academic institution, and in most high schools young women generally appear to have pursued the same course of academic studies as men.[4]

The impulse for home economics drew strength from other nineteenth-century sources, however. Home economics, like industrial education for boys, also can be linked to the manual education movement that began to take shape in the 1880s. It was in the eighties that sewing and cooking first found their way into public school curricula, mainly in elementary and grammar schools, as the female component of manual training for boys. Contrary to the impression given by advocates of home economics later, and by such contemporary advocates of separate curricula for women as Boston's John Philbrick, these early courses were not primarily intended to give women training for the home. Indeed, unlike manual education for boys, educators rarely mentioned the identification of vocational aims for instruction in these skills. This may have been partly due to a Victorian aversion to the very suggestion that women should perform manual labor for a wage. As suggested earlier, many educators in this period embraced vocationalism cautiously, and only as a means of encouraging boys to remain in school. Enrollments were not a problem with girls, however, so there was little incentive to develop vocational programs for them. Rather, the point was to exploit the natural interest that girls would have in these subjects to help them develop their native dexterity and motor skills to the fullest extent possible.[5]

Early instruction on domestic topics also provided a means of transmitting scientific principles and, as such, constituted a part of the traditional academic curriculum. In 1888 an article about the Milwaukee Cooking School Association was featured in the annual report of the U.S. Commissioner of Education. While the report stressed the educational value of instruction in cooking, it did not suggest that making female students better housekeepers was in any way the object of these courses (which were being offered in public school classrooms). Rather, the educational side of the cooking classes concerned "general phenomenon relating to combustion, to the atmosphere, the effects of heat upon water," and other aspects of "scientific demonstration." In contrast to the educational objectives assigned to home economics after the turn of the century, there was no mention of girls learning the importance of family life, better hygiene, or more economical ways of managing the family budget. Instruction in the domestic arts was simply viewed as another context in which to realize generally traditional aims in education. A survey conducted in connection with a similar experiment in New Haven found that the mothers of girls enrolled in these courses were enthusiastic supporters of manual education, in part because their daughters showed "increased interest" in housework as a result. Yet this information was offered less as a new reason to support such courses at the time than as an explanation of the popularity of cooking classes, particularly among mothers.[6]

Leading proponents of manual training in secondary and higher education rarely mentioned women's education in the period prior to 1900. Calvin Woodward, for instance, nearly always framed his discussions of the need for manual training in terms of the education of young men, and enrollment in his famous school at Washington University was restricted to males. Insofar as women's education was discussed at all, it generally was included as an afterthought. This was perhaps most striking in the context of discussions of how manual education was an aid to industrial growth. If men learned manual dexterity and gained experience with industrial work through manual training, it was cited as an aid to industrialization. But sewing and cooking classes were rarely seen in the same light. As a result, manual training for women in the late nineteenth century developed as a sort of women's auxiliary to the manual training movement and generally did not find its way into high school curricula. Like manual education for boys, its chief pedagogical aim lay in the development of new contexts for the learning manual activity afforded, but educators failed to reflect upon measurable social benefits that may have resulted from it. In the eyes of some, sewing and cooking were simply things for women to do while their male counterparts were learning to be better industrial workers.[7]

One reflection of the greater interest expressed by educators and other proponents of manual education in boys was enrollments in these programs. Of sixty-six specialized industrial and manual training schools surveyed by the Commissioner of Education in 1896, only thirty-five offered courses in sewing and cooking. Many such schools excluded women altogether. Enrollments nationally in manual education courses that year paralleled this pattern: males outnumbered females by nearly 2 to 1. By 1902 the number of manual training schools in the United States had multiplied dramatically, to over 232, and a substantially larger proportion of these schools were open to both women and men. This was reflected in the male-to-female enrollment ratio, which was about 3 to 2, including both elementary and secondary schools. But the ratio of men to women in secondary manual education classes, where the social purposes of the manual training movement were clearest, remained close to 2 to 1. Manual training, particularly as it was connected with vocational concerns, was a male-dominated curriculum throughout the opening decade of the twentieth century.[8]

As manual training gave way to industrial education in the late nineteenth and early twentieth centuries, it became more vocationally oriented. This was partly the consequence of agitation from groups such as the National Association of Manufacturers and organized labor, along with other supporters of industrial education who gathered to form the Society for the Promotion of Industrial Education (NSPIE) in 1906. Part of the impetus for this new organization came from a widespread impression that American youth lacked the skills required to facilitate further industrial growth in the United States. Schoolboys in the United States, it was felt, needed training commensurate with the requirements of modern industry. Where manual training had urged a generalized education with emphasis on manual dexterity and the development of mechanical comprehension, industrial education sought to fit young men to the needs of industry. This was a subtle shift insofar as males were concerned, for the manual training movement had been permeated with undertones of industrial purpose from its inception. But the more explicit concern with vocational ends raised troublesome questions about what industrial education for women ought to entail.[9]

Perhaps the biggest problem facing educators pondering industrial education for women was the matter of determining just which occupations women needed training for. At its second annual meeting in 1908, the NSPIE called for the development of a comprehensive program of vocational education in American cities, linked to local industry and designed to equip young men to work upon leaving the school. Educators, however, were uncomfortable with the prospect of preparing women for jobs in industry, particularly inasmuch as industrial job opportunities for women were limited to begin with. Some argued that schools could help prepare women for employment in the garment industry or as domestic servants and cooks. But the garment industry was relatively small outside of a few large cities—in particular New York, Rochester, and Chicago—and domestic service, although deemed important, hardly seemed worthy of an elaborate program of industrial training. Besides which, many educators—most of them male—were uncomfortable with the idea that women should be educated for any industrial role that would take them away from their families. To the extent that educators saw rising rates of female employment as a threat to the family, they hit on a common solution to their dilemma: a women's proper occupation was the care of her children and her home.[10]

This simple formulation became the cornerstone of a movement to make home economics the female equivalent of industrial education for males. In 1908, furthermore, it was an idea whose time had clearly arrived. That year witnessed the formal organization of the American Home Economics Association (AHEA) by a group of interested educators in Saranac Lake, New York. This meeting was the culmination of a series of annual summer conferences held at nearby Lake Placid through the previous decade. The women and men who participated in these meetings saw themselves as shaping a new academic disciple organized around the theme of domesticity. Their purpose was to promote the study of domestic issues as a means to improving "the conditions of living in the home, the institutional household and the community." Home economics, the term adopted by the new organization to describe the study of housekeeping, included cooking and sewing but added a wide range of additional issues. In addition to the traditionally female concerns of the manual training curriculum, home economics included the study of family consumption (or household economics), nourishment, family relations (calling upon psychology and sociology), and personal hygiene. According to proponents of home economics, the object of this avowedly broad approach to the matter of homemaking was to prepare women for their roles in sustaining what they believed to be the keystone of modern industry and civilization: the American family.[11]

The organizers of the AHEA numbered among thousands of

reform-minded middle-class Americans in this period who linked the growth of industry, the rapid expansion of cities, and their associated problems of poverty, overcrowded living conditions and ill health with a general decline in national morality. To the individuals who launched the AHEA, the American family lay at the center of this maelstrom and was threatened with destruction unless some substantial effort was made to save it. This, moreover, was hardly a philanthropic concern, for the family was also seen as the very means by which morality and order could be restored to American life in the twentieth century. The family, after all, was the context in which all previous generations of Americans had acquired their sound values and respect for authority. And what better place could there be to combat disease and malnutrition if not the family? Many of the early enthusiasts of home economics even believed that poverty itself could be circumvented by the proper management of household resources. The effort to promote the study of home economics, in that case, came to assume the dimensions of a general reform movement. In the words of one of the AHEA's early leaders, Ellen Richards, the "upheaval in educational ideals" associated with the introduction of home economics to secondary education was "nothing less than an effort to save our social fabric from what seems inevitable disintegration".[12]

The family, in that case, was determined to be the true aim of women's work, and homemaking the "natural" vocation for women in the new industrial order. These ideas, of course, were perfectly consistent with the nineteenth-century ideology of domestic feminism, and in many respects, the women and men who championed home economics in this period were heirs of the domestic feminist legacy. The principal difference between the nineteenth-century advocates of improved women's education and the champions of home economics, however, was the general social reform impulse that animated the latter group. While the domestic feminists had been especially concerned with establishing women's intellectual and social equality, participants in the home economics movement were interested in equipping women to address a variety of social problems from the vantage point of the home.

The leaders of the home economics movement were concerned with improving women's status, but felt the key to this lay in cultivating a peculiarly female contribution to social reform. In this regard they can be linked to a larger group of reform-minded women in this period whom historian William O'Neil has described as "social feminists." Like earlier women reformers, advocates of home economics remained interested in questions of equity. Much of the domestic feminist tradition of upholding a separate but equal female "sphere," after all, was sustained in the home economics movement. But champions of home economics also endorsed a separate course of study for women in high schools and colleges, a recommendation that most domestic feminists in the nineteenth century had vigorously opposed. In the space of less than a half century, it appears, the viewpoint of a sizeable group of educated, middle-class women on a critical issue in female education had changed dramatically.[13]

This shift in perspective reflected the different set of circumstances that existed at the turn of the century. By 1900 coeducation had been nearly universally accepted, and the ideas of Edward Clarke and other opponents of sex equity in education had been widely repudiated. In the early years of the twentieth century, moreover, the nation wrestled with problems of immigration, rapid urbanization, growing disparities in wealth, and the appearance of radical social movements. In the wake of the general social reform movement which developed in response to these problems, Ellen Richards, Christine Frederick, and other leaders of the home economics movement proposed to equip women with the specialized skills and knowledge they would need to make the home a bulwark against social decay.

Historian Nancy Cott has argued that a tension existed between the emphasis that women reformers placed on equity in these years and their concern with augmenting the special roles women could play in social reform. Organizers of the home economics movement clearly emphasized the peculiar contributions women could make to social improvement while retaining their traditonal roles as wives and mothers. In this regard, they stood opposed to more radical activists for women's rights such as Charlotte Perkins Gilman, who believed that women should be freed from such traditional roles (although Gilman also believed that housework should be made more efficient, an important theme in home economics). The home economics movement, consequently, generally represented the conservative wing of the women's movement at this time. The principal goal of its most prominent leaders was to shore up and extend the nurturing abilities of wives and mothers as a strategy of large-scale social reform.[14]

Other conservative women's reform groups endorsed such goals and lent their support to the home economics movement. Both the General Federation of Women's Clubs and the National Congress of Mothers devoted time and resources to the general promotion of instruction in home economics as a strategy for social reform. While the home and family life continued to be identified as women's special sphere of authority and interest, feminists were less preoccupied with issues of equity in education than they had been some forty years earlier. Now the domestic sphere was seen as more than simply an arena for women to exercise their abilities; it was a vital link in the struggle to sustain American civilization in the face of mounting social problems.[15]

The fact of identifying the importance of domestic issues in social reform, however, did not prima facie establish the need for a special course of study focusing on the home. From the very start, proponents of home economics were required to contend with questions about why women suddenly needed training for housework when it had never been provided before in high schools. Generally speaking, the rationale for instruction in the domestic arts fell in two broad categories: first, women required instruction in homemaking because they no longer learned it at home, and secondly, homemaking itself was infinitely more complex as a result of industrialization and urbanization. For both of these reasons, champions of home economics argued that it was the job of the schools to prepare women for their tasks as wife and mother.

While some educators and social reformers celebrated the growth of female labor force participation as evidence of the openness of American society, others were concerned that women were losing touch with their roles as wives and mothers. The latter group pointed to the rising incidence of female teenage employment, speculating that, while these young women were at work, they missed valuable exposure to the work habits and household skills exhibited by their mothers. The home, they argued, had historically been the context in which women learned the art and science of running a household and rearing a family. The danger in large numbers of women leaving the schools to work was the possibility that they would not be prepared for their "true" occupation as homemakers. Advocates of home economics instruction pointed out that most woman only worked four or five years before getting married. Hence, the principal work of women's lives was housework, and the schools should assume responsibility for guaranteeing that they knew how to carry it out. After home economics courses had become widely accepted in principle (if not in practice) these arguments were also used in support of establishing home economics continuation schools, aimed explicitly at working women. If women were unable to learn to be good mothers and wives, it was the duty of educators to see that they got the opportunity in school.[16]

The other major argument in support of home economics was that homemaking had become more complex with the development of modern civilization and that learning housework at home—delimited as it was by growing female labor force participation—simply was not adequate to the task of training good mothers. This issue drew much greater attention from supporters of home economics than the matter of working women being unable to learn household skills, undoubtedly in part because it attributed sophistication to the field and highlighted the importance of the home as an object of social reform.

The argument typically began with identifying the family as a vital center of essential social activities. The most basic of these, the production of household goods and their consumption, drew the most attention from the AHEA through the first decade of its existence. Although supporters of home economics recognized that industry had taken many household tasks out of the home and had invented new machines to make housework easier and faster, they insisted that modern housewives needed even more training than their mothers had. Indeed, women's growing reliance on machinery and consumption goods produced outside the home was often cited as a circumstance that dictated the need for such instruction. "Tomorrow, if not today," declared Ellen H. Richards in 1911, "the woman who is to be really mistress of her house must be an engineer, so far as to be able to understand the use of machines, and to believe what she is told".[17]

Some reformers stressed the economic effects of improved homemaking. The seemingly small efficiencies gained from better management of household budgets, they argued, could contribute to more efficient use of society's resources if practiced on a massive scale. Some maintained that if women could learn to prepare meals cheaply and trim household expenses, families could save money and help contribute to capital formation. Others suggested that such savings could be invested in a wide range of goods and services, ranging from houses to higher education. Frank Gilbreth, who along with Fredrick Taylor was a chief proponent of scientific management in industry, even suggested that women consider the use of time and motion studies to organize household tasks most productively. Gilbreth's wife Lillian and Christine Frederick became leading proponents of a scientific management perspective within the home economics movement. One of their most basic points was that housekeeping was essentially like any other job and subject to the same rules of rationalization as other more traditional forms of work. Perspectives such as theirs helped to establish homemaking as a legitimate occupation for women, a productive role with genuine economic consequences.[18]

Other supporters of home economics stressed the importance of a proper family environment for raising children. They argued that women, in their roles as mothers, played a critical role in regeneration of society. In this regard, women were made responsible for the nation's human capital, with an eye to developing both the skills and the character in future generations necessary for continued social and economic development. The most basic quality, however, was moral. Here, the advocates of home economics were perfectly consistent with the ideology of domestic feminists in the nineteenth century. Above all else, the women's function in the social order revolved around moral development. Few home economics spokespersons captured this vision as completely as Ellen Richards, who argued that the fundamental question was a matter of character.

> This material machine of ours is manufactured in the home, from the habits of life formed there. All the sciences must be made to contribute to the problems of better living conditions which render possible the truer production of human energy, which in its most valuable form, creates, organizes, combines and controls all other forces. The future of America does not lie in railroads, in machines, in commerce, in agriculture. The future of our republic will be determined by the character of American homes.[19]

A wide range of other considerations accompanied the view that the family was the vocational sphere of women. The question of nutrition, for instance, received a great deal of attention in the various home economics periodicals at this time. If American industry was to benefit from strong and healthy workers, the argument went, proper nourishment at home and in school was necessary. The same was true of personal hygiene and household cleanliness. These questions were also connected with the larger issue of public health, particularly combating disease. Home economics reformers in the opening decades of the century believed they had found sufficient evidence for concern about the conditions under which families lived. Like other reformers concerned with living conditions in the big industrial cities of the Northeast and Great Lakes regions, they worried about how poor living conditions would affect children raised in such settings. The result was a series of efforts at public education about matters of hygiene and nutrition, aimed at improving standards of living in areas where poor and overcrowded housing existed.

One recurrent theme in the first decade of the AHEA's existence was the problems of immigrant families. Advocates of "American standards" in matters of nutrition and cleanliness never tired of complaining that immigrant women did not appreciate the importance of proper sanitation. The issue, as these reformers typically saw it, was not one of poverty alone. Most supporters and practitioners of home economics believed that any family could improve its standard of living if only women were mindful of the need to do so and employed the proper techniques of homemaking. The problem with immigrant women in particular was generally seen to be ignorance, possibly aggravated by an unwillingness to learn. Investigators routinely assumed that the middle-class housekeeping standards they were familiar with should stand as criteria by which others were to be assessed. Evidence of any deviation from such standards was interpreted as fundamentally irrational. Such was the sentiment of educators at a conference on the education of immigrants in New York in 1931.

> The immigrant woman is ignorant of the value of fresh air, and in our campaign of education we have to make the mother of a family realize that ventilation prevents sickness and that sickness means expense before she will attempt to ventilate her home. The educator has to create a horror of flies by drawing attention to the flies on the filth in the street, and then showing how they convey germs into the house. Such a thing as ventilating clothing or comforters or pillows is unknown, and the educator shows that unheard of things are possible by assisting at the first bed cleaning.[20]

This passage indicates the importance home economics supporters assigned to personal hygiene and cleanliness, but it also reflects their steadfastly moralistic perspective. No where did they make reference to social structure or the unequal distribution of income when discussing such problems as overcrowded and run-down housing, disease and malnourishment, or even the ignorance of proper means of ventilation. Their remedy for these problems focused resolutely on the woman's role as a household worker: if she could be made to understand the importance of proper nourishment and a clean and sanitary living environment and could be given an appreciation for the proper spiritual development of her children, the American family could be saved from the dangers posed by modern industrial society. If urbanization and economic development had made society more complex, they argued, women required training in ways to cope with their new environment. And the most basic element of such efforts was giving these women proper values. What most advocates of home economics failed to consider was that many—perhaps most—working-class women lacked resources much more basic to survival than education in middle-class standards of domesticity.

As shown below, home economics courses became an important

dimension of women's education in this period, but they appear to have been least popular in the industrial cities of the Northeast where most immigrant working-class families lived. Eventually, the attention of home economics educators turned to other issues. The reforming zeal of the home economics movement gave way to a modulated, academic discussion of problems in family life, especially in the period after World War I when immigration slowed dramatically and public attention shifted away from social reform. All told, the movement's ability to hold the attention of large numbers of working-class women—the group identified as needing help most—appears to have been hampered by an underlying flaw in its vocational premises. Home economics as a matter of curricular reform began with the notion that family life could be improved if housework were subjected to the same rules of production and management as all other forms of labor. The key difference between housekeeping and other types of work for women, however, was one that advocates of home economics failed to emphasize but, in the last analysis, may have been most important to working-class families: women were never paid for keeping their own homes.[21] Homemaking was one career that offered no direct returns to an investment in secondary schooling.

If many—perhaps most—women in the United States in this period failed to consider home economics as an occupation (and their judgment was corroborated by the behavior of employers), in what way was the home economics movement a response to changes in women's work? As indicated above, part of the sentiment in support of home economics instruction was derived from the growth of teenage female employment and fears that women were entering matrimony unprepared for the responsibilities of motherhood. Secondly—and more importantly—however, was the commitment of educators to the idea that homemaking was the only *appropriate* vocation for most American women. The term "vocation," when employed in reference to home economics, was meant to convey a sense of women's calling rather than the more modern notion of a particular occupation. A woman's life's work, supporters of home economics argued, was her family.

This was not, of course, a new argument, but it held new implications for educators in the opening decades of the twentieth century. Unlike domestic feminists in the nineteenth century, home economics educators did not emphasize the purely intellectual dimensions of women's education. Like other educational reformers in the Progressive era, their purposes were decidedly practical. And it was in this connection that they encountered problems. One of the chief advantages of the industrial education movement was supposed to be the opportunities it afforded students to find remunerative employment after finishing school. There was a big difference in this regard, however, concerning men and women. If the industrial education movement was committed to preparing men for their careers in paid employment, home economics educators felt the schools ought to be equally committed to providing women with specialized training for *unpaid* labor.

The chief social benefits most advocates claimed from home economics were, in fact, economic in nature, suggesting that its supporters did indeed see it as training for a variety of work. Their biggest problem, it seems, was a matter of convincing female high school students to share this vision. Like many other social reformers at this time, the leaders of the home economics movement were much better at identifying problems and devising programmatic solutions for them than they were at persuading the public to support their efforts. Enrollments in home economics courses grew rapidly between 1910 and 1920, and by the latter date nearly one out of three women enrolled in high school in the United States were taking courses in home economics. As shown later, however, home economics educators faced difficulty in some parts of the country persuading skeptical women high school students to enroll in their classes. Some of the problems these champions of women's "true" vocation encountered can be comprehended in light of other school programs concerned with women's work. Advocates of home economics were required to contend with a variety of other changes in the curriculum competing for the attention of female high school students.

Commercial Education: A Vocational Groundswell

One of the most important and least understood elements of the high school curriculum at the start of the twentieth century was education for office work, widely referred to by contemporaries as commercial education. Historians have neglected to emphasize the importance of commercial education, perhaps because contemporary commentators devoted comparatively little attention to it. Home economics, industrial education, and vocationalism all received a great deal more commentary than the development of the commercial curriculum. Commercial subjects generally were not included under the rubric of vocational education, perhaps because office work was such a new category of employment. As historian Harvey Kantor has noted, commercial education courses also drew a largely middle-class clientele, and the thrust of the vocational education movement was aimed at working-class youth. Besides which, many vocational educators were interested in attracting more boys to school, and commercial employment was rapidly becoming dominated by women at this time. Commercial courses, in that case, were often treated as a separate branch of the high school curriculum rather than as part of vocational education. Yet, when educators occasionally did discuss education for business, they usually began with an acknowledgment of its phenomenal growth and its close association with the labor market.[22]

Commercial education was among the fastest growing areas of study in high schools across the country in this period. This was undoubtedly a consequence of the rapid growth of clerical work. With the feminization of clerical employment, moreover, commercial education became an important aspect of the development of a distinctive female high school curriculum. In this regard, it presents one of the clearest examples of the manner in which women's education responded to changes in the labor market.[23]

Commercial education was by no means a new aspect of the high school curriculum at the turn of the century. Courses in book-keeping and other branches of accounting had been regular fare in many nineteenth-century high schools. These courses were considered to be of intellectual as well as vocational purposes, though one underlying aim clearly was to prepare young men for careers in business. It was not until the last decade of the nineteenth century that other business-related courses began to be offered in high schools across the country: commercial geography, principles of business, and most important for women, typewriting and stenography. The latter two courses developed in direct response to technical innovations then beginning to revolutionize office work, changes that presaged the movement of women into the clerical labor force. The two decades which followed 1890 witnessed a dramatic expansion of commercial education in the nation's public high schools.[24]

Prior to 1900 most vocationally oriented business education courses were not offered in the public schools. In the 1870s and 1880s, a network of private business schools grew up in American cities to provide training for men and women seeking to go into the world of business. These schools developed the first courses in typing and stenography when typewriters were still a novelty and clerical work was dominated by men (indeed some schools were sponsored by typewriter companies eager to promote the use of their products). Unregulated and subject to no higher authority than their ability to draw students, these schools flourished in the period prior to the development of the commercial course in public schools.

Public educators railed against what they considered to be the unscrupulous recruiting methods employed by some of these schools: open solicitation of prospective students in the public schools, often with exaggerated accounts of the value of attending a business school. Investigators charged with determining the quality of education offered in these institutions reported that some were run by men intent upon deliberately cheating people. No doubt some such fraudulent institutions existed. Yet there also were many well-established schools with hard-earned reputations for effective instruction in the various branches of commercial education. Apart from occasional flashes of information revealed in surveys conducted to uncover evidence of fraud in these schools, little is known about the educational opportunities they offered. Prior to 1890, however, fully 80 percent of all commercial instruction in the country was conducted by private business schools.[25]

The three decades following 1890 witnessed a dramatic rise in public school enrollments in commercial courses. Between 1893 and 1910 the proportion of all public high school students enrolled in such courses more than doubled, jumping from 5 to over 11 percent of the entire high school population. From 1910 to 1930 enrollments in business courses grew less dramatically, but the number of students taking these classes continued to increase substantially. By 1928 roughly one out of every six high school students in the United States was enrolled in business courses. The period between 1890 and 1930 was characterized by rapid overall growth in high school enrollments, of course, so the growing share of total enrollments commanded by the commercial courses represented a rapidly growing constituency for this branch of the public high school curriculum. In absolute numbers public school enrollments in business courses increased by nearly 2,000 percent between 1890 and 1920, from fewer than 15,000 to nearly 300,000. Impressed with this massive influx of students into commercial classes, at least one contemporary suggested that the growth of commercial enrollments contributed much to the overall expansion of the high school population in this period.[26]

Most of this growth in commercial enrollment occurred in public high schools. Between 1890 and 1920 the proportion of all commercial students enrolled in private business colleges dropped from about 80 percent to less than 50 percent. Business students enrolled in the public schools increased from less than 20 percent to about 45 percent of the national total. Thus, while private business schools continued to do a brisk business in preparing students for careers in office work, the public schools increasingly encroached on their domain. Public school enrollments, moreover, expanded more rapidly than those of the business schools. Consequently, a much larger share of the overall growth in commercial education in this period is attributable to the development of high school business course than to the private business schools. Business education was increasingly associated with the public high school in the popular mind.[27]

The shift to business education in the public schools, of course, probably reflected students' concern with quality and costs. Educators claimed that the public schools maintained higher standards than the private business schools and thus prepared their students better for business careers. High school courses generally were longer than those in the business colleges, and high schools had the advantage of offering a wide range of other courses to consider as electives. Of course, they also were free. This point was probably especially important. In time the business schools came to be seen as ancillary to the public schools, a direction to turn if a student wanted to drop out of school and pick up a few office skills quickly before entering the job market. As more public high schools offered commercial courses, it became more difficult for the private business schools to compete with them for the growing commercial course clientele. By 1920 (and probably earlier), the era of the private business school had clearly passed, and commercial education was firmly implanted in the highly differentiated public high school curriculum.[28]

When educators did discuss commercial education in the high school, they generally started with acknowledgment of its rapid expansion and turned to a series of recommendations for improving the business curriculum. These recommendations were often the same from one school district to another. Perhaps the most important concerned an interest in fitting commercial education more perfectly to the needs of the local business community. The Committee on Business Education of the Kingsley Commission, a prominent National Education Association panel charged with recommending reforms for secondary curricula, suggested that surveys be conducted by local school authorities to determine the best combinations of courses to offer, along with the establishment of cooperative education programs involving local businessmen. Other studies of business education agreed. While most educators did not classify commercial education under the general rubric of vocational education, they did believe that it had to be fitted closely to the requirements of local labor markets. The Kingsley Commission report even went so far as to suggest that business courses be offered early in the four-year high school course in order to give dropouts an opportunity to acquire business skills before leaving school. Despite their arguments that commercial education was valuable both for intellectual and vocational purposes, educators often suggested reforms in commercial education that were principally designed to make it more practical and efficient as a form of job preparation.[29]

Given the rapid pattern of growth in commercial enrollments in this period and the concerns of business educators, it is clear that the commercial curriculum developed largely in response to changes in the demand for white-collar labor. Enrollments increased most rapidly at the very time that the clerical labor force increased most dramatically, and educational spokespersons concerned themselves with finding ways of better fitting commercial education to the labor market. Unlike their counterparts in home economics, moreover, commercial educators rarely campaigned for higher enrollments in their courses. They did not need to. Rising enrollments usually were a natural consequence of increasing office employment. Business education bore a unique relationship to the labor market, in that case. It developed as a response to a growing demand from educational consumers, from students and, to a smaller extent, from businessmen, for training that would enable them to pursue careers in office work.[30]

Women, of course, constituted the majority of new entrants to the clerical labor force, and they also substantially outnumbered men in commercial education courses. Although there were slightly more girls than boys enrolled in high schools across the country throughout this period, in 1920 girls outnumbered boys by better than 2 to 1 in shorthand and typewriting and held a 3 to 2 advantage in bookkeeping. These were the largest and most widely offered commercial courses in the country, and generally speaking, they were dominated by women. The same male-to-female ratio characterized these courses seven years later, the last point before 1930 at which the Commissioner of Education's statistics permit such comparisons. If clerical labor was becoming women's work in the opening decades of the twentieth century, in the twenties business education was dominated by woman as well.[31]

If business educators were aware of the preponderance of women in their classes, they rarely made reference to it. They did, however, comment repeatedly on the different career patterns men and women followed in business. And some argued that distinctive male and female business curricula ought to be established to accommodate these differences. A survey of sixty-six high school principals in 1917 found that nearly two-thirds believed businessmen wanted different training for girls and boys. Boys, it was felt, required preparation for careers in administration and management, while women needed training for relatively short-term employment as secretaries and typists. Consequently, men needed a broad education commensurate with the responsibilities they were to assume, while the technical aspects of office training were suitable for women and their generally short working careers. Surveys of the occupational status of men and women in business confirmed these perceptions. One of the best known such surveys found that in Cleveland, "regardless of the positions in which boys and girls started commercial life, boys worked into administrative positions," while women remained secretaries or clerks until they left the office to be married. As a matter of better adapting commercial education to the needs of business, in that case, nearly all the major commentators on business education from 1910 to 1920 called for separated commercial training for women and men.[32]

Despite the unanimity displayed by business education leaders on the question of a separate commercial curriculum for women, there is little evidence that such proposals were seriously considered by most educators. A survey of 112 schools with between 100 and 200 students enrolled in commercial courses in 1917 found that nearly 98 percent made no distinction in requirements for boys and girls. Detroit appears to have been one of the few cities in the country to have experimented with establishing different sets of requirements for men and women taking commercial courses. Other cities that separated men and women often did so because their public high schools were sex-segregated to begin with. Boston, for example, sponsored a female commercial high school, which offered courses leading to jobs as saleswomen, telephone operators, and a wide range of other tasks identified with educated women. For most school systems, however, such segregation was both prohibitively expensive and contrary to popular tradition. Whether for reasons of economy or principle, men and women continued to pursue the same courses of commercial study in high schools throughout this period across most of the United States. The impact of the marketplace upon the development of commercial education was substantial but was not strong enough to bring educators to formally differentiate the business course by sex.[33]

Commercial education was a unique development in American education at the close of the twentieth century's second decade. Almost wholly the result of interest generated by the expansion of job opportunities in business, this branch of the curriculum mushroomed into significance by the very force of its enrollments. What contemporaries failed to emphasize was that commercial education was also largely female. Stenography, the fastest growing of the commercial courses after 1910, was more than 85 percent female by 1927. The orientation of commercial courses to the needs of the business community, the prevailing theme in the business education literature of the period, meant that commercial education—insofar as it trained students for office work—was increasingly women's education, at least in certain of its parts. In the face of labor market pressures, it appears that a formal policy of sex segregation in business courses would have been redundant. Women were entering these courses more rapidly than their male counterparts. Commercial education appears to have been one area of the high school curriculum where formal policy was in fact made needless by the association between school and work.[34]

Industrial Education for Women

At the heart of the industrial education movement, of course, was the matter of training teenagers for jobs in industry. In practice this meant training men for industrial jobs, largely because most women did not aspire to become industrial workers. And as indicated earlier, those women who did seek employment in factories usually left school too soon to benefit from specialized industrial training. This situation was further aggravated by the narrow range of industrial occupations then open to women, and the generally unskilled nature of the jobs women held in industry. Yet, despite these obstacles, schools for industrial education for women were established in some American cities in this period. Intended to provide incentive for working-class women to remain in school, these institutions shared important social and moral purposes in addition to their technical function of training women for factory jobs. The chief measure of their success was their small enrollments and the tendency of most contemporaries to confuse female industrial education with home economics. If commercial training was an educational success story, the opposite was true of industrial education for women.[35]

Most comprehensive high schools did not train women for industrial employment. Rather, industrial education for women was typically conducted in separate schools designed specifically for that purpose, and these were few in number. Specialized industrial training for women in this period was limited to large cities capable of supporting highly differentiated school systems and affected relatively few women, or to cities with large numbers of women employed in industry. In the second decade of the twentieth century, many of these schools were organized to reach working women who had already left school. Often conducted in the afternoon or evening, these were called continuation schools and were intended to provide women workers with an opportunity to acquire job-related skills. School systems in industrial cities conducted surveys of local industry to determine the types of training that ought to be offered in such schools. The Commissioner of Education's Annual Report in 1914 listed such surveys in Troy, New York, Grand Rapids, Michigan, Philadelphia, and New York City. In each of these cities, schools for training female industrial workers were established.[36]

Not surprisingly, industrial schools prepared women for relatively few jobs. The only significant urban industry that employed women on a large scale in this period was the garment trades. Hence, most of the industrial component of women's industrial education was related in some way to sewing. Some schools offered courses in commercial cooking and painting as well. This, of course, made the female industrial course quite similar to home economics and helps to explain why contemporaries often confused them. To the extent that female industrial schools also endeavored to offer instruction in home economics, the distinction between the two courses blurred even further.

This confusion pointed to one of the chief difficulties that programs for women's industrial education encountered in this period: the work that women performed in industry was often very similar to the work they performed at home. This was a function of the general division of labor between men and women in modern society. Those types of labor that required skills transferred from the home were usually labeled women's work. The principal differences lay in the conditions under which work was performed once it became a form of employment. Most industrial courses, consequently, stressed factory methods of production. Women were taught to sew on machines, for instance, in New York's Manhattan Trade School and how to stitch together gloves by industrial methods. The object of the course was to bring each girl's work up to prevailing trade standards and guarantee her placement in the industry. The chief difference between schools such as this and the home economics course in the comprehensive high school, in that case, was the narrow vocational orientation of industrial training.[37]

For the most part, the women who received industrial training did not find employment as skilled workers. Of nearly a thousand requests for girls from employers submitted to the Manhattan Trade School in 1914, over two-thirds were for operatives in the various branches of the garment industry. Since fewer than 500 girls graduated from the school each year, its alumnae constituted a tiny fraction of the more than thirty thousand women working in the New York garment industry. Most unskilled women workers in this period either did not want industrial training or could not afford the opportunity costs associated with prolonged attendance. Of course, industrial training of the sort offered by trade schools clearly was not necessary to find employment in industry. It is possible that schooling enabled women to hold on to the jobs or to advance to skilled positions. But studies conducted in 1914 found it impossible to trace graduates of the Manhattan Trade School through their industrial careers because so many were laid off at the end of each season. This alone suggests that formal training offered women little advantage in the struggle for stable work at a livable wage. Given this, it is no wonder that relatively few women were interested in industrial training classes.[38]

Unlike their male counterparts, women in industrial schools were confronted with a rather narrow range of career opportunities. Few of them, moreover, intended to make industrial employment their life's work. Most women in industry in this period performed tasks that were learned relatively easily on the job. There is little evidence that schooling added anything to their industrial careers. Perceived widely as being unnecessary, female industrial education attracted few students. Women who wanted to work in factories simply dropped out of school and went to work. Many probably felt that working in the garment industry and related employments was bad enough to start with and certainly not worth struggling through more school. For those women who did enroll in these courses, however, schooling was most definitely related to work. But their small numbers were a revealing measure of the irrelevance of formal education to the needs of female industrial workers in this period.[39]

The Changing Face of Coeducation

The development of distinctive female courses of study in the opening decades of the twentieth century affected all aspects of women's secondary education. Coeducation had become a celebrated feature of public schooling in the United States by the turn of the century. In 1900 the Report of the Commissioner of Education declared the United States to be a world leader in the matter of providing education "without distinction of sex." Yet in the years that followed boys and girls moved through school in curricula that became increasingly differentiated along lines of gender. While schools remained coeducational for the most part, vocational courses taken by large numbers of high school students demanded that the sexes be separate. One effect of the growing interest in vocationalism in the public schools, in that case, was the development of a distinctive women's curriculum.[40]

Coeducation continued to be a matter of considerable controversy in the opening decades of the twentieth century, even though relatively few educators appear to have questioned its wisdom explicitly. While educational leaders including the U.S. Commissioner of Education and most state and city superintendents remained strong supporters of coeducation in principle, an odd assortment of academics, religious leaders, and educators spoke out against teaching boys and girls together in high schools. Several of the nation's largest cities continued to maintain sex-segregated secondary school systems throughout this period, and most urban private schools were either for girls or boys. This suggests that there was continuing opposition to coeducation, even though there is little evidence of public support for efforts to change the general policy of coeducation in most public high schools.[41]

In 1901 the U.S. Commissioner of Education declared coeducation, "or the education of youth of both sexes in the same schools and classes," to be a "marked characteristic" of American education. Two decades later, the same claim could not be made, at least with regard to secondary education. Teenage men and women continued to attend the same schools in most American cities, but took courses increasingly dominated by one gender or the other. By 1920, for instance, roughly one out of three high school girls were enrolled in home economics courses, and about twenty percent of all high school males took manual training. These, moreover, were only the most extreme cases of sexual differentiation in high school courses. In stenography, which was taught in more schools than manual training, women outnumbered men by three to one. In typing classes enrollments favored women by a two to one margin. And on the academic side, boys outnumbered girls by about three to two in physics and held a slight edge in most branches of mathematics, despite the fact that more women than men were enrolled in high schools. In the early twentieth century, it appears, the modern differentiation of the curriculum along gender lines finally became evident in American secondary education.[42]

If this sort of sexual differentiation in public high schools failed to abrogate coeducation altogether, it certainly altered its spirit. While the figures cited above reflect enrollments at a given point in time, they suggest that most men and women had at least some courses in high school limited to their own gender. If nearly a third of all women enrolled in high schools in 1920 were in home economics classes, much larger numbers must have taken home economics at some point in their high school careers. The same undoubtedly was true of manual training for teenage boys. The effect of this was to link girls and boys with different high school curricula, despite the fact that in many courses—perhaps most—they continued to sit in class together. The vocational nature of the segregated courses accounted for this new distinction. The vocational education movement in secondary education focused the attention of educators on the issue of preparing students for their likely careers after school. And few observers could escape the conclusion that high school boys and girls were destined for radically different types of work.

It was not simply a few courses that distinguished high school curricula for boys and girls, in that case, but the manner in which educators viewed their education. It established a different set of expectations regarding the education of men and women that shaped the content of the curriculum as well as its form. Even traditional academic courses were tailored to better reflect the presumed interests of male and female students. Educators began to think about changing science and mathematics courses to focus on issues thought to be appropriate for one group or the other.

This tendency seems to have affected women's education more than it did men's. Some courses simply were no longer required of women, as they were deemed of little utility in a domestic setting. Physics, for example, was often cited as a branch of science with few practical uses around the home. Some educators even argued that men and women should have separate classes in some subjects to augment the different purposes they had in education. For example, the high school in Marinette, Wisconsin, offered separate courses in chemistry for boys and girls. According to the superintendent of schools, girls chemistry was "built up largely around the chemistry of the home, of cooking, food values, and adulteration in their detection, while that of the boys classes is like that of physics, more technical and 'scientific,' calculated to be of most service to them in higher institutions and in the arts and crafts." Other schools proposed similar curricular distinctions. Although it is unclear how many of these suggestions were actually followed—indeed they often prompted spirited opposition—they reflected a belief that the education of men and women should be different.[43]

There is evidence that female enrollments in some traditional academic courses—math and science in particular—actually began to decline in this period. According to one study, female enrollment rates in algebra fell by nearly a third between 1900 and 1928, and enrollments in physics dropped by about 80 percent. These figures undoubtedly varied a great deal from one school—and area—to another. But the general decline from the high levels of female enrollment in these types of courses in the nineteenth century is striking. The division of the high school curriculum into separate male and female components, regardless how subtle, conveyed an important message. If there were certain subjects that young women simply must have studied, there were others they did not need. The decision to push female students in one direction simultaneously meant excluding them from other parts of the curriculum. The home economics movement and the introduction of domestic themes throughout women's secondary education, in that case, spelled an end to the nineteenth-century tradition of gender equity in American high schools.[44]

Even though the majority of American secondary schools remained coeducational, the opponents of coeducation finally realized their goal of highlighting separate male and female aims in education in the years following 1900. Curiously, however, this victory was not achieved through appeals to morality or concerns about health. Rather, it was the Progressive preoccupation with vocationalism—linking education with the division of labor in the larger society—which led to the transformation of women's schooling.

Several of the period's most prominent educators were in the forefront of the controversy over coeducation, and the sexual division of labor figured prominently in their thinking. G. Stanley Hall, the champion of masculinity in education, argued that distinctions between boys and girls ought to be pushed to "their uttermost" by the schools, in order to "make boys more manly and girls more womanly." Hall believed that the most important social role played by women was in the home and shared concern with other educators that schooling was discouraging women from embracing their domestic duties. David Snedden was another advocate of sexual differentiation in education. A prominent educational sociologist who served for a time as Superintendent of Education in Massachusetts, Snedden felt that courses for women in high school should be fitted to their vocational requirements. He suggested that special courses in "applied" chemistry and physics be developed to suit women's interest in housework.

Other commentators urged that the mathematics requirements for women be relaxed, simply because little training beyond arithmetic was deemed necessary for homemaking. In all instances the underlying rationale for devising a distinctive curriculum for women was the same: women were to be trained to be effective wives and mothers. Men, on the other hand, were to be prepared for a variety of productive roles in the wage economy and, hence, required a different sort of education. If coeducation ceased to be a universally celebrated principle of American education in the opening decades of the twentieth century, it was partly because educators were increasingly concerned about the link between schooling and the labor market.[45]

Private secondary schools in the United States during this period were a bulwark of resistance to coeducation. Between 1900 and 1930 roughly half of the country's private secondary schools were restricted to either young men or women. There was surprisingly little variation in this statistic over time. In 1910 about 49 percent of all students in private secondary schools attended schools exclusively for either boys or girls, a figure that corresponded to the proportion of sex-segregated schools in the private sector. By 1929 the number of students in segregated schools had increased to 56 percent of the total private school enrollment, while the number of schools limited to either boys or girls remained about the same. This pattern characterized both male and female enrollments, although boys were slightly more concentrated in gender-exclusive schools at the end of the period than were girls.[46]

Interestingly, women enrolled in private secondary schools do not appear to have been affected by the same vocational concerns as their counterparts in public high schools. In 1929 less than 2 percent of all women attending private high schools were enrolled in home economics courses. Enrollments in manual or industrial training were negligible. The only area in the curriculum of private schools that exhibited sexual differentiation on the order of that seen in the public schools was commercial education, which included about 10 percent of the total private secondary school enrollment. Otherwise women in private schools took essentially the same courses that men did. If the content of these courses varied from boys to girls schools, it generally was not designed to suit the homemaking interests of the girls or the industrial objectives of the boys. This may have been due to the rather elite character of many private schools. Private schools in this period delivered academic training of the sort required for admission to college or—as had been the case in the nineteenth century—a career in teaching. In 1929 fully 80 percent of all students in private schools were enrolled in academic courses. Unlike the pattern in public secondary education, the rejection of coeducation in private schools does not appear to have been linked to vocational concerns.[47]

Sex segregation in private secondary schools may have been due to a number of factors. In the first place, it may have been partly a reflection of the clientele of these schools. Privately supported education, after all, has always been especially sensitive to the wishes of its consumer public. If separate schools for boys and girls flourished in this period, perhaps it was because the families who patronized them simply preferred gender segregation.

There are other explanations for gender segregated private secondary schools, however. Many of the private schools included in the Bureau of Education statistics in this period were religious schools, which drew on high- and low-income constituencies alike. The largest and most significant of these groups, of course, was the Catholics. In 1910 over a third of all private high schools included in the Bureau of Education survey were Catholic, more schools than any other religious category including "nondenominational." Catholic secondary schools accounted for slightly more than 27 percent of the nation's total private school enrollment. The proportion was almost certainly much higher if urban schools alone are considered. In a national sample of schools in some sixty cities, over a third of all private schools were Catholic in 1900. By 1920 the number had jumped to more than two out of three of all private schools with enrollments over one hundred. Very few of these schools were coeducational. In both years more than 90 percent of all Catholic high schools in these cities were segregated by sex. And as the number of Catholic schools increased, the coeducational proportion of private sector high schools dropped. Indeed, the growth of Catholic secondary education in the opening decades of the twentieth century offset a drift toward coeducation in other private high schools. Much of the apparent rejection of coeducation in private schools, it seems, may have been linked to the attitudes of a particular group in American society.[48]

Catholic educational leaders were among the most vociferous opponents of coeducation in this period. Much of their opposition to men and women attending high school together associated with Catholic moral standards. "The argument of propriety is all sufficient in my judgement," answered one Catholic rector when asked why he was against coeducation in 1901. "There are dangers at an earlier period of life in our grammar schools: how much greater are such dangers apt to be in high schools?" The dangers to which he referred, of course, concerned the interaction of young men and women. In the minds of most Catholic educators, at least with regard to teenagers, there was safety in separation.

One of the most widely cited Catholic opponents of coeducation was Thomas Shields, a priest and professor of psychology at the Catholic University of America. Drawing heavily on G. Stanley Hall, Shields argued that men and women were "complements of each other, not duplicates," and therefore required different types of education. To arguments linking coeducation with equality and progress, Shields responded with sociological axioms about differentiation of structure and specialization of function to buttress the argument for separate women's schools. Shields did not argue that a separate education for women was necessary strictly for vocational purposes, his concern was one of preserving "all that is finest and sweetest and noblest in woman" from the dangers of coeducation. But if arguments against coeducation rested in part on the notion that women and men performed different social roles, Catholic leaders were willing to incorporate such ideas into their position. The critical factor in their view was the matter of maintaining proper morality at school through

It would be wrong to imagine, however, that Catholics were the only group opposed to coeducation in this period. In addition to leading educators such as Hall, Snedden, and Edward Thorndike, local public school officials in some parts of the country voiced their opposition to coeducation as well. The location of these exceptions to the norm of educational school policies corresponded to no general regional pattern, and shared little in common in the way of their industrial or demographic characteristics, other than size. Most of them had long-standing policies of sex segregation dating from the establishment of public education. But all continued to defend their policies of maintaining separate boys and girls schools well into the twentieth century.

As indicated in chapter 1, Boston was probably the period's best-known sex-segregated school system. But other big-city school districts on the East Coast also maintained separate schools for boys and girls—most notably New York and Philadelphia. Other districts with sex-segregated high schools were scattered across the country haphazardly—Louisville, Atlanta, Chicago, Cleveland, and Charleston. As had been the case in the nineteenth century, the reasons given for such policies varied considerably. Some emphasized morality, others the different vocational aims of boys and girls, and still others the beneficial effects of separate schools on male school performance. Although segregated public school districts were fewer in number than they had been some fifty years earlier, the very existence of such systems—particularly among some of the nation's largest school districts—helped to further confound the idea that coeducation was a positive virtue in its own right.[50]

If there was any single community characteristic most closely associated with the maintenance of sex-segregated schools in this period, it was size. Big cities were better able to afford the added expense of separate schools for boys and girls, whereas smaller places were often required to adopt coeducational policies because it was a way of maximizing cost efficiency. With the rise of vocationalism, some cities established specialized schools for girls. Boston, again, was a leader in this respect. By the second decade of the twentieth century, high school–age women in Boston could choose between a female Latin (or academic) school, a girls' commercial high school and a female trades school. The same was true in New York. Educators in these cities argued that such schools served the scholastic and vocational needs of both male and female students better than the comprehensive coeducational high school then coming into fashion.

Educators in other cities invoked the same principle, although few places matched the level of differentiation in sex-segregated schools exhibited in New York or Boston. Both Cleveland and Chicago, for instance, experimented with establishing separate schools for girls and boys in this period. Smaller communities could ill-afford the cost of erecting new schools to serve only men or women. Yet for larger school systems, faced with the prospects of expansion to begin with, establishing sex-segregated schools was less problematic. Differentiation, as a function of size, seem to have helped to undermine coeducation in many of the nation's leading school systems.[51]

While most educators continued to cling to the rhetoric of coeducation—and the presumed equality of opportunity it gave women —between 1900 and 1920 there was a decided drift away from coeducation both in the outlook of certain leading educational spokesmen and in educational policy. As has been argued by other students of this process, this was partly associated with concern for "propriety" and a proper moral environment in the schools, as well as concern for providing a more masculine environment for teenage men and improving overall school performance. But the effect of the development of a distinctive female curriculum in these years must have been an important factor as well. Even in most schools that claimed to be coeducational, women and men attended different classes and pursued fundamentally different educational goals. And it was just a short leap from differentiation within the school to differentiation on the system-wide basis, across schools.

The differences that characterized men and women's vocational education in this period, moreover, helped to highlight other factors that militated against coeducation. If boys performed better in all-male schools, it was in part because courses could better be adopted to their goals and interests. The movement of women into the labor force and the recognition of household labor as a legitimate field of study changed the high school curriculum dramatically in the opening years of the twentieth century and helped to shake the traditional American commitment to coeducation.[52]

American high schools in 1920 were quite different from what they had been like just thirty years earlier. A vast array of practical courses had appeared in the schools, dividing their clientele according to background and interest. There were very few references to coeducation in American secondary schools among educational leaders after 1910, except to argue that separate schools and/or curricula should be established for men and women. Gone was the laudatory tradition that had proclaimed the United States a world leader in the matter of educating men and women together. In its place emerged a concern for instilling women with a sense of their responsibility as homemakers and boosting the educational achievement of men. If the nineteenth-century high school provided young women with a widening field of life choices, high schools in the twentieth century offered a considerably more restrictive view of possible roles for women—even if many still studied essentially the same curriculum as the men. Whether implicitly or explicitly, women were told that certain roles were acceptable for them to pursue and that others were more appropriate for the boys. The spirit of equity and openness that characterized nineteenth-century high schools, it appears, was lost.

American educators began to question coeducation at about the same time large numbers of women began entering the labor force. Although cultural and religious sentiments militated against coeducation as well (not to mention the thinking of early psychologists), the recognition that women played a number of peculiar productive roles in society led many educators to believe that they should receive a particular form of education. Educational policy, it seems, was in this regard decisively related to the development of the female labor force, and the identification of women with a narrow range of productive activities associated with home and family.

Regional Patterns of Female Participation in High School Courses

If a distinctive female curriculum appeared during this period, how did women students respond to it? Did women everywhere enroll in these programs, or did different courses appeal to different groups or to women in different areas? Beyond the issue of the development of home economics, commercial courses, and industrial education, there is the matter of who was interested in these courses. In this connection it is relevant to consider regional enrollment patterns for each of the major curricular areas discussed above. By linking enrollments with the regional areas identified earlier, inferences can be made about the ways in which new subject areas such as home economics or commercial education appealed to women, and how they were related to regional economic or demographic characteristics. It is possible in this way to test whether these courses met some of the stated objectives of educational reformers. Did home economics, for instance, grow in popularity as a response to the effect of industrial society on the family? Did business education, as was often charged by its critics, develop without regard to the needs of local businessmen? These issues can be addressed, if not conclusively resolved, with the analysis that follows. A more detailed discussion of the way in which programs such as these developed in selected local settings is offered in chapter 5.

Home economics was the curricular innovation most educators in the early twentieth century identified with women. As indicated above, enrollments in home economics grew rapidly in the second decade of the century, such that most women who attended high school by 1920 were almost certain to take it sometime in the course of their school careers. These developments suggest that the efforts of reformers in the AHEA to promote home economics, particularly among women from working-class background, were generally successful. The rapid growth of enrollments in domestic science in public high schools and their slow advance in private schools would seem to indicate that working-class girls were indeed drawn to homemaking as their chosen vocation in significant numbers.

Table 4.1   Percent of All Female Public High School Students
             Enrolled in Domestic Science Courses in 1910 by Regions

REGION	PERCENT
North Atlantic	2.54
South Atlantic	11.32
North Central	6.29
South Central	8.89
Western	7.98
U.S. total	5.90

Source: Annual Report of U.S. Commmission of Education, 1910.

The opposite, however, appears to have been the case. Tables 4.1 and 4.2 present data on the regional distribution of women enrolled in home economics courses in 1910, 1922, and 1928. Throughout this period the highest rates of participation in such courses existed in the South and in the predominantly agricultural plains states. Enrollments in home economics were lowest on the other hand, in the most industrialized areas of the country, where most urban working-class girls lived. As indicated in Table 4.2, states with large urban populations, such as Massachusetts, New York, and Illinois, had very low female enrollment rates in home economics classes. Arguments from reformers about the virtues of education for homemaking notwithstanding, this suggests that home economics did not appeal very strongly to the immigrant working-class constituencies of urban high schools in this period. Home economics appears to have found its widest audience in the nation's agricultural regions, where relatively

Table 4.2 Percent of All Female Public High School Students Enrolled in Domestic Science Courses in 1922 and 1928 in Selected States and Regions

	1922	1928	1928*
Northeast			
Massachusetts	19%	33%	9%
New York	16%	14%	7%
Connecticut	20%	32%	15%
Rhode Island	13%	29%	9%
Great Lakes			
Ohio	26%	29%	23%
Illinois	25%	25%	13%
Michigan	26%	28%	16%
Wisconsin	20%	27%	22%
South			
Mississippi	34%	38%	32%
North Carolina	21%	32%	28%
Alabama	26%	31%	27%
Louisiana	46%	47%	38%
Plains			
Iowa	34%	35%	26%
Kansas	36%	39%	26%
Missouri	23%	24%	13%
South Dakota	23%	24%	17%
West			
California	32%	37%	18%
Oregon	27%	26%	15%
Washington	39%	37%	21%
U.S. total	26%	30%	19%

*Women enrolled in home economics only.
Sources: Biennial Survey of Education, 1924 and 1930.

few women pursued working careers outside of the home prior to marriage. Jane Bernard Powers has argued that home economics was an especially important aspect of the Country Life educational movement at this time, an effort to reform rural education. This may account for some of the popularity of these courses in agricultural regions of the country. Women in these areas also may have identified more strongly with their roles as wives and mothers than women elsewhere, simply because there were fewer opportunities for employment outside the home. But the women who in the eyes of reformers needed such schooling most desperately, and who had the least exposure to traditional domestic skills, appear to have been least interested in taking home economics.[53]

Evaluated on its own terms, in that case, as a means of helping working women to learn how to be better housewives, the home economics movement enjoyed only limited success. Women living in areas with the highest enrollments in home economics probably needed such training (insofar as it was needed at all) less than women living in the nation's urban, industrialized regions, where large numbers of women left school to enter the job market. But they crowded into home economics courses nonetheless. This feature of the new women's education that emerged in the second decade of the twentieth century appears to have merely reproduced many of the differences distinguishing women in the nation's major regions. If women were generally interested in becoming homemakers, they took home economics in high school. If women in other areas were most concerned with getting a job upon leaving school, it appears that they did not take domestic science courses. Women's career outlooks in this period, it seems, shaped their choice of high school studies in ways that contemporary educational leaders found it difficult to anticipate.

Table 4.3   Percent of All Female Public High School Students
            Enrolled in Business Courses, 1910

REGION	PERCENT
North Atlantic	17.04
South Atlantic	6.74
South Central	3.31
North Central	8.04
Western	12.90
U.S. total	10.75

Source: Annual Report of U.S. Commissioner of Education, 1910.

If women in the nation's urban, industrial areas were not taking home economics in high school, what were they taking? A clue to this question can be found in Tables 4.3 and 4.4, which feature data on female enrollments in business courses for the states and regions discussed above. As indicated in these tables, there was wide regional variation in enrollment levels in these courses. Enrollments were highest in the Northeast and on the West Coast, highly urbanized areas that presumably had high demand for women with business training. By the end of the 1920s nearly a third of all female high school students in the three industrial New England states were enrolled in business courses.

Table 4.4   Percent of All Female Public High School Students
Enrolled in Business Courses (Typing), 1922 and 1928, in
Selected States and Regions

	1921–22	1927–28
Northeast		
Massachusetts	32%	31%
New York	23%	26%
Connecticut	26%	30%
Rhode Island	27%	34%
Great Lakes		
Ohio	13%	18%
Illinois	22%	26%
Michigan	20%	28%
Wisconsin	17%	22%
South		
Mississippi	5%	5%
North Carolina	3%	4%
Alabama	4%	9%
Louisiana	12%	9%
Plains		
Iowa	8%	16%
Kansas	10%	19%
Missouri	14%	16%
West		
California	26%	30%
Oregon	19%	28%
Washington	19%	24%
U.S. total	17%	21%

Note that women enrolled in typing includes women in most other business courses.
Sources: Biennial Survey of Education, 1924 and 1930.

Because this measure captures only those girls enrolled in these courses at any one time—and many high school students attended school for two to three years—this indicates that most women in high school in these areas prepared themselves to one extent or another for careers in business. The same situation appears to have existed in New York, California, and Illinois, states with large urban populations and highly diversified economies. With the exception of California, female enrollments in home economics in each of these states was below the national level. Women there enrolled in business courses instead. Thus, while their cohorts in the South and plains states crowded into cooking, sewing, and housekeeping courses, women in the nation's highly industrial and urbanized regions took bookkeeping, stenography, and typing.[54]

Occasionally, educators acknowledged the problems of keeping women interested in home economics in the face of rising enrollments in commercial courses. In a revealing article published in 1921, a domestic science teacher in Philadelphia lamented that "homemaking courses do not hold the girls in school." Declaring that such courses were "entirely extraneous to commercial work and (were) only of mild interest to the girl who gets enough practical domestic science education at home," she concluded that the vast majority of girls in her school were most interested in getting a "nice respectable job" as soon as possible. Judging from the regional patterns reflected in Tables 4.3 and 4.4, this was probably true of other high schools in large eastern, midwestern, and western cities.

Home economics had little to offer a generation of women concerned primarily with getting the best job they could and who were concerned with acquiring saleable skills as quickly as possible. A number of leading educators commented on the tendency of women in the nation's largest cities to drop out of school upon finishing their commercial courses, or to switch to private commercial colleges when commercial courses in the public schools were filled. If women viewed high school in largely vocational terms, as training for rewards in the labor market, it is little wonder that they were not interested in enrolling in home economics.[55]

This further confirms, of course, the close association between women's interests in education and the labor market in this period. If relatively few women were enrolled in commercial education courses in the South, it probably was because women in those states had relatively little opportunity for white-collar employment. In those areas where women faced greater opportunities for white-collar careers, enrollments in commercial education mushroomed. Educators concerned with commercial education in this period never tired of charging that business courses needed to be made more responsive to the requirements of local business conditions. Yet it appears that the general pattern of growth exhibited by female enrollments in business courses matched the expansion of white-collar employment quite well.

It may have been true that many women did not receive particular types of training demanded by businessmen in different contexts (such as the operation of new business machines), but women prepared themselves for careers in office work in those areas of the country where the demand for women office workers was highest. If most educational reformers in this period failed to concern themselves with the growth of commercial education, it was because enrollments in commercial courses expanded independently of educational reform. Women took courses in school that they thought would help them find a job. In cities of the Northeast and West, this meant business courses. Commercial education was almost certainly the period's clearest case of education responding directly to the dictates of the labor market.

The third area of the specialized female curriculum that emerged in the opening years of the twentieth century was industrial or manual education. As indicated earlier, the proportion of female high school students enrolled in these courses dropped in this period, while male enrollments in manual training increased significantly. Tables 4.5 and 4.6 present figures for the regional distribution of enrollments in manual training for both men and women in public high schools in 1910 and 1922. In both years male enrollments in these courses followed a regional pattern that seems generally to have corresponded to the distribution of American industry in this period. Enrollments were lowest in the South, where industry was least developed, and highest in the Northeast and far West, where job opportunities in industry were greatest.

Table 4.5   Male and Female Enrollment Levels in Manual Training Courses in Public High Schools, 1910, by Regions

REGION	FEMALE	MALE
North Atlantic	3.5%	12.7%
South Atlantic	3.7%	16.3%
South Central	1.7%	7.6%
North Central	1.7%	11.2%
Western	3.9%	13.3%
U.S. total	2.6%	12.0%

Source: Annual Report of U.S. Commissioner of Education, 1910.

Table 4.6 Male and Female Enrollment Levels in Manual Training
Courses in Public High Schools, 1921–1922, by Selected
States and Regions

	FEMALE	MALE
Northeast		
Massachusetts	1.0%	18.8%
New York	1.7%	13.4%
Connecticut	–	16.0%
Rhode Island	9.8%	34.1%
Great Lakes		
Ohio	3.4%	27.0%
Illinois	0.3%	27.6%
Michigan	0.2%	20.0%
Wisconsin	0.3%	30.0%
South		
Mississippi	0.4%	7.3%
North Carolina	–	5.0%
Alabama	0.2%	20.0%
Louisiana	–	5.2%
Plains		
Iowa	0.4%	31.0%
Kansas	0.8%	25.0%
Missouri	1.0%	17.2%
West		
California	10.%	27.1%
Oregon	0.6%	14.5%
Washington	0.3%	34.0%
U.S. total	1.0%	21.0%

Sources: Biennial Survey of Education, 1924 and 1930.

The high rate of male participation in manual training courses
reported for the South Atlantic states in 1910 was almost entirely due to
the extremely high enrollment rates in industrial education in Maryland in this period. Other Atlantic seaboard southern states recorded
very low rates of male enrollment in these courses. The states with the
highest male enrollment rates in manual training in 1922, of course,
included a number of the nation's most highly industrial areas. Ohio,
Illinois, and Wisconsin were all located along the Great Lakes industrial

core area which emerged as the nation's manufacturing center during this period. Male enrollments in manual training were well above the national level in each of these states. It was also high in the Plains states and in California, where agriculture was more capital-intensive (or mechanized) than in the South, and in parts of the Northeast, where industry had long been an important aspect of the region's economy.

Yet if male enrollments in manual training seem to have corresponded to the regional distribution of industry, female enrollments may have been slightly less responsive to the demands of employers for industrial training. As indicated in Table 4.6, female enrollment rates in manual training courses were not uniformly high in those states with high enrollment levels for boys. Illinois and Wisconsin, for example, were both highly industrial states with low rates of female interest in manual education. Yet the highest rates of female participation in these programs did occur in the nation's industrial core area: Ohio and Rhode Island both exhibited high female enrollment levels in manual training courses. Conversely, of course, the lowest levels of interest in manual training were in the South. Alabama appears to have been an exception to a general southern pattern of low rates of participation in manual training courses for both men and women, perhaps because of the steel industry there. Several Southern states had no industrial education program for women whatsoever. Female interest in industrial education also appears to have been low in the plains states and on the West Coast, where industry was not as developed as in the East.

This general pattern seems to reflect, once again, the requirements of employers, but the fit between female enrollments in manual training and industry was not as tight as it was in the case of commercial education. In some industrialized states, such as New York or Massachusetts, female enrollment levels in these programs matched or exceeded the national rate of participation, while the male enrollment rates were lower than the national standard. This may have been due to the presence of particular industries (the garment industry in New York or Boston, for example), or even a single program in the schools. The numbers of women represented by the figures in these tables were so small that variations such as this are to be expected. Generally speaking, the regional pattern of development exhibited by female industrial education programs appears to have reflected the same sort of response to the labor market displayed in the cases of other educational programs for women.

Insofar as they responded to the development of vocational programs for women in the high schools, teenage girls in this period appear to have been cognizant of their future roles as workers, wives, and mothers. The regional distribution of enrollments in the programs considered above suggests that each of the various vocational education reforms initiated in this period were associated with different social and economic contexts. Home economics, probably the most important national reform effort aimed specifically at female high school students, had its greatest effect in the South, where the problems it was intended to address may have been least important. In the South, and in other agricultural areas of the country where home economics courses were widely popular, women left the schools to take up careers as homemakers. In the Northeast and the industrial Midwest, on the other hand, where women left school to work in offices and factories, enrollments in home economics courses were lower than elsewhere. Women crowded into commercial education courses in these settings to acquire the skills needed for office jobs. A smaller number, though generally more than elsewhere in the country, enrolled in manual training courses for jobs in industry.

The development of vocationalism, at least insofar as it concerned women, was dictated in large measure by high school students themselves. Vocationalism was indeed the principal theme in educational policy in this period, but the type of schooling a young woman was likely to receive was highly dependent upon her immediate social and economic context. Women in the South had fewer opportunities to consider careers in office work and enrolled in home economics, while their counterparts in the Northeast responded to the immediate demands of the labor market by enrolling in different vocational courses.

The failure of home economics in northeastern urban settings led some reformers to call for the establishment of special continuation schools for working women or for women leaving the labor force to take up housekeeping. These efforts never amounted to much in the way of actual programs but reflected a recognition on the part of some educators that high school girls planned their school careers around their own interests. "Effective homemaking education," David Snedden declared in 1920, "can only be given when 'motive' is ripe." The fact that so few women felt motivated to take home economics in the urbanized northeastern industrial states underscores the importance of the labor market in the development of women's education in this period. If the development of women's work had indeed threatened the traditional American family in these settings, the schools were powerless to bring women back to their domestic roles. The most that educators could do was to prepare women for the tasks they were to face immediately upon graduation.[56]

Conclusion: Educational Policy and Women's Work

A strong vocational impulse shaped secondary education for both men and women in the opening decades of the twentieth century. The major reforms of the period—and the most important changes in women's education—were concerned primarily with meeting the demand for different kinds of female labor and with addressing popular anxieties about changes in family structure and women's roles. High school enrollments indicate that many women were interested in the new vocational purposes of the high school, and participation rates in both home economics and commercial courses was quite high. The geographical distribution of enrollments in these programs, however, suggests that the regional differentiation identified in chapter 3 played a role in the development of educational policy. Vocational programs for women developed most widely in those areas where the labor market demanded the particular skills they offered. Urban industrial areas posed altogether different challenges to educators than the nation's agricultural areas in the South and West. By and large, curricula in the nation's high schools appear to have responded rather closely to the requirements of regional labor markets.

Perhaps the most important development in women's education following 1900, however, was the appearance of a distinctive *female* curriculum in American high schools. In the nineteenth century young men and women seem to have studied generally the same subjects. The new vocational orientation of secondary education after the turn of the century ended this tradition of gender equity. In this regard, constraint—not opportunity—was the dominant theme in women's education at this time. Vocational aims in education naturally reflected the general sexual division of labor in modern American life. Because educators could not (or refused to) imagine women playing the same set of productive roles as men, home economics was established as a female counterpart to industrial education for the boys. Where industrial education programs existed for girls, they were limited to training women for jobs in a narrow range of industries and for jobs typically reserved for women. In the case of commercial education, it was not necessary to formally segregate men and women, for the feminization of certain categories of clerical work eventually resulted in the feminization of business courses in public high schools (although many women undoubtedly viewed these courses as a welcome opportunity to learn valuable skills). In each of these cases, vocationalism was accompanied by a growing sexual differentiation *within* the high school curriculum that matched the division of labor in society at large. Moreover, there is evidence that this heightened level of gender awareness in high school vocational courses affected other areas of the curriculum as well. By the twenties Progressive educational reformers appear to have gone a long ways toward achieving their vision of a system of secondary education more perfectly attuned to the needs of the economy. One price of this change, however, was the loss of a tradition of gender equity which had existed in American high schools for nearly a half century.

Chapter Five

Varieties of Adaptation:
Local Patterns of Women's Education and Work

The new vocationalism in women's education did not develop in the same way everywhere, of course. Regional patterns of social and economic development shaped its growth, but there also were important local variations in the ways schools prepared women for work. In this chapter I explore the theme of diversity in female secondary education by examining schools and students in particular cities. This makes it possible to focus more carefully on ways in which women's education was related to the general division of labor. Opportunity and constraint, it seems, took different forms from one locale to the next in this period. The relationship between education and work varied significantly in different settings and hinged on a variety of economic, social, and cultural factors.

Local studies of women's education are necessary to address a number of issues for which data are not available on a national or regional level. It is not possible, for instance, to discuss the manner in which local school systems adopted the many curricular innovations in women's education in this period without choosing particular communities to study. Likewise, one cannot evaluate intercity differences in the way women were distributed among the various high school courses without examining individual school systems. And given the limited evidence concerning the backgrounds of high school students in this period, it is simply impossible to determine precisely which groups of women were enrolled in different courses without focusing on the cities for which such data are available. Each of these questions, of course, is important to understanding the ways in which education was related to women's work in various settings, and how it affected the division of labor. This chapter examines these and other issues that require examination of particular communities.

There is a wide range of factors to consider, of course, when comparing developments in different locales. Often there are problems of incompatibility in data sets, and questions of contextual circumstances peculiar to a given problem. Consequently, my discussion of education and women's work in particular cities falls into three parts, each dealing with a different set of issues. The first features a comparison of the development of secondary education in two cities, one in the Northeast and the other in the South. This approach permits consideration of differences in the way local school systems adopted curricular reforms in women's education in this period, differences mediated by social, economic, and cultural factors. As demonstrated below, important differences also marked the ways in which schools served local labor markets in the North and South.

Comparisons in the next two sections are somewhat less comprehensive and are dependent on data drawn from a narrower range of sources. The second one deals with intercity differences in the distribution of women between different curricula and the manner in which these differences were related to cities' industrial characteristics. Not surprisingly, there were important regional variations in female interest in different high school courses in this period as well. In the third section I examine the class background of women enrolled in various high school courses in this period, with particular attention to the women in commercial courses. With data on the backgrounds of high school women drawn from several surveys it is possible to determine whether indeed the high school afforded working-class women opportunities for social mobility. As suggested in earlier chapters, relatively few high school students in this period appear to have come from working-class backgrounds, including those in vocational courses.[1]

Education and Women's Work in Two Cities

Perhaps the most powerful method for demonstrating the ways in which two factors are related is through some form of comparative analysis. I begin this discussion of local variation in women's education and work by comparing the development of secondary education in two cities between 1900 and 1930. One purpose of this approach is to provide a closer look at the development of educational programs for women after 1900 than was possible in chapter 4. Another is to examine the role that local labor markets played in the development of secondary education in American cities at this time. In particular, I am especially interested in examining ways in which women's education was linked to divisions within the female labor force in each of these settings.

The two cities to be considered are Boston and Memphis. I selected these sites because they represented distinctive regional social and economic contexts: the industrial Northeast and agricultural South. Both exhibited characteristics of other cities in these regions in 1900. As will be seen below, these cities were marked by strikingly different patterns of educational development in the opening years of the twentieth century, particularly in programs intended for women. And it appears that differences in the educational opportunities in these cities were linked to underlying interurban differences in their economies and the development of local labor markets. Opportunity, it seems, was bound by a host of economic and social circumstances.

At the turn of the century, Boston and Memphis were cities identified in the popular mind with specific cultural, social, and economic qualities. Boston was one of the eastern seaboard's busiest ports. A city dominated by immigrants since the massive influx of Irish in the mid-nineteenth century, it was an important manufacturing center as well. Boston also was widely acknowledged to be the cultural center of New England, generally held to be the nation's oldest and most intellectually distinguished region. The latter point was especially important with regard to education. Boston shared in a proud Massachusetts tradition of universal public schooling dating from the seventeenth century. As suggested in chapter 1, education was valued highly in Boston and an unusually high level of public interest was devoted to its development.[2]

Memphis, on the other hand, was a prototypical southern river town. Established in the antebellum period as a Mississippi depot for cotton from the upper South, Memphis flourished in the age of the riverboats and the rapidly expanding cotton trade. This, of course, meant that the city's economy was dependent to a large degree upon the vicissitudes of the international cotton trade. It also meant that the local economy was dominated by commerce rather than industry. In the postwar period, local community leaders sought to end the city's dependence on cotton and to diversify its industrial base. Memphis, accordingly, became a leading community in the New South movement which developed in the 1880s and 1890s.[3] Like other southern cities in this period, however, Memphis had a poorly developed public school system by northern standards. It was not until the closing years of the nineteenth century that education became an important popular issue there. Boston and Memphis were quite different, in that case, but they were both important regional centers characteristic of their respective sections of the country. Differences that distinguished them at the turn of the century almost certainly characterized other major urban centers in the Northeast and the South at this time.[4]

From the standpoint of human ecology, perhaps the most basic difference between Boston and Memphis in this period was size. Statistics on population growth for these cities are presented in Table 5.1. Boston, like other important eastern seaboard cities, was quite large, even by national standards. In 1900 more than half a million people lived there, and Boston's suburban sprawl had already begun to draw neighboring communities into a highly integrated metropolitan area. By 1930 Boston's population had increased to 781,183, and its metropolitan area was nearly double that. Memphis, on the other hand, was a medium-sized city by national standards, although it was one of the largest cities in the South. In 1900 its population barely numbered 100,000, but by 1930 it had grown to slightly more than a quarter-million. Its rate of growth in this thirty year period (about 150 percent) was fast even for the South, where all major cities expanded rapidly—although it was substantially less than burgeoning Los Angeles in the West or Detroit in the industrial Northeast. After the turn of the century, Memphis began to acquire a substantial urban spread of its own, though it did not develop into as large and complex a metropolitan system as Boston.[5]

Table 5.1   Boston and Memphis, Population 1900–1930.

	1900	1920	1930
Boston	560,892	748,060	781,188
Memphis	102,310	162,351	253,143

Sources: U.S. Census, *Twelfth Census of the United States, 1900,* vol. 1, Population (Washington, DC: Government Printing Office, 1901); *idem; Fourteenth Census of the United States, 1920,* vol. 1, Population (Washington, DC: Government Printing Office, 1921); and *idem, Fifteenth Census of the United States,* vol. 2, Population (Washington, DC: Government Printing Office, 1933).

In 1900 Memphis retained many of the physical dimensions of the nineteenth-century cotton trading center it had been in the antebellum period. Most productive activities were located in the central city, and a substantial portion of the city's mercantile elite lived in close proximity to their businesses and warehouses. Boston, on the other hand, was a highly differentiated urban center with well-to-do and working-class districts located both within the city's core and at its outskirts, scattered around its many factories, warehouses, and service enterprises. The degree of differentiation in each city's economy at the turn of the century was reflected in their occupational statistics, presented in Table 5.2 Over a third of Boston's labor force was engaged in manufacturing, while less than a quarter of the workers in Memphis were. Larger numbers of women were employed as clerical workers in Boston as well. Because of its larger size and diverse economy, Boston had a more highly developed division of labor than Memphis, and a wider range of job opportunities for young men and women leaving school.[6]

Table 5.2 Sectoral Distribution of the Labor Force in Boston and Memphis, 1900–1930

	1900		1920		1930	
	Boston	Memphis	Boston	Memphis	Boston	Memphis
Manufacturing (male)	34.1	25.5	42.1	34.9	37.7	36.4
Trade and Transportation (male)	38.1	42.1	29.9	39.6	31.8	36.4
Manufacturing (male)	28.8	11.2	24.9	12.6	19.9	8.7
Clerical (female)	8.1	1.6	25.2	13.8	27.2	16.3
Domestic Service (female)	41.7	78.1	25.8	53.4	26.7	53.5

Sources: U.S. Census, *Twelfth Census of the United States, 1900*, Occupations (Washington, DC: Government Printing Office, 1904) Table 43; *idem, Fourteenth Census of the United States, 1920*, vol 4, Occupations (Washington, DC: Government Printing Office, 1923) pp. 1062–1065 and 1138–1140; and *idem, Fifteenth Census of the United States, 1930*, vol. 4, Occupations, by States (Washington, DC: Government Printing Office, 1933) pp. 755–756 and 1547.

This was particularly true regarding women workers. Even though the overall rate of female labor force participation was lower in Boston than Memphis, the proportion of Boston's working women employed both in manufacturing and clerical work was much greater than in Memphis. At the turn of the century, women were nearly three times more likely to work in a factory in Boston than Memphis. Nearly eight out of every ten working women in Memphis, on the other hand, worked as domestics. The variety of job opportunities for women was clearly greater in Boston than Memphis or most other southern cities. This suggests an important difference between female labor force participation in northern and southern cities: the variety of skills and aptitudes required for employment were quite different at the turn of the century.

Table 5.3   Female Population Distribution by Ethnic Groups in Boston and Memphis, 1900–1930

	1900	1920	1930*
Native			
Boston	25.6%	24.3%	67.8%
Memphis	34.4%	50.3%	59.8%
Native of Foreign Parentage			
Boston	36.5%	41.5%	(Included in above)
Memphis	10.7%	7.9%	(Included in above)
Foreign Born			
Boston	35.9%	31.9%	29.9%
Memphis	4.4%	3.1%	2.1%
Black			
Boston	1.9%	2.1%	2.2%
Memphis	50.7%	38.7%	38.1%

Sources: U.S. Census Population volumes for 1900, 1920, and 1930 (see note for Table 5.1)
* Calculated from total male and female population; female only figures may differ slightly.

Apart from the matters of city size and urban structure Boston and Memphis were distinguished by altogether different demographic characteristics. Data on the ethnic composition of each city are provided in Table 5.3. Like other large cities on the eastern seaboard in this period, Boston was a city of immigrants. In 1900, 72 percent of its population consisted of immigrants and their children; in 1920; 73 percent. The largest immigrant group, and the group traditionally associated with Boston in the popular mind, was the Irish. Less than a quarter of Boston's population were of white native-born parentage, and barely 2 percent were black. Memphis, on the other hand, had virtually no immigrants. Barely 11 percent of the city's population were of immigrant parentage in 1920, including those born abroad, and fewer than 4 percent were foreign-born. About half of Memphis' population was of white native-born parentage in this period, many having migrated to the city from the surrounding countryside. Between 1900 and 1920 the white native-born portion of the population increased nearly 50 percent, reflecting the magnitude of this movement. The remainder of Memphis's population was black, nearly half in 1900. Blacks, of course, were a large group in virtually all large southern cities at this time. And their presence appears to have affected the city's occupational structure significantly.

The fact of its large black population—and the racism black people were subjected to in the South—made Memphis quite different in character from Boston. Boston's immigrant population may have suffered discrimination, but immigrants were largely integrated into the mainstream of the community's economic, social, and political life. The same cannot be said of Memphis's black population. Disenfranchised, economically repressed, and subject to frequent spontaneous harassment, blacks in Memphis constituted a special caste in the city's social structure. This appears to have been one aspect of the city's social and economic life that bore important educational consequences.[7]

Boston and Memphis: Two Labor Markets

Like other regionally distinct cities in the United States, Boston and Memphis became more similar in the opening decades of the twentieth century. As indicated in Table 5.2, the occupational profiles of both the male and female work forces in Boston and Memphis converged with time. By 1930 both cities had roughly equal shares of their male labor force in each sector of the economy. This was largely due to the expansion of industrial employment in Memphis, one result of the effort to industrialize southern cities in the period after 1890. Most of Memphis's industry, however, was linked to the resources of the region immediately around it. Lumber and wood products accounted for more of the city's exports than any other industry throughout the opening decades of the twentieth century, followed by the cottonseed processing industry. Manufacturing in Memphis, in that case, did not entail complex assembly requirements or highly technical production processes. Local factories continued to draw upon separate pools of unskilled labor and workers trained in traditional woodworking crafts.

In Boston, on the other hand, a wide variety of manufactured goods were produced in local shops, ranging from shoes and clothing to ships and transportation accessories for New England merchants.

Thus, even though the number of men employed in industry in these cities was roughly the same, the skill requirements of manufacturing firms in Boston was considerably higher than in Memphis. Despite appearances of similarity, substantial differences distinguished the male labor markets in these cities as late as 1930.[8]

With regard to women's work, the situation in Boston and Memphis grew more similar with time but continued to be marked by important differences. Between 1900 and 1920 the proportion of women employed in domestic work and manufacturing in both cities fell substantially, and the number of women employed in clerical jobs increased. This, of course, paralleled a national trend. But it is significant that generally the same developments affected the career orientation of women in cities as different as Boston and Memphis. By 1930 more than one out of four working women in Boston and nearly one in six in Memphis were employed in some line of clerical labor.

Substantial differences, however, also continued to distinguish the female labor markets in each city. As late as 1930 over half of all working women in Memphis continued to work at jobs as domestics. And the white native-born rate of female labor force participation was considerably lower in Memphis than in Boston. Even so, the general trend of employing more women in offices in both cities was unmistakable. Since office work in this period was not subject to as many technological innovations as industry, the types of work performed by women in these cities probably was substantially the same.[9] And most forms of office work called for certain minimum standards of education and training.

These similarities notwithstanding, the clerical job market clearly loomed much larger in women's lives in Boston than Memphis. Despite the growth of white-collar employment, more women were employed as domestics in Memphis than in all other occupations combined. The female labor force in Boston, on the other hand, was nearly evenly divided between domestics, clerical, and manufacturing and the "trade" occupations (particularly sales). Thus, while women in both cities were moving into the white-collar labor force, the female work force was considerably more differentiated in Boston than in Memphis. This meant that a wider range of career opportunities were open to women there. As a consequence, the female labor force in Boston embodied a much wider array of skills than in Memphis. More women in Boston—and elsewhere in the Northeast—needed specialized training than in southern cities at this time, even in Memphis— one of the celebrated industrial centers of the "New South."[10]

Other differences in the female work force of Boston and Memphis reflected prevailing patterns of employment discrimination and an underlying ethnic division of labor. In Boston the largest group of working women was those of immigrant parentage, whether born abroad or in the United States (in 1900 the largest group was foreign-born women, in 1920 it was native-born women of foreign-born parentage). As indicated in Table 5.4 immigrant women from both of these groups were distributed among all major occupational groupings. Foreign-born women were concentrated in domestic service jobs and second-generation immigrant women were disproportionately represented in factory work and clerical employment, but neither of these groups was relegated to a single set of occupations or a particular type of work.

Table 5.4   Ethnic Composition of Various Types of Women's Work in Boston and Memphis, 1920

	NATIVE	NATIVE OF FOREIGN PARENTAGE	FOREIGN-BORN	BLACK
Boston				
Total Female Labor Force	24.3	41.0	31.5	3.1
Manufacturing	17.3	46.5	34.4	1.8
Clerical	32.5	55.2	11.9	0.3
Domestic	12.2	18.1	58.3	9.0
Memphis				
Total Female Labor Force	35.8	4.0	1.9	57.3
Manufacturing	47.6	4.5	3.2	44.8
Clerical	83.0	12.1	1.6	3.2
Domestic	8.2	.8	.5	89.0

Source: U.S. Census Bureau, *Fourteenth Census of the United States, 1920*, vol 4, Occupations, pp. 1062–1065 and 1138–1140.

Black women, on the other hand, were limited largely to domestic service employment throughout this period in both cities. As late as 1930, when large numbers of foreign women had moved into factory work or clerical employment in Boston, three out of four black women continued to work as domestics. In Memphis, where black women constituted well over half of the female work force, nearly nine out of ten were employed as domestics. The growth of female white-collar employment in both cities was limited virtually exclusively to white women. And although black women constituted nearly half of all the women employed in manufacturing in Memphis in

1920 and 1930, factory jobs only accounted for less than 10 percent of all the city's black women workers. In the South, as in many other parts of the country, domestic service was considered to be work for black women and came to be identified with them. The fact that Memphis had a large black population— meaning a large pool of available black women—probably accounted in part for the unusually large number of domestics employed there (and in cities throughout the South) in this period.[11]

To summarize, in that case, working women in both Memphis and Boston appear to have responded to changes that affected women's work across the country in this period. Important differences, however, continued to characterize the markets for women workers in these cities. Despite growing demand for clerical labor in Memphis, female employment in clerical, service (nondomestic), and manufacturing jobs lagged far behind that in Boston. The market for female labor in Memphis was stable during this period and continued to be dominated by domestic service work—virtually a monopoly of black women workers— through the third decade of the century. In Boston, on the other hand, the female labor force grew between 1900 and 1930. At the same time, working women in Boston performed a wider variety of tasks. In 1930 over a quarter worked in offices, thousands worked as big city store clerks, as purchasing agents, telephone operators, and other jobs associated with the burgeoning service sector of the economy.[12] Many of these jobs required training beyond the sort traditionally provided by the common schools—elementary schools—in Massachusetts. This labor market (like the one in Memphis) required a particular configuration of educational institutions.

Schools in Boston and Memphis

As suggested earlier, the school systems in Boston and Memphis were as dissimilar as the cities' underlying economic structures in this period. Boston's public school system was the oldest in the nation, and was much larger than its counterpart in Memphis. Memphis, like other southern cities, had a poorly developed educational system by northern standards. In 1900 public school expenditures in Memphis totalled less than $200,000, barely five dollars for every school-aged child in the city. The public schools in Boston, on the other hand, spent twenty-seven dollars per child. The rate of school participation was lower in Memphis than in Boston, so the amounts spent in each city on children enrolled in school was somewhat closer. But the difference in public commitment to education, at least insofar as it was expressed in the public school budget, was substantial.[13]

This was particularly evident with regard to secondary education. At the turn of the century, Memphis had only one public high school. Boston, on the other hand, had eleven. Boston, of course, was a much larger city, but differences extended to more than simply the number of schools. Until 1905 the city high school in Memphis only conducted classes to grade eleven.[14] In Boston most high schools offered a full four-year curriculum. The quality of secondary education, accordingly, was considerably lower in Memphis than in Boston, and because there was only one high school to attend, opportunities for secondary education were more restricted in Memphis than in most northern cities at this time. The greater number of high schools in Boston seem to have assured better accessibility to secondary education for students in outlying areas of the city. One result was substantially higher enrollment rates for teenagers in Boston than in Memphis.[15]

Table 5.5 Teenage Enrollment Rates, Boston and Memphis, 1900, 1920, and 1930

	1900 (15–20)		1920 (16–17)		1930 (16–17)	
	Male	Female	Male	Female	Male	Female
Boston	28%	30.3%	41.5%	44.8%	65.2%	65.2%
Memphis	18%	24.8%	34.5%	43.4%	61.5%	60.4%

Sources: U.S. Census, *Twelfth Census of the United States, 1900,* vol 11, Population (Washington, DC: Government Printing Office, 1902); *idem, Abstract of the Fourteenth Census of the United States, 1920* (Washington, DC: Government Printing Office, 1923); *idem, Fifteenth Census of the United States, 1930,* vol. 11, Population.

Teenage enrollment patterns in the two cities converged with time, but important differences continued to distinguish secondary education in these settings. In the opening decade of the twentieth century, school systems across the South grew dramatically. In Memphis some seventeen grade schools were built in this period, and in 1911 the new Central High School was established in the city's center. At the same time, a high school was finally provided for the city's black population.[16] By 1920, as indicated in Table 5.5, enrollment rates for sixteen- and seventeen-year-olds in Memphis and Boston were substantially the same. At that point public school expenditures in Memphis had increased to just over twenty dollars per school-age child, compared to nearly forty-three dollars in Boston. Although public school expenditures in Boston remained much higher, the 5 to 1 ratio that distinguished the two cities' educational spending at the turn of the century had diminished significantly. These were signs that the two school systems were becoming more similar. Yet other differences continued to distinguish secondary education in these cities. These distinctions concerned the type of education young men and women received rather than the amount, and it was in this regard that the effects of local labor market conditions were clearest.[17]

When the Memphis high school adopted a four-year curriculum in 1905 and added a commercial course as well as a college preparatory course, curricular features of public secondary education in the two cities were essentially the same. Young men and women could take commercial and academic courses together in the general course (although it appears that there was more flexibility to do this in Boston) or enroll in either an exclusively academic or commercial curriculum. Important differences were reflected in the choices individual students made. Of particular interest are enrollments in the commercial course, by far the most popular vocational program in northeastern big-city high schools.[18] More than other high school programs in this period, the growth of commercial education was singularly responsive to local labor market conditions.

The association between school and work was most immediately evident in Boston. Massachusetts was among the first states to embrace the doctrine of vocational education in this period, and the Boston public school system had a functioning set of vocational programs in place well before the turn of the century.[19] In addition to training in manual arts (the precursor to industrial education), the first commercial courses were introduced into the city's public high schools in 1897. Significantly, over 85 percent of the 117 students in two high schools who enrolled in these courses were women. Within two years commercial courses were offered in seven high schools.

Enrollments in these courses increased rapidly over the first decade of the twentieth century. By 1910 students in commercial courses in the city's regular high schools numbered between 13 and 25 percent of the total instructional load. Manual training and home economics, on the other hand, accounted for 9 percent of instructional time at one school and nearly 4 percent at another but was less than 2 percent at all others; they were not offered at all in four of the city's nine regular high schools.[20] This may have been partly due to the existence of special schools to accommodate boys and girls interested in these subjects; but the choices made by students in general high schools across Boston were clear. Vocational education in the large cities of the Northeast was largely subsumed by a general interest in commercial education.

In Memphis, on the other hand, quite a different pattern of course enrollments appears to have prevailed. In 1906 the city high school introduced a commercial course, partly in response to a growing national interest in such courses and in vocational education generally. Yet by 1910, a bare 82 students were enrolled in bookkeeping, less than a fifth the number taking geometry. This figure, less than 7 percent of the city's total high school student body, was substantially lower than in Boston, where enrollments in bookkeeping courses ranged between 8 and 13 percent in the comprehensive high schools. Even more telling was the enrollment level for the commercial course in the Shelby County High School, which served the area around Memphis in 1912. Less than 4 percent of the student body was enrolled in these courses as opposed to about 47 percent in the Latin course. Enrollments in home economics and agricultural courses were not substantially greater than those in commercial courses. At the end of the first decade of the twentieth century, it appears, the high school curriculum in Memphis was linked to a traditional notion of high school education as a branch of higher education.[21]

In the years following 1910, commercial enrollments in both Memphis and Boston expanded, but more rapidly in the latter than the former. By 1914 a survey conducted by the Women's Educational and Industrial Union concluded that over 62 percent of all women enrolled in Boston's high schools had taken commercial subjects. In 1928 a special report conducted by the Superintendent of Education found that some 50 percent of all high school students in the city were pursuing commercial courses. In 1928 the commercial course accounted for more public high school graduates in Boston than any other course. Interest in commercial education appears to have been high from the beginning of the second decade of the century on, and enrollments were sustained at a high level throughout the period.[22]

In Memphis, on the other hand, the growth of commercial enrollments was hardly as dramatic. Figures published in the 1913 Tennessee state school report indicate that enrollments in typing and stenography in Memphis were less than a third the number of women taking home economics. Indeed, commercial subjects appear to have been among the *least* popular courses in Memphis high schools at that time. In 1915 some 20 percent of the students in the Shelby County High School were enrolled in the commercial course, up significantly from three years earlier but still far below the levels then prevailing in Boston and other large northeastern cities. In 1919 the U.S. Office of Education conducted a survey of the Memphis schools, which revealed that, of 117 fourth-year students in the Central High School, only eleven, or less than 10 percent, were enrolled in the commercial curriculum. This contrasted sharply with figures from Boston, where 27 percent of all high school seniors were enrolled in the commercial course. At the city's newly established vocational school, some 56 percent of the 128 students interviewed were enrolled in the commercial course, most of them in their first year.[23] On the other hand, more students in Memphis High Schools were enrolled in the traditional academic courses than commercial courses through the 1930s. By the early 1940s this was even true at the city's vocational school. Commercial education courses, however, were more popular than other vocational or nonacademic subjects, particularly industrial education.[24] Yet the interest in these courses never approached the scale seen in major northeastern cities.

These differences point to the underlying influence of the local labor market. Nearly 30 percent of all women workers in Boston were in clerical work, and as noted earlier, clerical jobs typically paid more than other lines of work for women. The distinction between manual and white-collar work in Boston was important and appears to have affected the thinking of its young women. Thus, the incentives to enroll in commercial courses were high. In Memphis, by contrast, the female commercial labor force was growing but constituted only about one out of every six women workers in 1920. Most working women in Memphis toiled as domestic servants throughout this period, and a major distinction in the labor market—as well as in social life generally—was between work performed by black and white women. As shown below, this distinction found expression in the organization of the city's school system. But most working women performed manual labor in Memphis, regardless of their racial status. Incentives to pursue a career in commercial employment were smaller in Memphis than in the Northeast, and fewer women enrolled in commercial courses there. In the opening decades of the twentieth century, it appears, the development of the secondary curriculum followed the dictates of local labor market conditions in Memphis and Boston.

Differentiation in Two School Systems

There were yet other dimensions of these educational systems—related to local labor markets—that served to distinguish them. Chief among these was the manner in which the school systems differentiated as they grew. Faced with a growing demand for different types of specialized training in the high schools, the Boston School Committee established a wide variety of specialized high schools, each of which focused on a particular type of training. This was not the case in Memphis, although there was an extensive program of high school specialization there as well. In Memphis special schools were established for blacks, providing them with training deemed appropriate for the work they were expected to perform. In both cases special schools were established with a view to fitting particular groups of young men and women to different sets of tasks, but the pattern of specialization reflected basic differences in the objectives of educators in these two settings.

The first specialized schools in Boston were the boys' and girls' Latin high schools, elite academic schools requiring examinations for entrance, the first of which was established in the eighteenth century (the Girls' Latin Grammar School was opened a century later). In the opening decade of the twentieth century, a number of specialized vocational schools were started, reflecting the concern in Boston and throughout the urban Northeast for practical ends in secondary education. The first was The High School of Mechanical Arts, dedicated to the extension of mechanical and industrial training and limited to boys. This was followed in 1907 with the establishment of the High School of Practical Arts for girls and the High School of Commerce for young men.

Because it was designated for males, the High School of Commerce featured little emphasis on clerical skills. Its purpose was to prepare businessmen, not office workers. Apart from academic courses, particularly English, foreign languages, and mathematics, the most important subjects in the curriculum were bookkeeping and commercial geography. The High School of Practical Arts was intended for "girls who desire to make an intelligent study of the home from the standpoint of sanitation, decoration and care." This, of course, was a familiar theme in Boston, where John Philbrick had praised the virtues of sewing instruction for earlier generations of women. According to its catalogue, the school's clientele was supposed to include two "classes" of students: "those who do not intend to become self-supporting, but who desire the best possible training for homemaking" and "those who must become—at least for a time—self-supporting." The latter were to learn dressmaking, millinery, and other garment-industry–related trades. With this emphasis the High School of Practical Arts anticipated many features of the home economics movement.[25]

Within a year the superintendent commented on what he perceived as "a very strong trend of public sentiment in favor of specifically vocational instruction in the high schools." This was most clearly evident at that time in applications for admission to the High School of Mechanical Arts, some 600, more than twice the number the school could accommodate. But applicants for admission to the new High School of Commerce and Practical Arts also exceeded capacity, although not as much as in the case of the School of Mechanical Arts.

The High School of Commerce expanded especially fast in the years after 1908, such that by 1910 additional space was rented to accommodate more than two hundred students.[26]

The success of these schools, along with growing demand for yet more specialized vocational training, led educational leaders in Boston to establish more such schools in the second decade of the century, two for women and one for men. In 1910 a trade school for girls was established, featuring training for the garment trades. The chief difference between the Trade School for Girls and the High School of Practical Arts was the length and academic requirements of the course in the latter. The Trade School for Girls was designed to train young women for jobs in industry without having to go to high school. By 1913 enrollment in the trade school was several times that in the High School of Practical Arts. In 1914 yet another school was established for women—the Boston Clerical School. The Clerical School was intended to function as a sort of finishing school for young high school women who wanted careers in office work. Its two courses trained women for "office service," principally bookkeeping, and stenography, the latter being considered the more advanced of the two. Beginning with some ninety students in its first year, the school enrollment had grown to nearly three hundred by 1920.[27]

Other programs were tried by the Boston public schools as well, although no other special schools were established. In 1914 there was discussion of establishing a school for girls to learn to become saleswomen, inspired by the success of the Women's Educational and Industrial Union Sales School established some nine years earlier. Instead, it was decided to arrange special classes in salesmanship for women in the city's high schools and continuation schools (schools for women who had left school to work). A similar approach was adopted to train women for work as telephone operators.[28]

By the middle of the second decade of the century, Boston had a highly differentiated system of vocational education. A variety of schools and programs had been established to fit women to the requirements of the local labor market. And the flexibility of the elective system in the high schools permitted thousands of additional young women to prepare themselves for working careers. Indeed, as suggested by the popularity of the commercial course, more high school women in Boston were preparing to work after leaving school than were not. Interest in home economics courses, by contrast, was slow to develop. Even in the High School of Practical Arts, where home economics was supposed to be a major point of interest, more instructional time was devoted in 1910 to dressmaking, sewing, and millinery than to the household arts.[29] Young women in Boston were interested in courses of study and specialized training that would prepare them for the job market.

In Memphis, on the other hand, the local labor market appears to have exerted little influence on the development of the school system. Memphis had no specialized vocational schools comparable to the Mechanical or Practical Arts High Schools or to the Female Trade School or Clerical School. The city's only vocational school was not granted high school status until 1918, and as indicated earlier, most of its students were enrolled in commercial courses. By the late 1930s most vocational high school students were enrolled in traditional academic subjects. The local school board did not conduct any survey of the manner in which the schools suited the needs of local employers until 1919, when it requested an extensive review of the entire system by the U.S. Commissioner of Education. At that time, roughly a third of those students in the vocational high school who responded to the survey were enrolled in the industrial curriculum, all of them boys. Considering the absence of any sort of industrial course in the city's Central High School, this number was small compared to the large enrollment in Boston's Mechanic Arts High School. Eventually vocational courses were included in the offerings of the city's high schools, but academic subjects continued to draw the largest enrollments.[30]

There was one exception to this general pattern: the city's black high school. Although the manuals and bulletins of the Board of Education maintained that the curriculum in white and black schools was fundamentally the same, investigators conducting the federal survey in 1919 found quite the opposite. Opportunities for secondary education had existed for black students since 1888, and in 1910 an old grammar school was christened the Kortrecht High School (Colored), providing expanded facilities for black secondary education. But the 1919 school survey found that the course of study at Kortrecht High was not differentiated into individual curricula. Rather, all students were required to take the same courses: "shop-work" for the boys and home economics for the girls. The course lasted only three years, and academic work was apparently kept to a minimum, for the survey reported that no courses in either American history or civics were offered in the high school (although it appears that most freshmen took ancient or medieval history). Students doubtless also took a smattering of courses in English and mathematics.[31]

This sort of curriculum was quite typical of the "industrial" education offered to black students across the country in this period, modeled on Booker T. Washington's experiment at Tuskegee, Alabama.[32] And it was especially well-suited to the work that both black men and women were expected to perform upon graduation: manual labor in factory or service jobs and domestic service. Jane Bernard-Powers has argued that home economics became a course of study specifically designated for minority women in a number of cities in this period. Black women enrolled in home economics courses in other southern cities, and Mexican-American women took special domestic science courses in the Southwest and Pacific states. Domestic training, Bernard-Powers maintains, was seen as appropriate for these groups of women because large numbers of them worked as household domestics. In this regard the Memphis school system was not unique. If black women worked almost universally as domestics in Memphis, local educators reasoned, what better training was there for them than instruction in domestic science? The very fact that educated black women were not considered suitable for clerical training in a major southern city reveals yet another connection between women's education and work at this time. If white secondary education in Memphis was not designed to fit the requirements of the local labor market, the city's black high school curriculum was.[33] Like the labor force itself, the schools in Memphis were divided between black and white.

Schools in Boston and Memphis, in that case, were characterized by fundamentally different patterns of organization. Both systems were functionally linked to the demand for different types of labor, but the manner in which the schools were adapted to these purposes was entirely different. In Boston schools were created to train young men and women to do particular jobs. In Memphis special schools were established for a particular social group and equipped to prepare them for the limited range of occupations they were permitted to pursue. In one system, schools were designed to facilitate the movement of young men and women into careers of their own choosing—however these choices were to be made—and in the other, schools were established to guarantee that students would move into an occupational system segmented along lines of race. Industrial and commercial expansion and associated demands for different types of labor was a major motivating factor in one system, racism and a highly discriminatory bifurcation in local labor markets in the other. Education adapted itself to two entirely different sorts of labor markets in these cases (not to mention associated opportunity structures) in quite different ways.

Women's Work and the High School Curriculum: Patterns of Adaptation

The foregoing discussion has suggested that important differences distinguished women's education from one urban context to the next in this period. In Boston, high school students poured into vocational classes, particularly those in commercial subjects, while schools in Memphis continued to emphasize a traditional academic curriculum for white students and a narrow vocational course for blacks. In the discussion that follows, I continue to focus on female enrollments in different high school courses, but I also expand my comparative analysis to a number of other cities in the Northeast, Midwest, and the far West. Unlike the opening section of this chapter, this analysis does not extend to differences in the manner in which local school systems were organized in this period. Rather, I limit my discussion to a single survey of high school attendance patterns, conducted by George Counts in 1920 and published in his book, *The Selective Character of American Secondary Education*.[34] This survey was one of a very few in this period that systematically examined the manner in which students were distributed across different high school courses. And it was the only one to do so in a number of urban contexts simultaneously. Counts's study, thus, offers a rare opportunity to further assess the relationship between women's work and high school enrollment patterns in this period.

While the object of Counts's study was an analysis of the backgrounds of high school students, he and his associates collected a wide assortment of data about American high schools in this period. His survey is particularly well-suited for use in a study such as this because it was limited to four cities, three of which represented distinctive regional patterns of urban development—Bridgeport (Connecticut), St. Louis, and Seattle.[35] The educational data Counts provided for each of these cities, moreover, can be linked with social and economic evidence for purposes of comparative analysis. These cities, after all, were characterized by different types of female labor markets, and each was associated with a distinctive economic function. The Counts survey, which gathered data on enrollment levels in different high school curricula, thus provides an opportunity to link enrollment patterns to intercity differences in employment and other economic indicators.

Table 5.6 presents data on the female labor force in these three cities, revealing the manner in which working women were distributed between the major occupational categories in each of them. A glance at certain of these categories reveals important differences between these cities. Bridgeport was a manufacturing town, dominated by a relatively narrow range of industries. In 1930 nearly 38 percent of the female labor force there was employed in manufacturing, most of them in factories producing clothing or electrical machinery. In Seattle, on the other hand, relatively few women worked in manufacturing. This pattern of female employment was characteristic of cities in the West, which typically had fewer women employed in industry than cities in the Northeast. Seattle was hardly a manufacturing center in this period and, consequently, had few of the industries that employed large numbers of women. Rather, it functioned as a central point for collection and distribution of goods and services for the entire Pacific Northwest. As a result, the occupational distribution in Seattle featured large numbers of women working in "trade" (both wholesale and retail) and the professions. As far as city function was concerned, Bridgeport and Seattle lay at opposite ends of the spectrum.

Table 5.6   Industrial Distribution of Working Women during 1930 in Four Cities

	BRIDGEPORT	ST. LOUIS	SEATTLE	BOSTON
Overall female labor force participation rate	28.5%	29.5%	29.1%	32.5%
Manufacturing	37.6%	23.4%	10.5%	19.1%
Clerical	23.4%	24.9%	27.1%	27.2%
Transportation/communication	2.1%	2.7%	2.6%	3.3%
Trade	8.2%	9.6%	14.8%	9.8%
Domestic service	16.5%	29.8%	28.8%	26.7%
Professional service	12.1%	9.5%	16.0%	13.8%

Source: U.S. Census Bureau, *Fifteenth Census of the United States, 1930,* vol 4, Occupations by States, pp. 277, 730, 910, and 1726.

St. Louis, although located in the border region between the industrial Northeast and the South, appears to have had a female occupational distribution quite similar to the large northeastern cities. The distribution of women workers across the categories in Table 5.6, for instance, was virtually the same in St. Louis and Boston in this period. Because of its close proximity to the South, St. Louis did have a considerably larger black population than most northern cities at the time. But unlike most southern cities, many women were employed in manufacturing and clerical jobs. In this respect, it resembled many industrial cities. Unlike Bridgeport, however, its local economy was not dominated by a narrow range of industries. St. Louis was not a specialized manufacturing center, and its working women were evenly distributed among the principal female occupational categories. On the other hand, a substantially smaller share of St. Louis's female work force was employed in trade and the professions than was the case in Seattle. Situated on the edge of the nation's industrial core area, St. Louis shared trade and service functions with a wide variety of other cities. It was a diversified manufacturing center serving a national market as well as its own immediate hinterland.[36]

Each of these cities, it appears, represented different patterns of urban development. Data collected from all three, thus, provide an opportunity to compare urban educational programs in each of several distinctive regional contexts, excluding of course, the South. Table 5.7 presents data on female enrollments in different high school curricula for each of these cities. Women in each, it appears, had different interests in secondary education. In Bridgeport, a specialized manufacturing center, fully half of all the women in high school were enrolled in the commercial course, while barely one in five were enrolled in the college course (another 27 percent were enrolled in the normal school course). In St. Louis, a larger city with a more diversified economic base, enrollments in the commercial course and the general or academic course were roughly the same. And in Seattle, a city with relatively little opportunity for manufacturing employment for young women and large numbers of women professionals, female enrollments in the college and academic courses together were more than twice as great as those in the commercial course. Women, it seems, went to school in these cities with altogether different purposes in view.

Table 5.7 Female Enrollments in Different High School Curricula, Three Cities in 1920

CURRICULUM*	BRIDGEPORT	ST. LOUIS	SEATTLE
Academic[†]	20.5%	44.1%	61.5%
Commercial	50.2%	40%	26.1%
Home Economics	–	9.4%	8.2%

Source: Counts, *The Selective Character of American Secondary Education*, chapter 8.

*Totals do not add up to 100% because some curricula were omitted, such as the normal school course and industrial arts.

†Including courses described as both "collegiate" and "general."

The most striking case of educational development in this small sample of cities, given the earlier discussion of Boston and Memphis, was Seattle. As in Memphis, female commercial enrollments there were relatively low, and most women were enrolled in one of the two academic courses. Indeed, Seattle, like other cities in the West in this period, was similar to southern cities with regard to female employment in manufacturing. Cities in both the South and West developed principally as trade centers for agricultural and resource-extractive hinterlands. That, however, was generally as far as most of the similarities went.

What made Seattle distinctive, along with other cities on the West Coast, was the relatively large portion of its female labor force employed in white-collar jobs (professional services, trade, and clerical work). In 1930 nearly 60 percent of the female labor force in Seattle was engaged in these types of occupations. In Memphis, on the other hand, nearly two-thirds of the city's working women were engaged in manual labor, more than half in domestic service alone. Many of the women who enrolled in Seattle's high schools, in that case, could aspire to employing their school-related skills in the job market, while most working women in the urban South had little need of formal schooling. This may explain in part why high school enrollment levels were higher in West Coast cities than elsewhere in the country. A relatively small number of high school women in Memphis and other southern cities could put their schooling to use in employment, particularly those enrolled in the academic course. Although the curricular distribution of female high school students in western and southern cities was similar in this period, the relationship of education to women's work was quite different in these settings.

The most important difference between Seattle and other cities in the Counts survey was the moderate level of female enrollment in commercial courses there. This is particularly remarkable in light of the large numbers of women employed in clerical work in Seattle. Even though clerical jobs commanded as large a share of the female work force there as in eastern cities, enrollment in commercial courses in Seattle were lower than in most cities in the east. Female school participation rates in Seattle were high, of course, and it is possible that some women who were enrolled in college and academic courses found employment in offices after leaving school.[37] This was far from inconceivable, particularly if women in these curricula had taken typing and stenography, either as electives or in one of the city's private business or secretarial schools. After all, educators and businessmen had long agreed that the most essential requirements for a successful career in clerical work (good manners, command of the language, spelling, grammar, and punctuation as well as typing) were only incidentally related to the commercial course. The relatively low level of female high school students enrolled in commercial classes in Seattle, in that case, may be a bit misleading, at least with regard to linking female secondary education to the demands of local labor markets.

A survey of the content of commercial courses in high schools across the country in this period revealed that the commercial curriculum generally differed little from the general or academic course. Only about 30 percent of the classes in most commercial curricula were explicitly vocational (these included typing, shorthand, and bookkeeping), the rest were standard "modern" academic subjects such as English, mathematics, and history.[38] Given this, it is possible that some employers may even have preferred women with a strong academic background to those with narrower vocational preparation, thinking that they were more competent spellers or grammarians.[39] Whatever the case, Seattle's experience makes it clear that high female employment in clerical jobs was not necessarily accompanied by high enrollments in the high school commercial course in this period. A high rate of female secondary school participation, even without large enrollments in commercial education, was apparently sufficient to satisfy the city's need for women trained for clerical labor.

Given that enrollment in the commercial course was not a prerequisite to clerical employment in many instances, perhaps the pattern of female enrollments in different high school curricula in Seattle was a reflection of women's interests in education rather than their concern with getting jobs. As indicated in chapter 2, this would be consistent with patterns of female enrollment in the latter nineteenth century, before female employment in offices became commonplace. It is possible, of course, that high female enrollment in the academic courses may have been linked to the large number of jobs for women in "trade" and the professions in Seattle. But employment opportunities in these areas were hardly great enough to account for the high level of female enrollment in academic courses there. Instead, it appears that many young women in Seattle chose their high school curricula without regard to their future employment prospects. In this respect, they seem to have been quite similar to many of the women discussed in chapter 2, and different from many of their contemporaries in eastern cities, who poured into commercial courses. Secondary education may have been seen as less an investment in future earning power in Seattle than it was an object of consumption, perhaps as a way of affirming status, or a matter of preparing young women to be well-informed mothers.

This pattern of high school enrollment stands in sharp contrast to Bridgeport, where fully half of all women in high school were enrolled in the commercial course. Many young women in Bridgeport, or for that matter in Boston and St. Louis, apparently thought of secondary education in vocational terms. An important difference between Seattle and the industrial cities of the Northeast, of course, was the size of the manufacturing sectors of their economies. As indicated in Table 5.6, more than 60 percent of the labor force in Bridgeport, males and females, were employed in industry, compared with about 41 percent of the labor force in St. Louis. As the Counts study indicates, average assessed income levels were lower in Bridgeport and St. Louis than they were in Seattle, just as income levels were generally less in the East than in the West at this time.[40] Thus, it is possible that families in the industrial cities of the Northeast were more dependent upon the earning power of their daughters than parents in the far West and urged them to enroll in courses that could land them a job upon leaving school.

As suggested in chapter 3, young women in eastern cities may have been forced to work by their family circumstances more often than their counterparts in the West. Faced with this situation, perhaps women in Bridgeport and other industrial cities viewed commercial education as a means of avoiding the lower wages, debilitating working conditions, and seasonal uncertainties of employment in industry. Young women in Seattle, on the other hand, may not have been as concerned with their occupational careers, partly because so few women there worked in manual occupations and because families there were less dependent upon their daughters' earnings. Generally higher levels of income, coupled with an occupational structure dominated by white-collar employment, may have made women in Seattle less preoccupied with vocational courses in the schools than their counterparts elsewhere.[41]

One relevant variety of evidence in assessing such explanations, of course, is information on the backgrounds of women enrolled in the high schools of these cities. If, for instance, a large proportion of the women enrolled in high schools in northeastern industrial cities were from working-class backgrounds, it could account for the larger numbers of women taking commercial courses in the East. Women from families with low incomes, after all, would clearly have had more reason to enroll in such courses than would their classmates from more affluent backgrounds.

Table 5.8 presents data on the occupational status of the fathers of women enrolled in high school in Bridgeport, St. Louis, and Seattle. A glance at the proportions represented by each major occupational group in the high schools of these cities, however, suggests that intercity differences in the backgrounds of female high school students in this period were not very great. The numbers of women whose fathers were employed as unskilled workers did not vary much from one city to the next and, in fact, were greater in Seattle than in either of the more industrial eastern cities. It is unlikely, in that case, that women in Eeastern cities enrolled in vocational courses because of their poor backgrounds. Some other explanation of intercity differences in curricular development must be found.

Table 5.8   Fathers' Occupations of Women Enrolled in High School, Three Cities in 1920

	BRIDGEPORT	ST. LOUIS	SEATTLE
Professionals and Managers*	41.8%	44.9%	42.5%
Commercial and Clerical	11.8%	18.5%	13.1%
Skilled Workers**	30.8%	22.5%	24.6%
Unskilled Workers†	9.6%	9.7%	11.6%

Source: Counts, *The Selective Character of American Secondary Education,* chapter 8.

* Including "proprietors" and "commercial service."

†Including "miscellaneous trades," "transportation service," "machine trades," "printing trades," "building trades," and "artisan proprietors."

What is especially striking about the pattern of female enrollments in Seattle at this time is the relatively large number of young women enrolled in *academic* courses there, as well as the rather high overall enrollment level for high school–age girls. In his study of vocational education in California at this time, Harvey Kantor has revealed high academic course enrollments in other West Coast cities, although his data are not broken down by gender. In a survey of career aspirations conducted among California high school students in 1927, nearly half the women expressed an ambition to professional positions, most of them in teaching.[42] This was clearly quite different from Bridgeport, where a bare 20 percent of the city's high school girls were enrolled in a precollegiate course of studies. In industrial settings, it appears, secondary education may have been seen as a matter of immediate vocational training, a way of improving one's status and augmenting family income, even for women from middle-class families. In cities such as Seattle, on the other hand, many women apparently went to high school for different reasons. For them secondary education may have been a way to learn more about the world, to prepare themselves for a professional position, and to eventually rear their own families. Secondary education for young women in Seattle at this time may have been viewed like it had been by women in the nineteenth century.

These intercity differences in curricular choice seem to have been unrelated to differences in social status. In all three cities the high school served a largely middle-class clientele. It is possible, however, that yet other factors may have accounted for the high level of interest registered in commercial education in eastern cities. Ileen Devault has suggested that young women from skilled workers' families enrolled in commercial courses because of status anxiety among skilled workers in a context of rapid industrial change. In many industrial cities in the East at this time, skilled workers were being displaced by technology and by inexpensive immigrant labor. Working-class neighborhoods were being transformed by the arrival of vast numbers of unskilled immigrant workers and their families. In this setting, DeVault has argued, middle-class families became particularly concerned with certifying or improving their social status, and getting a job in an office was often seen as a tangible sign of middle-class standing. This was especially evident among women from the families of skilled blue-collar workers.

Given DeVault's findings, it is reasonable to expect that commercial enrollments would be higher in industrial cities such as Bridgeport or Pittsburgh than in such places as Seattle or other West Coast cities. Indeed, a higher number of the students in Bridgeport were from skilled working-class families than any other city in the group. Perhaps commercial enrollments were high there because of the factors DeVault has identified: concern about these women's future status in a setting of industrial change and cultural conflict. Women in Seattle, on the other hand, may have been less anxious to study commercial subjects simply because they felt less anxiety about their futures than middle-class women in industrial settings at this time. Choice of curriculum, it seems, may have been related to the circumstances of change that shaped status anxiety in the early twentieth century. Of course, it is very difficult to test this interpretation thoroughly, but if DeVault is correct, her argument may account for a large part of the curricular variation observed in Counts's study. Vocationalism and the movement of women into white-collar jobs—at least in some instances —may have been partly a consequence of the general process of social change that transformed the nation's industrial cities at this time.[43]

Education and Social Class: Women in Clerical Courses

The foregoing, of course, raises the question of how women's social and economic background affected the likelihood of their enrolling in particular courses at this time. It makes sense, after all, to guess that working-class women (whether from skilled or unskilled working-class backgrounds) were more likely to enroll in vocational courses; they often were interested in finding employment as soon as possible. It also makes sense, on the other hand, to surmise that middle- and upper-class women were more likely to be enrolled in collegiate or academic courses than were working-class women. Because of their own social status, many of these women probably were interested in pursuing professional careers before they left the labor market for marriage. Using evidence from Counts and a number of more recent studies, it is possible to identify the social backgrounds of the young women who enrolled in various high school curricula. And it is this sort of information that can help in making inferences about the social impact of secondary education.

The key question is whether the new vocational curriculum of the twentieth-century high school attracted a new clientele. The most important single element of the new curriculum, of course, was the commercial course. As suggested earlier, these courses were especially popular in the cities of the Northeast, where thousands of young women poured into classes on typing, stenography, and bookkeeping each year. The distinctive characteristic of cities in the Northeast was their industrial base, and the large numbers of unskilled workers employed in manufacturing there. As high school enrollments rose in the opening decades of the twentieth century, larger numbers of children from working-class families in these cities were drawn into the schools. In cities dominated by manufacturing employment, such as Bridgeport, women from working-class backgrounds came to constitute a substantial portion of the high school's student body.

This raises a number of intriguing questions. At bottom is the matter of determining just how many of these working-class women were actually enrolled in the commercial course. A job as a clerical worker, after all, represented a significant improvement in the status of many working-class women—particularly those whose fathers were unskilled laborers. And this may have constituted an important incentive for these women to stay in school. To what extent, in that case, did business courses provide opportunities for social mobility to women from working-class backgrounds?

In the past few years, several studies which have ventured explanations for the rise of high school enrollments in American cities in this period. Most of these accounts agree that education came to be viewed as a vehicle for upward mobility in the opening decades of the twentieth century, particularly as large numbers of young men and women began to move into white-collar jobs. Such jobs would hold special appeal to the sons and particularly the daughters of working-class men, who often sought alternatives to the difficult, dangerous, and low-paying work their parents performed. At least one historian of this process has argued that many such students enrolled in the then burgeoning commercial courses and that they constituted the bulk of the new clientele brought into the schools because of these classes.[44]

Did commercial education indeed account for the growth of high school enrollments in this period? Were commercial courses dominated by a working-class clientele? These questions along with the issue of whether the high school curriculum in this period was organized along class lines, can be addressed with data from Counts's study of high schools in 1920 and a survey of "Women in Office Service," conducted in Boston by the Women's Educational and Industrial Union (WEIU) in 1914.[45] Both of these surveys provide information on the backgrounds of women enrolled in other noncommercial courses as well. As shown below, questions such as these pose special conceptual problems associated with different terms employed in the analysis. In part, the very definition of "class" and "mobility" shape the conclusions of this sort of discussion.

Perhaps the easiest question to consider is the matter of whether the high school curriculum was differentiated in this period in order to serve girls from different social classes. This was one of the issues Counts hoped to address with his study, and his data are well-suited to identifying the backgrounds of women enrolled in different high school courses.[46] Table 5.9 presents the distribution of female high school students from different types of backgrounds among various curricula in Bridgeport, St. Louis, and Seattle. These women were classified according to the occupational status of their fathers, which were grouped into several broad categories. These groups were generally distinguished by the types of work they performed, by the control each group exerted over the work process, and by educational requirements and income. White-collar workers typically enjoyed greater autonomy, higher income and greater status than manual laborers, and skilled workers earned more and enjoyed higher social standing than unskilled workers. The group with the highest status was women with fathers who were professions or well-to-do businessmen and managers (including men described as "executives" today). Women from families headed by unskilled blue-collar workers stood at the bottom of the social scale. Counts devised these categories to determine whether indeed high school students' backgrounds were related to their standing in school.

Table 5.9 Curricular Distribution of Female Students from Different Occupational Backgrounds in Three Cities, 1920

	PROPRIETORS, PROFESSIONALS, AND MANAGERS	COMMERCIAL AND CLERICAL WORKERS	SKILLED WORKERS	UNSKILLED WORKERS	TOTAL	OVERALL PUBLIC HIGH SCHOOL ATTENDANCE RATE
Bridgeport						
College	66.8	14.8	9.2	3.2	20.5	
Commercial	30.9	11.2	39.6	12.7	50.2	
Total	41.8	11.8	30.8	9.6		18.7%
St. Louis*						
General	51.4	21.1	13.5	7.3	44.1	
Home Economics	51.2	20.1	18.5	7.6	9.4	
Commercial						
4-year	38.2	16.1	28.1	12.7	21.6	
2-year	25.4	15.1	41.8	13.8	18.4	
Total	44.9	18.5	22.5	9.7		17.8%
Seattle						
College	54.6	15.1	15.6	7.5	35.8	
General	59.8	13.9	26.1	11.6	25.7	
Home Economics	34.1	13.9	25.6	16.0	8.2	
Commercial	30.2	9.3	28.4	16.9	26.1	
Total	42.5	13.1	24.6	11.6		28.8%

Source: Counts, *The Selective Character of American Secondary Education*, chapter 8
* White students only.

As indicated in Table 5.9, women from different backgrounds appear to have been associated with different high school curricula in this period. In all three cities women with fathers working in white-collar jobs were disproportionately enrolled in academic or collegiate high school courses. Women from working-class families, on the other hand, were much more likely to be enrolled in commercial courses than their higher-status schoolmates. To the extent that academic courses were held in higher esteem than the commercial course, this suggests that high school students in this period were differentiated along class lines in school.

This did not mean, however, that different high school courses were characterized by different classes of students. While women from high status backgrounds clearly dominated the academic courses, work-ing-class women did not constitute a majority in commercial courses. The bulk of high school students in this period came from white-collar family backgrounds. Thus, while there was clearly some curricular dif-ferentiation along class lines, the commercial course was by no means the special province of working-class women in this period.

In Boston it appears that the high school commercial course drew fewer students from well-to-do families than in other cities. As indicat-ed in Table 5.10, the WEIU survey found that less than 10 percent of all women enrolled in business courses there had fathers employed as professionals or substantial businessmen. More than three out of four of them were from the families of skilled blue-collar workers or white-collar office workers. Some 43 percent of the women enrolled in day-time commercial courses in Boston were from the families of blue-col-lar skilled workers, men employed in industry and service jobs. This figure is generally consistent with those reported for this group in Bridgeport and St. Louis in Counts's survey and with the findings of Ileen Devault's study of commercial students in Pittsburgh.[47]

Table 5.10   Occupational Background of Girls in Boston Public High
              School Clerical Courses, 1913

TOTAL (N = 552)	DAY SCHOOL (N = 244)	EVENING SCHOOL (N = 308)
Unskilled or personal service workers 15.5%	12.3%	18.2%
Skilled or public service workers 45.1%	43.4%	46.4%
Government or business white-collar workers 29.3%	31.9%	27.2%
Professionals and businessman (real estate, insurance agents, bankers, brokers, entrepreneurs) 71%	9.8%	4.9%

Source: From WEIU, *The Public Schools and Women in Office Service,* p. 163.

The major difference in the backgrounds of women interviewed in both surveys, in that case, was the size of the group with fathers employed in white-collar or clerical work, both in business and gov-ernment. In Boston nearly a third of all women enrolled in daytime business courses were from this occupational background. Women from presumably similar backgrounds in Counts's cities, on the other hand, accounted for a much smaller share of the high schools' commercial students.

This difference may have been due to the importance of white-collar work in Boston, which was a major regional center of trade in this period. But given the generally uniform expansion of clerical employment in all large northeastern cities, such an explanation seems improbable. It is more likely that this difficulty springs from the manner in which occupational categories were defined in these surveys. If Counts included occupations in his "commercial and clerical" category that were listed in the "professional and businessmen" group in the WEIU survey, much of the difference noted above could be explained as a matter of definition alone. Indeed, if the professional and managerial and clerical categories in both surveys were combined, the results would have been a single white-collar category of roughly equal proportions. This broad category accounted for between 40 and 50 percent of all women enrolled in commercial courses in these cities.

Because of the difficulty in distinguishing between the two white-collar occupational groups in these surveys, I use a single white-collar category in the discussion that follows. This permits data from both surveys to be considered simultaneously, without sacrificing the analytical advantages of having two white-collar categories. In any case, the distinction between women with fathers employed in different types of white-collar work is not essential to determining whether commercial courses contributed to social mobility in this period.

The critical issue, it appears, is the problem of classifying women from working-class families. If women with fathers employed in blue-collar occupations are classified as working class, about half of all women in high school business courses in American cities in this period were from working-class backgrounds. But important differences distinguished skilled blue-collar workers from unskilled workers. As indicated in Table 5.9, the largest group of working-class women in commercial courses in this period were the daughters of skilled workers: men who worked in the building trades, as skilled mechanics, machine operators, and the like, and who enjoyed substantially higher incomes than unskilled workers.

Historians have long acknowledged the differences between skilled, largely native-born workers and unskilled laborers, many of whom were immigrants. Women from the families of skilled workers, all other things being equal, enjoyed a higher standard of living and greater status than their cohorts from the families of unskilled workers. Because wage rates for skilled workers were generally rising, these men often aspired to middle-class status and eschewed a strong identity with the mass of unskilled (and often largely immigrant) laborers. Their children, conscious of differences in income and culture, may have identified with the interests, values, and goals of other "middle-income" groups in the schools, such as the sons and daughters of the growing corps of white-collar workers. This process was enhanced, no doubt, by the growing differentiation of the urban landscape, as middle-income skilled tradesmen began to move to suburban communities in larger numbers in this period. Despite their working-class origins, there can be little doubt that many families in this category saw themselves as distinctly "middle-class".[48]

Though often subtle, these distinctions are important for assessing whether the move to clerical work represented social mobility for working-class girls in this period. Barely one female secondary student in ten had fathers employed as unskilled workers. For these girls the prospect of a job in an office held the promise of substantial social mobility. Clerical workers earned considerably more than women in unskilled industrial labor, and being a form of skilled labor itself, office work carried a good deal more prestige as well (status enhanced, no doubt, by the relatively short workweek and the relatively quiet, clean work environment characteristic of clerical jobs). Women from unskilled working-class families, in that case, could almost certainly enhance their status by finding employment as office workers.[49]

For the daughters of skilled workers, on the other hand, clerical work held fewer advantages of enhanced social ability. Wages for skilled workers in this period were relatively high, and their families were typically less dependent upon their daughters earnings than were those of unskilled workers. Thus, the financial advantages of clerical work probably exerted less pull among women with skilled fathers than among those with unskilled parents.[50] Similarly, clerical work held out less opportunity for improved prestige for women from skilled working-class backgrounds than for other working-class women. Many daughters of skilled workers in the period could lay claim to middle-class status by virtue of their income and identification with particular neighborhoods. Clerical work hardly represented social mobility for these women.

For the daughters of skilled blue-collar workers, employment in an office was a career commensurate with their families' middle-class standing. As Ileen Devault has noted, it represented an affirmation of status that they enjoyed as a consequence of higher income and emerging urban patterns of residential segregation. As indicated earlier, most women who worked as clericals left the labor force at an early age, and few had illusions about making office work a career. Clerical employment for them, as with other types of work for immigrant and black women, was an interlude between adolescence and marriage. Being of such short duration, such a job was not likely to appreciably enhance their status. If jobs in office work had not been available, many of these women probably would not have entered the labor force at all. Most of them certainly would not have taken jobs as factory workers or domestics. Because it was not economically imperative that they work, these women had little reason to accept a job unless it confirmed their current status.

There is evidence that the families of women who worked as clericals were less dependent upon the girls' income than were those with daughters in other occupations. A comparison of two surveys of working women in this period indicates that women clerical workers contributed less to their families than women working in manufacturing. In 1910 a federal survey of wage-earning women discovered that nearly 90 percent of young women employed in New York City's garment industry contributed all of their earnings to their parents. About 85 percent of the women working in retail and department stores did the same, displaying a strong responsiveness to family need. The WEIU study of women in office service in Boston, on the other hand, reported that only 40 percent of women clerical workers turned all of their pay over to their parents each week.[51] Even though this comparison is based upon surveys conducted at different times and in different cities, it suggests that financial need was not as important a motivation for women entering clerical service as for those women working in manual or industrial occupations. This probably was because a substantial number of women employed as clerical workers lived in households with sufficient income to permit them to keep some of their pay.

This inference is supported by the WEIU's finding that female office workers from immigrant families were more likely to contribute their pay to family uses than their counterparts of native parentage. While WEIU researchers attributed this to family loyalties endemic to immigrant culture, it also may have been due to the generally low-income level endured by these families.[52] As indicated earlier, a much higher proportion of immigrants were employed as unskilled workers than native workers, and many of the families of these women may have needed additional income simply to meet basic living expenses.[53] Employment as clericals was an improvement in status for these women, and enabled them to contribute considerably more to their families' income than they could have as industrial workers. On the other hand, the fact that most native women who worked as office workers kept some of their pay suggests that economic need was less a factor in their decisions to work after graduation than for most immigrant women. If these women did not need to work, how great an improvement in status could employment as a clerk, stenographer, or secretary have been? Although it is unclear whether clerical workers from immigrant families were indeed more needy than their native counterparts in this period, the foregoing suggests that most women who found work as clericals did not do so out of economic necessity.

A final indication that clerical employment probably did little to raise the status of middle-income working-class women has to do with popular perceptions of the commercial course in high schools. Students and educators alike generally viewed business courses as inferior to the academic curriculum. In addition to large numbers of working-class students, these courses typically drew students with fewer academic skills than those in the academic classes.[54] If clerical work was preferable to industrial employment and thereby attracted large numbers of working-class women, it was disdained by most women from professional or managerial backgrounds. As Harry Braverman has suggested, office employment was degraded in this period from the status of a middle-class "craft" or profession to a number of discreet tasks requiring little responsibility and offering no prospects of promotion. In a word, clerical work was "industrialized" as larger numbers of women became office workers, and as clerical courses began to become more popular.[55] The clerical course, it appears, drew a constituency appropriate to the new status and income levels associated with office work. Given this, it is difficult to see how the movement of large numbers of middle-income working-class women into white-collar work of this sort can be interpreted as evidence of social mobility.

There is little evidence, in that case, that enrollment in the clerical course and employment in office work was a major source of social mobility for working-class girls in this period. The daughters of some unskilled workers may have benefited from the growth of clerical employment, but the vast bulk of the women who were enrolled in commercial courses in this period were from middle-income backgrounds, the daughters of skilled blue-collar workers, white-collar workers, and professionals and businessmen. This was largely due to the small number of women from unskilled working-class backgrounds in any high school curriculum in this period. As indicated earlier, relatively few of the children of poor working-class families were able to attend school. The high school clerical course could not help women who were not in a position to enroll in school.

For women who were able to attend high school, getting a job as clerical workers probably did not appreciably improve their social standing. Indeed, there is evidence to suggest that women enrolled in clerical courses in the high schools suffered a lower status than their peers enrolled in the academic courses. This hardly supports the notion that the high school functioned as an engine of expanding occupational opportunity for the poor and unskilled. Only women who could afford to go to school to begin with could make use of secondary education in the labor market. By the second decade of the twentieth century, social class seems to have operated as an important constraint in the lives of young women.

If the evidence cited above is indicative of trends elsewhere in the country, it appears that the development of the commercial course may have hardened rather than relaxed class lines in the female labor force. If the principal beneficiaries of the expansion of clerical work and the expansion of the commercial course were middle-class women, the career patterns of women from working-class families probably changed little during the period under consideration. Conditions that led the daughters of unskilled workers to leave school at age 14 to work in the 1890s probably exerted the same influence twenty years later.

These findings suggest that the chief source of the expansion of female high school enrollments in these years were middle-income occupational groups, the very same families that sent their daughters off to work in offices after they left school. Additional evidence must be considered before these findings can be elevated to the status of generalizations about the relationship of education to female labor force participation in this period. But the results of these surveys suggest that the Progressive period and the great expansion of secondary education that accompanied it did not appreciably diminish class distinctions in early twentieth-century American cities.

Conclusion: Education and Local Labor Markets

Intercity differences in social and economic development were decisively linked to the growth of secondary education for women. This was yet another dimension of the dialectic between opportunity and constraint described in earlier chapters. The strong vocational orientation of women's education in this period, it appears, was restricted to the Northeast. Although vocational programs existed in other cities, they were neither as well supported nor as popular in the South and West as in the nation's industrial core area. If vocationalism offered women new opportunities in employment, its effects were delimited by the realities of local labor markets.

My discussion of Boston and Memphis suggests that differences in the purpose of education in this period were manifest in different patterns of school system organization, as well as in the size of vocational courses. Data drawn from George Counts's survey of secondary education in a number of cities point to a distinctive West Coast pattern of school enrollment, which appears to have subordinated vocational concerns in favor of popular interest in academic education. And evidence on the background of female high school students in this period, drawn from cities in all regions except the South, indicate that very few daughters of poor working-class families could afford to take advantage of the opportunities offered by the schools. If the growth of white-collar employment transformed women's work in this period, most working-class women were excluded from benefits of these changes. In this regard, women's secondary education can be said to have helped reproduce the existing social (and geographic) division of labor. The opportunities offered by a widening field of women's education, it seems, were delimited by the harsh realities of social class.

These conclusions, of course, have been based upon analysis of women's education and women's work in a limited number of cities. The foregoing discussion was intended to offer examples of lines of research related to the broad analysis performed in earlier chapters, not conclusive answers to the questions posed. These findings, in that case, can be interpreted as a starting point for subsequent explorations of the relationships of education and work in American cities during this period. Given the relationships identified in this study, additional consideration of the manner in which secondary education was linked to the labor market could be fruitful indeed.

Conclusion

The terms of opportunity and constraint in women's secondary education shifted significantly in the years between 1870 and 1930. In the decades following the Civil War, young women entered a world of unprecedented educational opportunity. They studied a curriculum essentially the same as that given the boys and, by all available measures, performed as well or better than their male classmates. For most of these women, the high school was not a gateway to a working career, but a way of preparing themselves for a wider vision of traditional female roles. Eventually, however, the expansion of women's education did allow women to enter new occupations, particularly the rapidly growing fields of teaching and clerical work. This, it appears, portended important changes in women's schooling.

There can be little doubt that women's education in the United States underwent a profound transformation in the opening decades of the twentieth century. This was partly a consequence of changes that affected all of American secondary education at that time. Enrollments rose dramatically, old curricula were swept aside and new ones implemented, and new modes of organization were adopted by city school systems in an effort to accommodate a host of new purposes. As secondary education became a more commonplace dimension of American experience, it was more closely associated with the labor market. Schools, as never before in American history, were called upon to ready young people for the world of work, and this meant that the sexual division of labor was extended into the high school curriculum. Opportunity remained an important theme but was delimited by a number of fixed conceptions about women's work and social roles.

The development of a distinctive *female* curriculum in American secondary schools, of course, represented a sharp break with tradition. A generation of talented and dedicated women educators had

211

campaigned long and hard for equality in education during the nineteenth century. It is difficult to say how many of them would have reacted to the development of a separate set of courses for women students in the twentieth century, but some (such as Anna Brackett) probably would have found it quite distressing. The division of labor and its attendant specialization, however, was often seen as a unmitigated blessing during the Progressive era, and in the schools "social efficiency" meant developing curricula tailor-made to meet the interests of diverse constituencies. In the early twentieth century, "domestic feminism" gave way to a new interest in celebrating and developing uniquely female skills and knowledge, with a good deal less concern about the issue of gender equity or broadening women's access to new careers among certain women reformers.

As a group, educators seemed willing to entertain the notion of gender equity in education as long as women made little use of their schooling in the labor force. Once large numbers of young women began working, however, voices were raised in favor of specialized training in domestic science and other particularly "female" studies, so that future American families would not be jeopardized by the spectre of working women. As soon as opportunity for women shifted to the labor market, it seems, constraints were introduced in education. Educators, most of them men, were in favor of gender equity as long as it provided them with high enrollments and a steady supply of teachers. But when women began to utilize their skills in the labor force, educators (including many women) exhibited a new interest in defining a sex-specific curriculum.

At the same time that the thinking of educators about women's education shifted, there is evidence that the attitudes of women *students* also may have changed in this period. In the nineteenth century relatively few women appear to have attended high school to enhance their careers. Even those who eventually became teachers (such as Nellie Clark in Detroit) seem to have gone to school simply to learn more about the world and to enjoy themselves. The high school seems to have represented an important new step in the personal development of these women, but not one which turned them away from traditional roles. With the growth of female employment in white-collar occupations, particularly clerical work, this may have changed somewhat. In the opening decades of the twentieth century, some young women appear to have entered high school with one eye on the labor market. This would account for the rapid rise of enrollments in certain courses. Many women, particularly those who lived in the nation's highly urbanized areas (where white-collar employment opportunities existed), paid little heed to the advice and admonitions of educators and other social commentators. The prospect of work was an alluring alternative to staying at home or getting married immediately after school. Despite the efforts of leading educators and other figures to mitigate this tendency, the growth of female labor force participation—especially among young middle-class women—was a major factor in the transformation of female education. An important contradiction existed between the changing aspirations of these women and the concerns of educators interested in preserving traditional female roles.

But even with these changes, the growth of female labor force participation in these years did not pose the immediate threat some commentators feared. Only a small number of these women remained in the labor force for more than a few years. For most, going to school (and taking the commercial course) and working afterwards may have comprised an experience similar to those described in the nineteenth century diaries and letters analyzed in chapter 2. Throughout this period school and work represented a transition period between childhood dependence and marriage. Both offered a wider field of experience to draw from later in life, but neither represented a fundamental change in female roles of the sort denounced by many contemporaries.

It is not clear, in that case, whether vocationalism caused more young women to attend high school. Of course, the popularity of the clerical course, despite the efforts of educators to persuade women to take home economics and other courses, is evidence of the attraction which these new jobs held. But high school enrollment levels for women were high even in parts of the country where clerical employment was relatively scarce. As indicated in chapter 5, female high school enrollment rates were similar in Boston and Memphis during the twenties, despite the different labor markets in these cities. And the rise of vocationalism in women's secondary education does not appear to have changed the clientele of the high schools during this period. It is not apparent, consequently, just how great an impact vocationalism had on *students* in this period. While the availability of attractive jobs may have accounted for increased enrollments in some areas, for many middle-class women high school may have remained an interesting and potentially exciting challenge to occupy their teenage years. For these women vocationalism may simply have been a matter of switching curricula to afford them an opportunity to pursue a short and exciting work career before eventually marrying.

In any case, the relationship between education and women's attitudes about work and traditional female roles remains unclear. Future studies will have to focus more carefully on ways in which women's ideas about these issues changed in this period. The material

I have compiled on this score is suggestive of certain tendencies but is hardly conclusive. By and large I have limited the focus of this study to explaning changes in women's education and its relationship to work. Other scholars will have to take up the difficult but important task of determining how these changes affected—or reflected —more fundamental shifts in women's lives.

The evidence I have assembled points to a number of ways in which the development of women's education between 1890 and 1930 corresponded closely to the growth of the nation's economy. As indicated throughout the study, regionally distinctive enrollment patterns characterized female school participation across this period, and curricular differences from one part of the country to another appear to have corresponded with regional differences in women's work. As seen in chapter 3, school-leaving rates closely matched regional patterns of female labor force entry in this period. And women from different ethnic and class backgrounds left school and entered the labor force at distinctive intervals. All of this suggests that women went to high school—or left school altogether—in this period in response to identifiable social conditions, particularly regional levels of social and economic development and class and ethnic background. Women's education was inexorably influenced by the development of women's work. It also came to reflect the prevailing division of labor within the female labor force.

It is important to note, however, that the relationship between education and women's work was reciprocal. Education may have helped shape women's work in important ways during this period as well. First, the growth of women's employment in teaching, clerical work, and other white-collar occupations may simply not have been possible without the growth of female secondary school enrollments in the nineteenth century. By the start of the twentieth century, nearly twice as many women graduated from public high schools as men, but many of these female high school graduates did not work. In this regard, these educated women comprised a vast pool of underutilized labor. And it was the availability of this group of women that made the expansion of female white-collar work possible after the turn of the century.

The reciprocal relationship between education and women's work was evident in yet other ways as well. Because schooling was required for many of the best paying and highest status jobs for women, education became an important determinant of which groups of women would enjoy the benefits of these positions. In other words, the social division of labor *within* the female labor force was tied to women's education in this period. Only the white middle-class women who could afford to attend high school, including the daughters of skilled workers, enjoyed access to the attractive nonmanual jobs then becoming available to women. Education was becoming a key distinction that separated one group of women workers from another.

It is important to emphasize the fact that the high school remained a relatively elite institution throughout this period. Perhaps the most clearly identifiable group of women in this study are those who were *excluded* from school. If there was any one contextual factor that affected female school enrollment rates most in this period, it probably was employment in manufacturing. As indicated chapters 2, 3, and 5, and in countless contemporary accounts, women from poor working-class families—and particularly immigrants—were typically forced to leave school in order to find work in factories or as domestics. School enrollment in cities where large numbers of women were employed in manufacturing remained low throughout this period. The expansion of educational opportunities was of little consequence to those women who were unable to take advantage of them.

The basic *ability* to attend school, in that case, was the principal means by which the clientele of the high school was selected in this period. As George Counts pointed out, this was not a meritocratic process. The fact that those women who could least afford schooling were forced to drop out earliest and that secondary education was a prerequisite for most of the best-paying and comfortable jobs in this period, meant that the overwhelming majority of women who moved into clerical positions were from middle-class white backgrounds. The concentration of immigrant and black women in manual labor intensified at the same time. Although additional research on the composition of the female labor force in this period is necessary to explore the parameters of these trends, the results of the research presented here suggests that schooling did not function as a vehicle of social mobility for most women. Indeed, in this regard women's secondary education served to help reproduce the social division of labor within the female labor force.

The new vocationalism in women's education, in that case, made female schooling responsive to the division of labor in American life in a number of ways. It distinguished women's schooling—and women's skills and knowledge—from men's; at the same time, it helped to distinguish one group of women workers (and probably one class of women) from another. Because it developed in response to conditions that differed from one part of the country to another, it also helped to distinguish women from one region to the next. Rather than fostering the democratic vision promulgated by the champions of the nineteenth-century high school, whose rhetoric proclaimed a "people's college" where rich and poor attended together, the high school of the twentieth century made specialization and separation its watchwords. The result was an end to what may have been one of the most promising—even if largely unintentional—experiments in equality yet attempted in American education.

Several themes of contemporary significance emerge from this study of women's education and work between 1870 and 1930. All are related to the questions of opportunity and constraint. First, the experience of women in this period demonstrated the important role that education could play in widening women's sphere of activities. It established new areas of opportunity. The growth of women's education in the latter nineteenth century helped create a skilled pool of women workers who could move into clerical and other nonmanual occupations as they developed in the early twentieth century. It also helped to establish an expanded vision of possibilities for young women. A number of social scientists have observed that formal education is consistently associated with the propensity of women to work in a variety of social settings. This is a lesson of great significance today, as the number of women enrolled in higher education recently has surpassed the number of men. The growth of women's education has created today, as it did eighty years ago, enormous pressure to expand women's occupational and social roles.

On the other hand, the growth of women's education has also aggravated the existing social division of labor, highlighting the distinctions between men's and women's work and providing additional opportunities for a select strata of women—while limiting them for others. In other words, it has helped delineate constraints. While women's education seems to be a little less narrow today (home economics and clerical training courses still exist, however) the latter point is no less true today than at the turn of the century. At the same time that women have assumed new roles in business, government, and the professions, disproportionately more women, most of them single mothers, crowd the welfare rolls than ever before in recent American history. The distinction between educated and uneducated women is probably at least as great—or greater—today than when women were first entering offices, department stores, and schools. Education for women, in that case, has functioned as a double-edged sword. At the same time it has widened women's roles, confounding to an extent the sexual division of labor, it has erected new barriers between different groups of women. In this regard, the development of women's schooling until recently even may have helped to inhibit the growth of a viable women's movement in this country. Recognizing this puts a new challenge before the next generation of educated women: overcoming the barriers that have divided women in their quest to surmount the sexual division of labor. The challenge is one of making women's education truly liberating in the future.

Statistical Appendix:
Teenage School Attendance
in the Latter Nineteenth Century

Historians Carl Kaestle, Maris Vinovskis, Michael Katz, and Ian Davey have provided important insights into the social forces that shaped school enrollment in the nineteenth century. They have also offered a series of instructive examples of how multiple classification analysis (MCA) can be used to study school participation in the past. Table A-.5 provides the elements of an MCA table compiled from two adjacent tables in Kaestle and Vinovskis' book, *Education and Social Change in Nineteenth Century Massachusetts*. Table A.6 presents data from Katz and Davey's article, "School Attendance and Early Industrialization in a Canadian City," published in 1978. The focal point of both tables is teenage school participation in the nineteenth century. Using a large sample of teenagers drawn from federal census manuscript returns, Kaestle and Vinovskis identified eight independent variables they believed may have been associated with teenage school enrollment. Under each variable heading in Table 2.1 are listed the various categories of analysis, or subgroups of the population defined by particular characteristics. In its summary measures of association, MCA expresses the extent to which school enrollment varies systematically across the categories of each variable. The strongest variable in Table A.5, in that case is age, since there was a clear, linear relationship between age and school enrollment among nineteenth-century teenagers. The fraction of all teenagers in school, expressed in the unadjusted and adjusted mean columns, was smaller for each successively older age group. This is perfectly sensible, of course, and not very surprising. Age traditionally has been a primary criteria for determining which members of a given society are eligible for schooling. And as Kaestle and Vinovskis themselves point out, the study of school participation among teenagers in this period is largely an inquiry into patterns of school-leaving. While the decision to include age as an independent variable in the analysis contributes little to understanding social and economic forces associated with enrollment, it does help to clarify the relationship of other factors in the equation to teenage school participation. It is in connection with these other variables that the relationship between school enrollment and the social structure is most evident.

Class and ethnicity are the background factors to which historians have given the most attention when considering patterns of school enrollment in the nineteenth century. Class, generally defined by the occupational status of a child's father, is of interest because education was a valuable attribute in nineteenth-century society, even if not as valuable as it is today, and access to it may have been an important factor in determining individual social and economic status. Class and economic status are important factors in Katz and Davey's analysis.If class did shape school participation, in the eyes of some scholars, schools may have helped to reinforce or legitimize inequality in American society. Educational historians have also been interested in class because one of the public school system's most celebrated purposes was to bring children from all social and economic backgrounds together. To the extent that class was a major determinant of enrollment, this lofty goal was compromised. Ethnicity, on the other hand, is usually defined by the ethnic background or nativity of a child, and has drawn the attention of historians because of the negative feeling sometimes expressed in immigrant communities toward American public schools. Of course, the failure of the schools to accommodate immigrant children, or to expose them to prevailing elements of American culture, constituted yet another departure from the frequently expressed purposes of American public education in this period. Accordingly, Katz and Davey (and Kaestle and Vinovskis for that matter) devoted much of their attention to identifying the effects of both class (occupational background) and ethnicity on teenage school participation in nineteenth-century Massachusetts.

As indicated in Table A.5, the ethnicity and class variables were the strongest factors, aside from age, in the 1880 MCA run. Kaestle and Vinovskis found ethnicity to be a more important factor than class throughout their analysis of enrollment. But both variables were associated with enrollment in a clear linear fashion. This is evident in examining the adjusted mean column for each variable. The children most likely to be in school in this age range were the daughters and sons of professionals, the vast majority of whom were native-born, and whose participation rates appear to have been higher than 50 percent. The children of white-collar and skilled workers attended at a comparatively high rate as well, even after the effects of ethnicity had been controlled. The lowest rates of teenage school participation were those registered by the children of foreign-born and unskilled (or semiskilled) workers. This probably was because working-class families were less able to afford the relatively high opportunity costs of sending teenage children to school in this period, when opportunities for industrial employment abounded in Massachusetts. Additionally, some groups of immigrants—and Catholics in particular—found the curriculum of the public schools objectionable, or disagreed with the nativist biases of many educators at that time. They kept their children out of school, it appears, as a consequence. Thus, in the case of both of these variables, the structure of school participation generally mirrored the larger social structure; the social groups enjoying the greatest prestige and power also were able (and willing) to send their teenage children to school in the greatest numbers. The general pattern of teenage school participation in late nineteenth-century America, it appears, was dictated in part by the realities of social class and the value different ethnic groups assigned to formal education. The results reported in Table A.6 also support this view.

There are a range of other factors in Tables A.5 and A.6, but none is as important to understanding teenage enrollment patterns— conceptually or statistically—as ethnicity and parental occupational background. Kaestle and Vinovskis included gender in their analysis as an independent variable. Katz and Davey performed separate analyses for males and females. As indicated both in the summary measures of association and the two means columns in Table A.5, there was very little difference in the enrollment rates of young men and women in Massachusetts at this time. But the gender variable is interesting precisely because it reveals such little distinction in male and female patterns of school participation. This suggests that the overall pattern of teenage enrollment in this period was the same for boys and girls. While it is possible that the relative weight of the elements in the 1880 MCA might change if separate runs were made for girls and boys, the overall pattern of association between the class and ethnicity variables and teenage school enrollment clearly would not. For both young women and men in late nineteenth-century, the question of whether or not to attend school as a teenager was closely associated with questions of income and the perceived value of education. Judging from the results obtained by these scholars, for some groups of women a high school education evidently carried considerably less value than it did for others.

The other tables in this appendix provide additional information about the statistical analyses performed in chapter 2.

Table A.1   Correlation Matrix—39 State National Analysis

	(1)	(2)	(3)	(4)	(5)	(6)	(7)
1900 Female high school enrollment (1)	***						
1900 Male high school enrollment (2)	0.95	***					
"Trade" employment (3)	0.66	0.57	***				
Urbanization (4)	0.49	0.52	0.79	***			
Income (log) (5)	0.78	0.74	0.87	0.72	***		
Percent of all teachers female (6)	0.73	0.77	0.55	0.62	0.65	***	
Teacher-student ratio (7)	0.71	0.72	0.43	0.38	0.45	0.63	***
Fertility change, 1870–1900	0.45	0.32	0.51	0.09	0.51	0.10	0.28
1890 Female high school enrollment	0.90	0.92	0.47	0.48	0.64	0.79	0.71
Northeast	0.38	0.50	0.39	0.65	0.41	0.63	0.47
South	-0.73	-0.67	-0.76	-0.57	-0.79	-0.59	-0.64

Critical value = +/- 0.37

Table A.2   Regression Analysis—39 State National Analysis with Income Variable

INDEPENDENT VARIABLES	B	STANDARD ERROR	PROBABILITY	PARTIAL R
1890 Enrollment	1.1941	0.1988	0.0000	0.5299
Percent of all teachers female	-0.0097	0.0523	0.85427	0.0011
Income (log)	0.0948	0.0237	0.00036	0.3327
Teacher-student ratio	0.8070	0.3816	0.04236	0.1226
Change in fertility	0.0055	0.0180	0.76357	0.0029
Northeast	-0.0185	0.0094	0.05839	0.10759

Dependent variable: female high school enrollment rates, 1900; N = 39; adjusted R^2= .89; constant = -0.1600; standard error of estimate = 0.0189.

Table A.3 Regression Analysis—39 State National Analysis with "Trade" Employment Variable

INDEPENDENT VARIABLES	B	STANDARD ERROR	PROBABILITY	PARTIAL R
1890 Enrollment	1.4328	0.2034	0.00000	0.61
Percent of all teachers female	0.0004	0.0527	0.99340	0.00
Teacher-student ratio	0.5158	0.3824	0.18682	0.05
"Trade" employment	0.3808	0.1019	0.00073	0.30
Fertility change, 1870–1900	0.0065	0.0185	0.72752	0.00
Northeast	-0.0207	0.0097	0.04112	0.12

Dependent Variable: Female High School Enrollment, 1900; N = 39; adjusted R^2= .88; constant = -.0092; standard error of estimate = 0.01933.

Table A.4 Regression Analysis—28 States, Excluding the South

INDEPENDENT VARIABLES	B	STANDARD ERROR	PROBABILITY	PARTIAL R
1890 Enrollment	1.3914	0.3100	0.00020	0.4897
Urbanization	-0.0426	0.0253	0.10682	0.1191
Income (log)	0.1346	0.0329	0.00053	0.4429
"Trade" employment	-0.0930	0.1749	0.60034	0.0133
Teacher-student ratio	0.2867	0.4305	0.51264	0.0207
Percent of all teachers female	0.0220	0.0552	0.69475	0.0075

Dependent variable: male high school enrollment rates, 1900; N = 28; adjusted R^2 = 0.81; constant = -0.2576; standard error of estimate = .0168.

Table A.5 Multiple Classification Analysis
—Essex County, Massachusetts, Teenagers, 1880

VARIABLE AND CATEGORY	N	UNADJUSTED MEAN	ETA	ADJUSTED MEAN	BETA
Age			0.29		0.55
13	198	0.87		0.86	
14	236	0.66		0.68	
15	212	0.50		0.49	
16	223	0.32		0.32	

222   *Statistical Appendix*

Table A.5   *(continued)*

VARIABLE AND CATEGORY	N	UNADJUSTED MEAN	ETA	ADJUSTED MEAN	BETA
17	184	0.23		0.24	
18	218	0.14		0.13	
19	209	0.09		0.08	
Community			0.03		0.10
Salem	292	0.41		0.43	
Lawrence	434	0.30		0.37	
Lynn	373	0.38		0.35	
Rural	381	0.55		0.48	
Literacy of Parent			0.02		0.02
Illiterate	137	0.19		0.37	
Literate	1,343	0.43		0.41	
Gender			0.00		0.02
Male	699	0.40		0.39	
Female	730	0.41		0.41	
Work/Consumption Index*			0.01		0.10
0–19	234	0.42		0.43	
30–34	203	0.31		0.34	
50 and up	350	0.34		0.40	
Ethnicity			0.06		0.19
First generation	258	0.18		0.25	
Second generation Irish	339	0.36		0.36	
Second generation Other	170	0.38		0.37	
Native of native parent	713	0.51		0.49	
Occupation of Parent*			0.05		0.12
Professional	156	0.56		0.55	
White-collar and skilled	325	0.49		0.46	
Semiskilled and unskilled	607	0.33		0.37	
No father, mother unemployed	183	0.26		0.33	
Age of Parent*			0.00		0.05
40–44	334	0.42		0.38	
45–49	340	0.42		0.43	
50–54	310	0.40		0.42	
55–59	160	0.35		0.43	

From Kaestle and Vinovskis, *Education and Social Change in Nineteenth Century Massachusetts*, pp. 87–88. *Dependent variable: Enrollment in school, ,en and women age 13 to 19; (N = 1,480; R^2 = 0.38; grand mean = 0.40.*

*Several categories missing, see original tables for complete data, in Kaestle and Vinovskis, *Education and Social Change in Nineteenth Century Massachusetts*, pp. 86–87.

Table A.6 Multiple Classification Analysis of Female School
Participation in Hamilton, Ontario, 1871

VARIABLE AND CATEGORIES	ETA	ADJUSTED MEAN	BETA
Place of Birth (Father and Child)	0.17		0.12
Ireland-Ireland		0.54	
Ireland-Canada		0.42	
Scotland-Scotland		0.44	
Scotland-Canada		0.47	
England-England		0.46	
England-Canada		0.54	
Canada-Canada		0.62	
Religion	0.13		0.13
Church of England		0.40	
Catholic		0.52	
Presbytarian		0.55	
Methodist		0.70	
Baptist		0.52	
Economic Rank (percentile)	0.19		0.11
0–20		0.49	
40–60		0.44	
80–90		0.58	
90–100		0.60	
Occupation of Father	0.24		0.20
Profession		0.73	
Commerce-middle		0.64	
Construction trades		0.50	
Semiskilled		0.46	
Laborers		0.40	
No father		0.39	
Property and Children	0.12		0.06
1–2 Children, rent		0.42	
1–2 Children, own		0.54	
3–4 Children, rent		0.49	
3–4 Children, own		0.54	
5+ Children, rent		0.49	
5+ Children, own		0.48	

Derived from Michael B. Katz and Ian Davey, "School Attendance and Early
Industrialization in a Canadian City," *History of Education Quarterly*, 17, no. 2
(Summer, 1978), pp. 277; 282–283. Dependent variable: school enrollment,
women age 13–16; N = 998; R^2 = 0.24; grand mean = 0.49.

Table A.7 Multiple Classification Analysis—Teenage Women in Cities, 1900, with "Generation" Variable instead of Ethnicity

Public Use Sample

VARIABLE AND CATEGORY	N	UNADJUSTED MEAN	ETA	ADJUSTED MEAN	BETA
Age			0.27		0.49
13	185	0.80		0.77	
14	203	0.62		0.61	
15	196	0.37		0.37	
16	171	0.30		0.30	
17	172	0.23		0.23	
18	186	0.12		0.13	
19	195	0.06		0.09	
Region			0.01		0.08
Northeast	675	0.33		0.36	
Southeast	109	0.34		0.32	
North Central	392	0.37		0.36	
South Central	87	0.42		0.33	
West	45	0.58		0.54	
Father's Occupation			0.02		0.16
High white-collar	211	0.47		0.52	
Low white-collar	126	0.41		0.40	
Skilled labor	287	0.37		0.35	
Unskilled labor	397	0.33		0.31	
Farmer	19	0.22		0.24	
Father not present	268	0.29		0.32	
Position in Family			0.04		0.13
Older— small household	124	0.53		0.44	
Younger— small household	50	0.32		0.38	
Older— medium household	358	0.40		0.36	
Middle— medium household	133	0.38		0.39	
Younger— medium household	131	0.31		0.35	
Older— large household	204	0.32		0.31	
Middle— large household	90	0.42		0.41	
Younger— large household	67	0.39		0.41	

Table A.7 *(continued)*

VARIABLE AND CATEGORY	N	UNADJUSTED MEAN	ETA	ADJUSTED MEAN	BETA
Other relatives	72	0.35		0.41	
Unrelated teenagers	79	0.03		0.17	
Race			0.00		0.04
White	1224	0.36		0.37	
Black	84	0.30		0.28	
Generation			0.06		0.21
Native—native parents	551	0.47		0.47	
Native—foreign father	62	0.39		0.42	
Native—foreign mother	147	0.42		0.34	
Native—foreign parents	357	0.29		0.27	
Foreign born	191	0.13		0.22	

Dependent variable: enrollment in school, women age 13–19; N = 1,308; R^2 = 0.35; grand mean = 0.36.

Notes

Introduction

1. *Annual Report of the Board of Education of the City of Newburgh, 1896* (Newburgh, NY: Carter & Co., 1897), p. 52

2. Despite a recent surge of scholarship in both women's history and the history of education, women's education in the latter nineteenth and early twentieth centuries has received little attention from historians. A number of studies have focused on American women at this time. They have dealt with a wide range of issues, from prominent women reformers to the changing condition of women in everyday circumstances. For an overview of recent scholarship in women's history covering this period, see Lois Banner, *Women in Modern America: A Brief History*, 2nd ed. (New York: Harcourt, Brace & Jovanovich, 1984), chap. 1 to 4.

Relatively little has been written, however, about the development of women's secondary education at the turn of the century. While a number of excellent studies have looked at the growth of women's higher education, few have examined the high school as a factor in women's lives. See, for instance, Lynn D. Gordon, "Annie Nathan Meyer and Barnard College: Mission and Identity in Women's Higher Education, 1889–1950," *History of Education Quarterly* 26, no. 4 (Winter 1986): 503–23; Roberta Frankfort, *Collegiate Women: Domesticity and Career at the Turn of the Century* (New York: New York University Press, 1977); Sheila Rothman, *Woman's Proper Place: A History of Changing Ideals and Practices, 1870 to the Present* (New York: Basic Books, 1978), chap. 1. For discussion of this point, see John L. Rury, "Education in the New Women's History," *Educational Studies* (March 1986): 1–15.

Of course, the years between 1870 and 1930 also were a time of tremendous growth and change in American secondary education. Educational and social historians have devoted a great deal of study to the development of American high schools during these years, but few of them have given much attention to the issue of gender in education. Important studies of secondary education during this period include Lawrence Cremin, *Transformation of the School: Progressivism in American Education, 1870–1957* (New York: Knopf,

1961); Edward A. Krug, *Shaping the American High School, 1880–1920* (New York: Harper & Row, 1964); David B. Tyack, *The One Best System: A History of Urban Education in the United States* (Cambridge: Harvard University Press, 1976); and William Reese, *Power and the Promise of School Reform: Grassroots Movements in the Progressive Era* (Boston: Routledge and Kegan Paul, 1986).

Neither women's historians nor educational historians have examined the development of female secondary education. As a consequence, relatively little is known about the development of a key dimension of young women's lives—and an important aspect of American education—during this period of history.

3. See the studies cited in the previous note regarding the urban focus of educational reform. For a suggestive study on women in the city, see Barbara Berg, *The Remembered Gate: Origins of American Feminism* (New York: Oxford University Press, 1978). On the general development of education in cities at this time, see John L. Rury, "Urbanization and Education: Regional Patterns of Educational Development in American Cities, 1890–1910" *Michigan Academician* (Summer 1988): 261–80.

4. The best overview of this process is Elyce Rotella, *From Home to Office: U.S. Women at Work, 1870–1930* (Ann Arbor: UMI Research Press, 1981), chap. 1, 2, and 3.

5. Thomas Woody, *A History of Women's Education in the United States*, vol. 2 (New York: Science Press, 1929), p. 16.

6. Barbara R. Bergmann, *The Economic Emergence of Women* (New York: Basic Books, 1986), chap. 1, 2, and 3.

7. Geraldine Clifford, "Marry, Stitch, Die or Do Worse: The Education of Women for Work," in Harvey Kantor and David Tyack, eds., *Work, Youth and Schooling: Historical Perspectives on Vocationalism in American Education* (Stanford, CA: Stanford University Press, 1982).

8. See the discussion of this in Valarie Kinkaid Oppenheimer, *The Female Labor Force in the United States: Demographic and Economic Factors Governing Its Growth and Changing Composition* (Westport, CN: Greenwood Press, 1976), chap. 4. For an interesting discussion of this point in late twentieth-century Great Britain, see Madeline MacDonald, "Socio-Cultural Reproduction and Women's Education," in Rosemary Deem, ed., *Schooling for Women's Work* (London: Routledge and Kegan Paul, 1980), pp. 13–25.

9. Émile Durkheim, *The Division of Labor in Society*, trans. by George Simpson (New York: The Free Press, 1933), chap. 1.

10. For an interesting portrait of one of the period's most active champions of this concept, see Walter Drost, *David Snedden and Education for Social Efficiency* (Madison, WI: University of Wisconsin Press, 1967).

11. Oppenheimer, *The Female Labor Force in the United States*, chap. 3. For a more generalized and theoretical perspective, see Shirley Dex, *The Sexual*

Division of Labor: Conceptual Revolutions in the Social Sciences (New York: St. Martins Press, 1985), chap. 4.

12. On American regional development, see Harvey Perloff, Edgar S. Dunn, Eric F. Lampard, and Richard F. Muth, *Regions, Resources and Economic Growth* (Baltimore: Johns Hopkins University Press, 1960).

13. For an interesting discussion of women's education in Great Britain at this time, see Josephine Kamm, *Hope Deferred: Girls' Education in English History* (London: Methuen, 1965), chap. 15.

Chapter 1. Women at School: The Feminization of American High Schools, 1870-1900

1. On the early academies and seminaries for young women, see Thomas Woody, *A History of Women's Education in the United States*, vol. 1 (New York: Science Press, 1929), chap. 8 and 9. For high school and college statistics of enrollment, see U.S. Commissioner of Education, *Annual Report, 1900–1901*, vol. 2 (Washington, DC: Government Printing Office, 1902), in the Statistical Appendix.

2. A good summary of this perspective can be found in Catherine Clinton, *The Other Civil War: American Women in the Nineteenth Century* (New York: Hill and Wang, 1984). Also see Barbara J. Harris, *Beyond Her Sphere: Women and the Professions in American History* (Westport, CT: Greenwood Press, 1978), chap. 2; and Jane Rendall, *The Origins of Modern Feminism: Women in Britain, France and the United States, 1780–1860* (New York: Schocken Books, 1984) Chs. 2, 3, and 4. My use of the term "domestic feminism" is similar to Catherine Clinton's, and different from earlier uses of the term—most notably that of Daniel Scott Smith, who coined it to describe early efforts at birth control and resistance to patriarchy among American women. See Smith's article, "Family Limitation, Sexual Control, and Domestic Feminism in Victorian America," in Mary S. Hartman and Lois W. Banner, eds., *Clio's Consciousness Raised: New Perspectives on the History of Women* (New York: Harper and Row), pp. 119–36.

3. Emma Willard, *An Address to the Public, Particularly to the Members of the Legislature of New York Proposing a Plan for Improving Female Education*, 2nd ed. (Middlebury, NY: J. W. Copeland, 1819), pp. 7–10

4. Ibid., passim.

5. The best general overview of this new perspective on women's education can be found in Woody, *A History of Women's Education in the United States*, chap. 7. Also see Rendall, *The Origins of Modern Feminism*, chap. 4.

6. For an early expression of Beecher's thinking on female education, see her pamphlet *Suggestions Respecting Improvements in Education, Presented to the Trustees of the Hartford Seminary* (Hartford, CT: Packard and Butler, 1829).

Also see C. Beecher, "Female Education," *American Journal of Education*, 2, nos. 4 and 5 (April and May, 1827): 219–23, 264–69.

7. Elizabeth Alden Green, *Mary Lyon and Mount Holyoke: Opening the Gates* (Hannover, NH: University Press of New England, 1979) chap. 4, 5, and 6.

8. Patricia Smith Butcher, "Coeducation and the Women's Rights Press, 1849–1920," (Paper presented to Division F, American Educational Research Association, Washington, D.C., April 24, 1987), p. 3. On coeducation at Oberlin, see Ronald W. Hogeland, "Coeducation of the Sexes at Oberlin College: A Study of Social Ideas in Mid-Nineteenth-Century America," *Journal of Social History* 6 (Winter 1972–73): 168–69.

9. Anne Fior Scott, "What, Then, Is the American: This New Woman?" in her book, *Making the Invisible Woman Visible* (Urbana: University of Illinois Press, 1984), pp. 37–64. Kathryn Kish Sklar, *Catherine Beecher: A Study in American Domesticity* (New Haven, CT: Yale University Press, 1973), Parts 2 and 3.

10. Quoted in Richard P. DuFour, "The Exclusion of Female Students From the Public Secondary Schools of Boston, 1820–1920" (unpublished Ed.D. dissertation, Northern Illinois University, 1981), p. 129.

11. For an analysis of high school attendance in the latter nineteenth century, see David L. Angus, "A Note on the Occupational Backgrounds of Public High School Students Prior to 1940" *Journal of the Midwest History of Education Society* (1981): 158–181.

12. U.S. Commissioner of Education, *Annual Report, 1872* (Washington, DC: Government Printing Office, 1873), p. 474; and U.S. Commissioner of Education, *Annual Report, 1900–1901*, vol. 2 (Washington, DC: Government Printing Office, 1903), pp. 1923–139.

13. U.S. Commissioner of Education, *Annual Report, 1900–1901*, pp. 1923–39.

14. Maris A. Vinovskis, "Patterns of High School Attendance in Newburyport, Massachusetts in 1860," paper presented at the American Historical Association Annual Meeting in New York City, December 28, 1985. Reed Ueda, *Avenues to Adulthood: The Origins of the High School and Social Mobility in an American Suburb* (New York: Cambridge University Press, 1987), pp. 52–53.

15. *Thirteenth Annual Report of the Board of Directors of the St. Louis Public Schools*, 1867–68 (St. Louis: George Knapp and Co., 1869), p. 31.

16. Department of Public Instruction, City of Chicago, *Nineteenth Annual Report of the Board of Education* (Chicago: Bryant, Walker, and Craig, 1873), pp. 260–65.

17. See, for instance, *Fifty -Sixth Annual Report of the Board of Commissioners of the Public Schools to the Mayor and City of Baltimore* (Baltimore: Wm. J. C. Dunlany, 18845), pp. 83 and 96.

18. Cleveland Public Schools, *Forty-Third Annual Report of the Board of Education* (Cleveland: Robison, Savage and Co., 1879), p. 72.

19. *Thirty-First Annual Report of the Public Schools of the City of Springfield*(Springfield, IL: Springfield Printing Co., 1889), p. 23.

20. Cleveland Public Schools, *Forty-First Annual Report of the Board of Education* (Cleveland: Robison, Savage and Co., 1877), p. 77.

21. *Annual Report of the Public Schools of the City and County of San Francisco* (San Francisco: W. M. Hinton and Co., 1892), p. 86. Also see Public Schools of Chicago, *Fortieth Annual Report of the Board of Education* (Chicago: J. M. W. Jones Printing Co., 1895), p. 43.

22. U.S. Commissioner of Education, *Annual Report, 1888–1889*, vol. 2 (Washington, DC: Government Printing Office, 1890), p. 775.

23. See, for instance, Edward Krug, *The Shaping of the American High School, 1880–1920* (New York: Harper and Row, 1964), chap. 1 and 2.

24. Lawrence Cremin, *The Transformation of the School: Progressivism in American Education, 1876–1957* (New York: Alfred A. Knopf, 1961), chap. 2.

25. Department of Public Instruction, City of Chicago, *Twenty-Ninth Annual Report of the Board of Education* (Chicago: Jameson and Morse, 1884), pp. 28–29.

26. The best summary of research on the feminization of teaching in this period can be found in Myra H. Strober and Audri Gordon Lanford, "The Feminization of Public School Teaching: Cross-sectional Analysis, 1850–1880," *Signs: Journal of Women in Culture and Society*, 11, no. 2 (Winter 1986): 213–35. Also see John L. Rury, "Gender, Salaries and Career: American Teachers, 1900–1910," *Issues in Education* (now *American Educational Research Journal*) 4, no. 3 (Winter 1986): 215–35.

27. *Fortieth Annual Report of the Board of Education of the City of Detroit* (Detroit: J. F. Hadger and Co., 1883), p. 64. *Nineteenth Annual Report of the Board of Directors of the St. Louis Public Schools, 1873–74* (St. Louis: Democrat Litho and Printing, 1874), pp. 86–87. Department of Public Instruction, City of Chicago, *Twenty-Second Annual Report of the Board of Education* (Chicago: N.P., 1876), p. 46; *Annual Report of the Board of Education of the New Haven City School District* (New Haven: Tuttle, Morehouse and Taylor, 1881), p. 45.

28. On the structure of the female labor force in these years, see Lynn Y. Weiner, *From Working Girl to Working Mother: The Female Labor Force in the United States, 1820–1980* (Chapel Hill: University of North Carolina Press, 1985), chap. 1. Contemporaries clearly recognized the manner in which the prevailing sexual division of labor affected the status of women teachers. See, for instance, *Forty-Sixth Annual Report of the Board of Education of the City of New York* 1887 (New York: Hall of Board of Education, 1888), pp. 208–09.

29. U.S. Commissioner of Education, *Annual Report, 1891–1892* vol. 2 (Washington, DC: Government Printing Office, 1893), p. 783.

30. For discussion of Hall's views on the "feminization" of high schools, see John Clinton Maxwell, "Should the Education of Boys and Girls Differ? A Half Century of Debate," unpublished Ph.D. dissertation, University of Wisconsin, 1966, chap. 3. Also see Barbara Miller Solomon, *In the Company of Educated Women: A History of Women and Higher Education in America* (New Haven: Yale University Press, 1985), pp. 52–61.

31. Edward Clarke, *Sex in Education, or a Fair Chance for the Girls* (Boston: J. R. Osgood, 1873). For discussion of the importance of the teenage years, see p. 54. On Clarke's clinical examples of high school girls, see pp. 65, 98, and 102. For Clarke's conclusions about the probable effect of coeducation on the eventual fertility of young women, see p. 137. On the popularity and general impact of Clarke's work, see Sue Zschoche, "Dr. Clarke Revisited: Science, True Womanhood, and Female Collegiate Education" *History of Education Quarterly* 29, no. 4 (Winter 1989): 545–69. Also see Woody, *A History of Women's Education in the United States*, vol. 2, p. 274.

32. See, for instance, Julia Ward Howe, *Sex and Education: A Reply to Dr. Clarke's "Sex in Education"* (Boston: Roberts Bros., 1874), Eliza Bisbee Duffey, *N o Sex in Education: Or an Equal Chance for Both Girls and Boys* (Philadelphia: J. M. Stoddart and Co., 1874), and George F. Comfort and Anna Comfort, *Women's Education and Women's Health* (Syracuse, NY: G. W. Bardeen, 1874).

33. Quincy's ideas about women's education and the Girls' High School in Boston are discussed in DuFour, "The Exclusion of Female Students from the Public Secondary Schools of Boston," pp. 59–84. Quincy recognized the enormous demand for female secondary education in Boston, noting that applications for admission to the High School for Girls had more than doubled in its first year of existence. Displaying considerable prescience, he predicted that female high school enrollments would soon surpass those for the city's male high schools, largely because girls were less likely to drop out of school before graduation than boys. Quincy reasoned that since female secondary education was not necessary to train women for positions of social responsibility in business or the professions, the task of educating large numbers of young women in a public high school was an unreasonable expense for the taxpayers of Boston to bear.

34. Robert A. McCaughey, *Josiah Quincy—The Last Federalist* (Cambridge, MA: Harvard University Press, 1974), p. 111.

35. *Annual Report of the Boston School Committee, 1888* (Boston: Rockwell and Churchill, 1889), p. 32.

36. See, for instance, U.S. Commissioner of Education, *Annual Report, 1873* (Washington, DC: Government Printing Office, 1874), p. 139; idem, *Annual Report, 1887–88* (Washington, DC: Government Printing Office, 1889), p. 850; and *Fifty-Sixth Annual Report of the Commissioner of Public Schools to Mayor and City Council of Baltimore, 1884* p. 40.

37. Woody, *A History of Women's Education in the United States*, vol. 2, pp. 273–74.

38. For discussion of the concerns of educators and religious leaders about the moral dimensions of coeducation, see Arnold Jack Keller, "An Historical Analysis of the Arguments for and Against Coeducational Public High Schools in the United States," unpublished Ed.D. dissertation, Teachers College, Columbia University, 1971, pp. 132–60. Also see John L. Rury and Glenn Harper, "The Trouble with Coeducation: Mann and Women at Antioch, 1853–1860," *History of Education Quarterly* 26, no. 4 (Winter 1984): 481–503, and Hogeland, "Coeducation of the Sexes at Oberlin College," pp. 168–70. Also see the letters submitted by religious leaders on this point to the Boston "Committee on Coeducation" in *Boston School Documents*, Number 19, 1890, (Boston: Rockwell and Churchill, 1891).

39. Cited in DuFour, "The Exclusion of Female Students from the Public Secondary Schools of Boston", pp. 228–29.

40. See the reports from alumnae of these colleges in Julia Howe, ed., *No Sex in Education*. On the importance of the coeducation questions to contemporary feminists, see Butcher, "Coeducation and the Women's Rights Press, 1849–1920."

41. Rosalind Rosenberg, *Beyond Separate Spheres: The Intellectual Roots of Modern Feminism* (New Haven, CT: Yale University Press, 1982), pp. 15–18. Caroline D. Hall, "The Other Side," in Anna C. Brackett, ed., *The Education of American Girls* (New York: G. P. Putnam's Sons, 1874), pp. 160–64. On Catharine Beecher's view of the poor health of American women, see her *Letters to the People on Health and Happiness* (New York: Harper and Brothers, 1855). Also see *Miss Beacher's Housekeeper and Healthkeeper* (New York: Harper and Brothers, 1873).

42. Anna Brackett, *The Education of American Girls*, pp. 18–21.

43. Ibid., p. 82 (on the similarity of male and female needs in education) and pp. 98–105 (on the effects of poor female education on American children).

44. *Seventeenth Annual Report of the Board of Directors of the St. Louis Public Schools* (St. Louis: Democrat Litho and printing Co., 1872), p. 17.

45. *Nineteenth Annual Report of the Board of Directors of the St. Louis Public Schools* pp. 108–13. *Coeducation of the Sexes in the Public Schools of the United States*, Bureau of Education Circular of Information No. 2, 1883 (Washington, DC: Government Printing Office, 1883), pp. 8–23. In 1890 the Boston School Committee conducted its own national survey of local policies regarding coeducation. The results, which showed an overwhelming preference for coeducation, were published in *Boston School Documents, No. 19, 1890 (Boston: Rockwell and Churchill, 1890)*. On the extent of coeducation in 1900, see U.S. Commissioner of Education, *Annual Report, 1900–01* (Washington DC: Government Printing Office, 1901), pp. 1220–135.

46. Dayton Public Schools, *Annual Report of the Board of Education for the School Year Ending August 1877* (Dayton, OH: Journal Book and Job Room, 1878), p. 119; *Eighteenth Annual Report of the Kansas City Public Schools, for the*

Year 1888–89 (Kansas City, MO: Hudson, Kimberly Publishing Co., 1889), p. 73.

47. *Forty-Sixth Annual Report of the Board of Education of the City of Detroit, 1889* (Detroit: James Markey, 1889), p. 70; Cleveland Public Schools, *Fifty-Third Annual Report of the Board of Education* (Cleveland: The Plain Dealer, 1889), pp. 16–17.

48. See, for example, the report by the principal of a female high school in Baltimore, *Fifty-Fifth Annual Report of the Board of Commissioners of Public Schools to the Mayor and City Council of Baltimore* (Baltimore: John B. Piet and Co., 1883), p. 115, and the discussion of parental responsibilities in a report on physical education in Chicago, Department of Public Instruction, City of Chicago, *Thirtieth Annual Report of the Board of Education, 1884* (Chicago: George K. Hazlitt and Co., 1885), pp. 30–32. Also see the report on "Excessive Study" in *Annual Report of the Public Schools of the City and County of San Francisco, 1892*, p. 99. On the issue of concern over health at women's colleges at this time, see Sheila M. Rothman, *Woman's Proper Place: A History of Changing Ideals and Practices, 1870 to the Present* (New York: Basic Books, 1978), pp. 21–42.

49. Leading educators often commented on the popularity of coeducation as a matter of policy. "There is evidence of an increasing desire in the public mind to furnish women an education fully equivalent to the best education furnished men," wrote the U.S. Commissioner of Education in 1879. See his *Annual Report, 1879* (Washington, DC: Government Printing Office, 1880), p. 101. Nine years later newly appointed U.S. Commissioner of Education William Torrey Harris declared that "the overwhelming majority of all persons engaged in education in the United States are in favor of Coeducation." See his *Annual Report, 1888–89*, vol. 1 (Washington, DC: Government Printing Office, 1890), pp. 467–68.

50. For discussion of the nineteenth-century high school curriculum, see Krug, *The Shaping of the American High School*, chap. 1 and 2.

51. Jane Roland Martin, "Needed: A New Paradigm for Liberal Education," in Jonas F. Soltis, ed., *Philosophy of Education: The Eighteenth Yearbook of the National Society for the Study of Education* (Chicago: University of Chicago Press, 1981), pp. 37–59.

52. *Nineteenth Annual Report of the Board of Directors of the St. Louis Public Schools*, p. 106. Common Schools of Cincinnati, *Fifty-Second Annual Report for the School Year Encing June First, 1880* (Cincinnati: Wilstatch, Baldwin and Co., 1881), pp. 106–7. U.S. Bureau of Education, *Coeducation of the Sexes in the Public Schools of the United States*, pp. 20–23.

53. See, for instance, the high school curricula described in the following school reports: City of Chicago, Board of Education, *Chicago High Schools: Syllabus of the Course of Study, 1893* (Chicago: George Hazlitt and Co., 1893); Dayton Public Schools, *Annual Report of the Board of Education for the School Year Ending June, 1886* (Dayton: Hoffman Publishing Co., 1887), p. 128; *Annual Reports of the Board of Education of the City of Newburgh, N.Y., 1889* (Newburgh:

Strong Printing Co., 1890), pp. 110–12; *Annual Report of the Superintendent of Public Schools of Covington, KY, 1894–95* (Cincinnati: W. B. Carpenter, 1895), pp. 92–101. Also see Krug, *The Shaping of the American High School,,* chap. 1.

54. U.S. Commissioner of Education, *Annual Report, 1889–1890,* vol. 2 (Washington, DC: Government Printing Office, 1891), p. 1392.

55. S. Thurber, "English Literature in Girls' Education," *The School Review* 2 (June 1894): 321–36.

56. See the lists of books used in various Baltimore schools in the *Fifty-Fifth Annual Report of the Board of Commissioners of the Public Schools to the Mayor and City Council of Baltimore,* 1883, pp. 163–65.

57. On Philadelphia, see David Labaree, "The Making of an American High School: Central High School in Philadelphia, 1850–1950,"(unpublished Ph.D. dissertation, University of Pennsylvania, 1984); on Louisville, see *Report of Boys High School, Louisville, KY., 1898–99* (Louisville: Brandon Co., 1900), and Maxwell, "Should the Educations of Boys and Girls Differ?" p. 132. On New York, see the *TwentyNinth Annual Report of the Board of Education of the City and County of New York, 1870* (New York, NY: School Journal Printing, 1871), p. 6.

58. Discussion of this point can be found in Keller, "An Historical Analysis of the Arguments For and Against Coeducational Public High Schools in the United States," pp. 268–90. Also see U.S. Bureau of Education, *Coeducation of the Sexes in the Public Schools of the United States,* pp. 24–26, and *Sixty-Third Annual Report of the Board of Commissioners of the Public Schools to the Mayor and City Council of Baltimore 1891* (Baltimore: John Cox, 1891), pp. 47–50. For evidence of the strength of public opinion in favor of coeducation in a large eastern city, see the discussion of petitions and popular polls in local newspapers in Boston in 1890 in DuFour, "The Exclusion of Female Students from the Public Secondary Schools of Boston," pp. 244–45.

59. Anne Firor Scott, "The 'New Woman' in the New South," in *Making the Invisible Woman Visible,* p. 212.

60. U.S. Bureau of Education, *Coeducation of the Sexes in the Public Schools of the United States,* pp. 24–26.

61. See Common Schools of Cincinnati, *Forty-Second Annual Report for the School Year Ending June 1871* (Cincinnati: Wilstatch and Baldwin, 1872), p. 46; idem, *Fifty-Second Annual Report for the School Year Ending June 1881* (Cincinnati: Carpenter Printing Co., 1882), pp. 95–97; and idem, *Fifty-Sixth Annual Report for the School Year Ending June 1885* (Cincinnati: Wilstatch, Baldwin and Co., 1886), pp. 95 and 98. On the awarding of prizes to male and female students, see Common Schools of Cincinnati, *Forty-Seventh Annual Report for the School Year Ending June 1876* (Cincinnati: W. B. Carpenter and Co., 1877), pp. 58–59. "Report of the Principal of the High School," *Eighteenth Annual Report of the Board of Education, School District No. One, Arapahoe County, Colorado, 1892* (Denver: App-Stot Printing Co., 1892), p. 34. Also see State

of New York, *One Hundred Seventh Annual Report of the University of the State of New York, 1893* (Albany, NY: University of the State of New York, 1894), p. 378, for more commentary on the performance of women secondary students. The remarks of the professor from Texas can be found in "The Status of Women from the Educational and Industrial Standpoint," in U.S. Commissioner of Education, *Annual Report, 1897–98*, vol. 1 (Washington, DC: Government Printing Office, 1899), pp. 631–32.

62. For an example of this, see the list on page 84 of the *Sixteenth Annual Report of the Board of Directors of the St. Louis Public Schools.* The "deportment" grade referred to a "system of checks" recorded for "unnecessary trouble" occasioned by each student. This could include infractions as inconsequential as "talking out of turn," and was generally considered "a mark of thoughtlessness rather than of intentional disobedience." See the discussion of this in the *Twenty-First Annual Report of the Board of Directors of the St. Louis Public Schools, 1875* (St. Louis: Slawson Printer, 1876), p. 63. Ueda also observed that women students consistently performed better than the boys in the Sommerville high school. See *Avenues to Adulthood*, p. 172.

63. State of New York, *Ninety-Ninth Annual Report of the University of the State of New York*, 1886 (Albany, NY: University of the State of New York, 1886), p. 162.

64. U.S. Commissioner of Education, *Annual Report, 1888–89*, vol. 1 (Washington, DC: Government Printing Office, 1890), p. 465.

65. Ann Douglas, *The Feminization of American Culture* (New York: Alfred A. Knopf, 1977), p. 8.

Chapter 2. Participation and Purpose in Women's Education: Who Went to School and Why

1. Edward Krug, *The Shaping of the American High School, 1880–1920* (New York: Harper and Row, 1964), chap. 1.

2. Given the difficulties in establishing any line of causality in historical analysis, the limitations inherent in this sort of approach may be inevitable. But in the absence of more direct forms of evidence, examining the context of a given pattern of behavior—and determining just what was associated with it—can be a rather effective method of approaching the question why. For an interesting discussion of the issue of causality in social science research, see Hubert M. Blalock, Jr., *Causal Inferences in Nonexperimental Research* (Chapel Hill, NC: University of North Carolina Press, 1961), chap. 1.

3. See David Angus, "A Note on the Occupational Backgrounds of Public High School Students Prior to 1940," *Journal of the Midwest History of Education Society* 9 (1981): 158–83. Also see Krug, *The Shaping of the American High School*, chap. 8.

4. Michael B. Katz, "Who Went to School," *History of Education Quarterly* 12, no. 4 (Winter 1972): 432–54.

5. For discussion of rural-urban differences in school enrollment at this time, see John L. Rury, "American School Enrollment in the Progressive Era: An Interpretive Inquiry," *History of Education* 14, no. 1 (March 1985): 49–67. Also see John G. Richardson, "Town Versus Countryside and Systems of Common Schooling," *Social Science History* 11, no. 4 (Winter 1987): 401–32; Carl F. Kaestle and Maris A. Vinovskis, *Education and Social Change in Nineteenth Century Massachusetts* (New York: Cambridge University Press, 1980), chap. 5; and Lee Soltow and Edward Stevens, *The Rise of Literacy and the Common School in the United States: A Socioeconomic Analysis to 1870* (Chicago: University of Chicago Press, 1981), chap. 4 and 5.

6. While this does not allow the same level of precision regarding secondary enrollment levels as do aggregate statistics collected from the high schools themselves, it does afford the opportunity to determine which types of background characteristics were associated with teenage school participation in American cities at this time. The advantages of being able to perform this type of analysis, in that case, compensate for the imprecision associated with using census data to study patterns of secondary school enrollment. Even so, it is important to remember that the data used in this section of the study do not necessarily reflect patterns of high school attendance alone. For a general discussion of the difficulties in studying data on teenage school enrollment, see Kaestle and Vinovskis, *Education and Social Change in Nineteenth Century Massachusetts*, chap. 4.

7. In what was probably the most comprehensive analysis of this issue, Carl Kaestle and Maris Vinovskis argued that teenagers from immigrant families in late nineteenth-century Massachusetts were less likely to attend school than those from native backgrounds, even when occupational differences were controlled. Michael Katz and Ian Davey, on the other hand, have emphasized the importance of class variables (occupational background and wealth) in their studies of school participation in nineteenth-century Hamilton, Ontario. Tables summarizing the findings of both the Katz and Davey and Kaestle and Vinovskis studies can be found in the Appendix to this chapter. More recent studies have demonstrated the significance of both social class and ethnicity as factors associated with variation in teenage school participation, along with such other variables as home ownership, family size, and each child's position in the birth order. Despite these differences, all of these authors agree on the basic dimensions of nineteenth-century school participation: the teenage daughters (and sons) of immigrant and lower-class parents were less likely to attend school than those from more affluent and native origins. For a discussion of these studies see Harvey Graff, "'The New Math:' Quantification, the 'New' History, and the History of Education," *Urban Education* 11, no. 4 (January 1977): 403–40. Also see Rury, "American School Enrollment in the Progressive Era," pp. 49–50, for an updated list of such studies. For a comparative analysis of male and female teenage school

enrollment patterns in this period, see John L. Rury, "Urban School Enrollment at the Turn of the Century: Gender as an Intervening Variable," *Urban
Education* 23, no. 1 (April 1988): 68–88.

8. The quote is from Kaestle and Vinovskis, *Education and Social Change
in Nineteenth Century Massachusetts*, p. 99. Other studies cited include Michael
B. Katz and Ian Davey, "School Attendance and Early Industrialization in a
Canadian City: A Multivariate Analysis," *History of Education Quarterly* 18, no.
3 (Fall 1978): 271–93; Joel Perlman, "Working Class Home Ownership and
Children's Schooling in Providence, Rhode Island, 1880–1925," *History of Edu-
cation Quarterly* 23, no. 2 (Summer 1983): 175–91; and David Angus and Jeffery
Mirel, "From Spellers to Spindles: Workforce Entry by the Children of Textile
Workers, 1888–1890," *Social Science History* 9, no. 2 (Spring 1985): 123–44.

9. Kaestle and Vinovskis, *Education and Social Change in Nineteenth Century Massachusetts*, chap. 4.

10. For a description of the 1900 Public Use Sample, see Center for
Studies in Demography and Ecology, University of Washington, *United States
Census Data, 1900: Public Use Sample (ICPSR 7825)*. (Ann Arbor, MI: Inter-uni-
versity Consortium for Political and Social Research, 1981).

11. Judging from data collected by the Commissioner of Education, the
national high school enrollment rate among women was slightly more than
10 percent at the turn of the century. It was probably a good deal higher in
cities. See Table 2.2 below for more detailed statistics on this point.

This analysis of school attendance is different from previous studies in
yet other ways. Limiting the analysis to young women permits identification
of those factors especially important to female school participation in this
period. Of course, the Public Use Sample data are drawn from the 1900 census and therefore represent a different point in time than the nineteenth-century data other historians have used. As such, they also offer an opportunity
to examine the shape of school participation at the end of the period in question. For a discussion of this point, see Rury, "Urban School Enrollment at the
Turn of the Century," pp. 76–77.

12. On MCA see F. M. Andrews, J. Morgan, J. A. Sonquist, and L. Klem,
Multiple Classification Analysis (Ann Arbor: Institute for Social Research, 1973).

13. Other elements of my analysis are modifications of variables used
by other historians, most of them necessitated by the national scope of the
Public Use Sample. Where other studies have used "community" variables to
capture rural-urban differences in school enrollment, for instance, I have
developed a regional variable to measure the differences in attendance from
one part of the country to another. Similarly, because there are both black and
white women in the 1900 data, I have also included a variable for race. Factors that did not perform well in the nineteenth-century studies I excluded
from consideration in the 1900 analysis. See the discussion of these factors in
Kaestle and Vinovskis, *Education and Social Change*, chap. 4. I have modified

the father's occupation and ethnicity variables to include more categories than Kaestle and Vinovskis.

14. Angus and Mirel, "From Spellers to Spindles," pp. 131–40. For discussion on a somewhat different variable designed to measure family size as a factor in school attendance decisions, see Kaestle and Vinovskis, *Education and Social Change*, p. 91.

15. For a discussion of the many elements that have a bearing on the question of whether to attend school or work in these families, see the chapter titled "Families: Cycle, Structure and Economy," in Michael B. Katz, Michael J. Doucet, and Mark J. Stern, *The Social Organization of Early Industrial Capitalism* (Cambridge: Harvard University Press, 1982). Also see John Model, Frank Furstenberg, and Theordore Hershberg, "Social Change and Transitions to Adulthood in Historical Perspective," *Journal of Family History* 1 (Autumn 1976): 7–33.

16. The range of variation in enrollment levels was greater for both ethnic and occupational background variables than was the case in the 1880 analysis by Kaestle and Vinovskis, perhaps because of the larger number of categories employed for each factor. This was most evident in connection with the ethnicity variable. Eight different groups were included in the analysis of ethnicity in 1900, as opposed to just four in Kaestle and Vinovskis's analysis, a difference largely attributable to the national scope of the Public Use Sample. Similarly, I chose to separate lower white-collar from skilled labor in father's occupation, and this may have augmented the power of the occupational background variable somewhat. But in both cases the results obtained from an analysis of school enrollment using 1900 federal census manuscript data was generally the same as reported in Kaestle and Vinovskis's discussion of enrollment patterns in 1880.

17. For discussion of gender-related differences in the effect of class and ethnicity on female school attendance, see Rury, "Urban School Enrollment at the Turn of the Century." On the debates over the total number of teenagers enrolled in nineteenth-century high schools, see Maris A. Vinovskis, "Have We Underestimated the Extent of Antebellum High School Attendance?" *History of Education Quarterly* 28, no. 4 (Winter 1988): 551–67.

18. See the discussion of this point in Joel Perlmann, *Ethnic Differences: Schooling and Social Structure among the Irish, Italians, Jews, and Blacks in an American City, 1880–1935* (New York: Cambridge University Press, 1988), Conclusion. Also see Olivier Zunz, *The Changing Face of Inequality: Urbanization, Industrial Development and Immigrants in Detroit, 1880–1920* (Chicago: University of Chicago Press, 1982). This finding is also consistent with those of Kaestle and Vinovskis, *Education and Social Change in Nineteenth Century Massachusetts*, p 98. This pattern stands in sharp contrast, however, to those suggested in Paul Peterson, *The Politics of School Reform*, 1870–1940 (Chicago: University of Chicago Press, 1985), chap. 3 and 4, which argues that class background was an important determinant of high school enrollment for

boys and that ethnic background had little bearing on the allocation of school resources in selected American cities.

19. On this point, see David B. Tyack and Elizabeth Hansot, "Silence and Policy Talk: Historical Puzzles about Gender and Education" *Educational Researcher* 17, no. 4 (May 1988): 33–41.

20. Reed Ueda has identified a similar pattern of school participation among young women in his study of Sommerville, Massachusetts, at this time. See his *Avenues to Adulthood: The Origins of the High School and Social Mobility in an American Suburb* (New York: Cambridge University Press, 1987), p. 52.

21. Tyack and Hansot, "Silence and Policy Talk: Historical Puzzles about Gender and Education." Also see Elizabeth Hansot and David Tyack, "Gender in American Public Schools: Thinking Institutionally," *Signs: Journal of Women in Culture and Society* 13, no. 3 (FAll 1988), pp. 741–60.

22. Most social scientists learn early on that ecological analysis is fraught with potential pitfalls. The discussion that follows is no exception. In the data set I assembled for this section of the study, the unit of analysis—or the contextual entity to be studied—is defined at the *state* level. This means that a wide range of contextual factors can be identified, since the state was the most commonplace unit of data collection for federal agencies in this period. But it also means that a great deal of caution must be exercised in interpreting patterns of association identified below. Because states are rather large units of analysis, and often themselves contain a wide range of environments, it is possible that important patterns of association between contextual factors will be missed—or, worse yet, incorrectly identified—at the state level. In general, the larger the unit of analysis, the greater the possibility of the "ecological fallacy," the problem of identifying patterns of association incorrectly with ecological data. Because the data employed below are defined at the state level, great care must be exercised in interpreting the results of the following analysis. Bearing the limitations of such data in mind, however, ecological analysis can be a useful means of identifying general patterns of association which *may* reflect the behavior (and the thinking) of individuals. On problems in ecological analysis, see Blalock, *Causal Inferences in Nonexperimental Research*, chap. 4.

23. Contextual data on income and other factors are taken from Harvey Perloff, Edgar S. Dunn, Erick E. Lampard, and Richard Muth, *Regions, Resources and Economic Growth* (Baltimore: Johns Hopkins University Press, 1960), p. 650. Census data and educational statistics were drawn from summary tables provided in published census reports and the annual reports of the U.S. Commissioner of Education. For discussion of the poor data in the Commissioner of Education reports at this time, see David Tyack, "Ways of Seeing: An Essay on the History of Compulsory Schooling", *Harvard Educational Review* 46, no. 3 (August 1976): 360. These data, however, present a number of shortcomings. Perhaps the most important is a general underreporting of high school enrollment data in most U.S. Commissioner Reports

prior to 1890. The data given each year in these reports were taken from questionnaires completed by school officials across the country, but many schoolmen apparently never bothered to return the forms, and some schools undoubtedly were overlooked in the survey to begin with. Moreover, even as the number of reporting schools increased, many did not provide information on the gender of students. Thus, the high school enrollment data used for this study is most reliable for the years 1890 and 1900. The data for 1890 and 1900 appear to be considerably more complete than enrollment data in earlier reports. For this reason much of the ecological analysis herein will be restricted to 1890 and 1900 secondary enrollment data.

24. On regional differences in enrollment and social and economic development, see Rury, "American School Enrollment in the Progressive Era," pp. 52–66. Also see *idem*, "Urbanization and Education: Regional Patterns of Educational Development in American Cities, 1900–1910," *Michigan Academician* 20, no. 2 (Summer 1988): 261–79; and Richardson, "Town Versus Countryside and Systems of Common Schooling," pp. 408–16; and *idem*, "American States and the Age of School Systems," *American Journal of Education* 92, no. 4 (Winter 1984): 473–502.

25. As there were just thirty-six states included in the 1870 analysis (territories were excluded, as was the District of Columbia) only those values higher than 0.329 can be judged significant at the 0.05 level. In 1890 all thirty-nine states and the District of Columbia were included, so the critical value for significance is 0.312. Even in those cases where significance was not achieved, however, the direction and relative strength of the relationship can be telling.

I have put the term "trade in quotes to distinguish it from occupations—for both women and me—described as "trades" (such as the "garment trades" or "building trades"). "Trade" employment, as defined by the *census*, embraced a wide range of occupations involving the selling and distribution of goods.

26. For discussion of regional differences in the feminization of teaching, see John L. Rury, "Who Became Teachers: The Social Characteristics of Teachers in American History," in Donald Warren, ed., *American Teachers: Histories of a Profession at Work* (New York: Macmillan, 1989), pp. 9–48. Also see the discussion of regional differences in women's employment in chapters 3 and 5 of this book.

27. Reed Ueda found high school attendance to be an important avenue for the movement of young men into white-collar jobs in this study of one community in this period. See *Avenues to Adulthood*, p. 182.

28. The analysis of female high school enrollment levels to follow is different from the foregoing discussion in two critical respects. The first is conceptual, and has been touched upon above. Unlike feminization, which is a relative measure of female enrollment (compared to male enrollment), the absolute enrollment rate is determined by a range of factors, from the number

of secondary schools in each state to the interest of young women in getting a high school education. To get at the issue of why teenage girls might have wanted to attend high school, it is necessary to separate the effects of each of these various elements. The second difference concerns the data. As noted earlier, the information supplied the U.S. Commissioner of Education by local school authorities in the latter nineteenth century was notoriously incomplete, especially in the years prior to 1890. This is of less concern when considering issues such as feminization and graduation, since they are indexes calculated by comparing relevant groups of female students with other groups of students. In analyzing overall enrollment, however, the control group (or denominator) is the entire teenage population (or those age 15 to 19, as reported in the U.S. Census). Underreporting of high school enrollments, in that case, can seriously distort the effort to determine just what the overall enrollment rate was at any given time. For this reason, my analysis of enrollment rates is restricted to the years 1890 and 1900, when enrollment data are best and decennial census data are available for the determination of rates. This means that the treatment of enrollments below is not directly comparable to the discussion of feminization and graduation made earlier, since they concern different—albeit adjacent—periods of time. Even so, the two analyses are both located in the larger period under examination, the latter nineteenth century. In this respect, they complement one another, and together can provide a useful portrait of factors shaping the development of female secondary education in this period.

29. On multiple regression, see Hubert M. Blalock, Jr., *Social Statistics* (New York: McGraw Hill, 1972), chap. 17 to 19.

30. John L. Rury, "Urban Structure and School Participation: Immigrant Women in 1900," *Social Science History* 8, no. 3 (Summer 1984): 219–41; Miriam Cohen, "Italian-American Women in New York City: Work and School," *Labor History* 16, no. 3 (Winter 1975): 121–33.

The other elements of the analysis are relatively straightforward. One is a measure of pupils per teacher in each state, to indicate the overall level of development in each state school system. Another is the level of urbanization, a general measure of social and economic development. And the last is the per capita income of each state, a variable that may be related to the ability of parents to pay for extended education for their daughters (and to pay the higher tax bills associated with the appearance of public high schools). The income variable may also reflect differences in taste for education, regardless of cost, as studies have indicated that most high school students in this period were drawn from the ranks of the middle and upper classes. In any case, income is included in this analysis as a measure of the general ability to afford education and the particular value that higher-income families may have placed on secondary education for their daughters.

31. I have decided to include an 1890 enrollment variable to isolate the *difference* between 1890 and 1900 high school enrollment rates for each state as the dependent variable in this analysis. For discussion of the advantages of

this method, which was derived from the study of social mobility, see Peter Blau and Otis Dudley Duncan, *The American Occupational Structure* (New York: Wiley, 1967), pp. 195–99.

32. Clearly there is a good deal of interaction between the income, urbanization, and 'trade' employment variables in this analysis. "Trade" employment, however, turned out to be consistently important in repeated runs made with different combinations of variables. Consequently, I did not feel comfortable in ruling out all employment effects on enrollments.

For treatment of the timing of changes in women's work, see Elyce Rotella, *From Home to Office: United States Women at Work, 1870–1930* (Ann Arbor, MI: UMI Research Press, 1981).

33. On the question of motivation as an issue for historians, see Louis Gottschalk, *Understanding History: A Primer of Historical Method* (New York: Alfred Knopf, 1950), chap. 10.

34. See, for instance, Marilyn Ferris Motz, *True Sisterhood: Michigan Women and their Kin, 1820–1920* (Albany, NY: SUNY Press, 1983). Motz drew her material almost entirely from the Bentley Historical Library at the University of Michigan, where much of the material cited below is located.

35. Most of these women lived in Massachusetts or Michigan, as most of the material I used was drawn from collections in those states. No more than two of the women, however, attended the same school, and taken together the entire group represented a wide range of different communities and backgrounds. It is difficult to determine, in any case, just how representative these women are of all women attending high school in these years. For this reason less significance should be attached to particular statements they made than to general tendencies exhibited in the entire sample. I expect that a clearer picture of young women's thoughts and perceptions during high school will emerge as more such papers are examined by other scholars.

36. For an introduction to ethnographic method, see Harry F. Wolcott, "Ethnographic Research in Education" in Richard M. Jaeger, ed., *Complementary Methods for Research in Education* (Washington, D.C.: American Educational Research Association, 1988), pp. 185–216. Also see George D. Spindler and Louise Spindler, eds., *Doing the Ethnography of Schooling: Educational Anthropology in Action* (New York: Holt, Rhinehart and Winston, 1982), pp. 1–13.

37. On this point see James S. Coleman, *The Adolescent Society* (New York: The Free Press, 1961); Philip A. Cusick, *Inside High School* (New York: Holt, Rhinehart and Winston, 1973); and M. Brake, *The Sociology of Youth Culture and Youth Subcultures* (Boston: Routledge and Kegan Paul, 1980). See the discussion of this point in Ueda, *Avenues to Adulthood*, p. 152. For an interesting, if dissappointingly brief, discussion of the development of peer cultures among youth in this period, see Howard P. Chudacoff, *How Old Are You: Age Consciousness in American Culture* (Princeton, N.J.: Princeton University Press, 1989), pp. 102–6.

38. *Twenty-Sixth Annual Report of the Public Schools of the City of Spring-field, Illinois, 1884* (Springfield: State Journal Co., 1885), p. 24.

39. Dayton Public Schools, *Annual Report of the Board of Education for the School Year Ending 1885* (Dayton: Huffman Publishing, 1886), pp. 115–18.

40. Letter from Alice Devin to Anne Moore, November 6, 1871, Alice Devin Letters, 1870–1872, Bentley Historical Library, University of Michigan.

41. Diary of Lois Wells, 1882–1887, Schlesinger Library, Radcliffe College, January 1, 1882, and pp. 85–87.

42. Diary of Nellie Clark, University Archives, Walter Reuther Library, Wayne State University, January 5, 1894; February 1, 1894.

43. Letter from Alice Devin to Annie Moore, September 9, 1870, Alice Devin Letters. For examples of nineteenth-century educators' concerns about this question, see the complaints about women students overdressing for graduation exercises in Department of Public Instruction, City of Chicago, *Twenty-First Annual Report of the Board of Education for the Year Ending 1875* (Chicago, 1875), p. 147. Also see the discussion of these points in Ueda, *Avenues to Adulthood*, pp. 122 and 147.

44. Both quotes are taken from *Memorial to Mrs. Gayley Browne, 1895,* Women's League Collection (University of Michigan), Bentley Historical Library, University of Michigan.

45. See Carol Smith-Rosenberg, *Disorderly Conduct: Visions of Gender in Victorian America* (New York: Oxford University Press, 1985), Part 1.

46. For discussion of the changing nature of the high school in this period, see Krug, *Shaping the American High School, 1880–1920*, chap. 1.

47. Letter from Alice Devin to Annie Moore, November 6, 1871, Alice Devin Letters.

48. Letter from Vera Barton to Mrs. Matilda Douglas, February 12, 1893, Douglas-Nellis Collection, Benteley Historical Library, University of Michigan; Jeannette L. Gilder Papers, Folder One, Schlesinger Library, Radcliffe College; Diary of Nellie Clark, January 8, 1894.

49. Letter from Agnes Hankerd to her Parents, November 5, 1891, Birney-McClear-Hankerd Collection, Box 2, Bentley Historical Library, University of Michigan.

50. Diary of Nellie Clark, January 26, 1894.

51. Dayton Public Schools, *Annual Report, 1885*, p. 116; Diary of Nellie Clark, January 29, February 2, 1894.

52. Letter from Agnes Hankerd to her Parents, November 11, 1897, Birney-McClear-Hankerd Collection, Box 2.

53. Frances M. Quick, Autobiography, June 18, 1854, Frances Merrit Quick Papers, Box 1, Folder 3, Schlesinger Library, Radcliffe College.

54. For an overview of the ideology of domesticity that governed most women's lives in this period, see Carl N. Degler, *At Odds: Women and the Family in America from the Revolution to the Present* (New York: Oxford University Press, 1980), chap. 1 to 5.

55. Mary Bracken, "Influence of Women" (student essay), Smith Family Papers (Ontonagon County), Bentley Historical Library, University of Michigan.

56. Roberta Hawn, Student Essay, 1877, Wilber M. Brucker Collection, Box 12, Bentley Historical Library, University of Michigan.

57. Casassa's essay was published as "Woman and Education" in the *Annual Report of the Public Schools of the City and County of San Francisco, 1897* (San Francisco: The Hinton Printing Co., 1897).

58. Letters from Josiah Littlefield to his daughter Ellen, November 6, 1887 and December 16, 1895. Littlefield Family Papers, Bentley Historical Library, University of Michigan.

59. Letter from Edwin Phelps to his family, August 13, 1889, Jessie Phelps Papers, Bentley Historical Library, University of Michigan.

60. Ueda, *Avenues to Adulthood*, p. 121.

61. Diary of Nellie Clark, March 2, 1894.

62. Erik Erikson, *Childhood and Society* (New York: Norton, 1950), p. 261

63. David F. Allmendinger, Jr., "Mount Holyoke Students Encounter the Need for Life Planning, 1837–1850" *History of Education Quarterly* 19, no. 1 (Spring 1979), pp. 27–46; and Geraldine Jonich Clifford, "'Marry, Stitch, Die, or Do Worse': Educating Women for Work" in Harvey Kantor and David Tyack, eds., *Youth, Work and Schooling: Historical Perspectives on Vocationalism in American Education* (Stanford, CA: Stanford University Press, 1982). I found very little of the deliberate sort of planning by either parents or students described in Allmendinger's account and suggested by Clifford. I believe Allmendinger's Holyoke students may have represented a different set of circumstances— women who were intending to teach—and a different period, when secondary education for women was not quite so commonplace. The decision to send daughters to public high schools in the letter nineteenth century does not seem to have been as monumental as those described by Allmendinger. Still, the high school did afford young women an opportunity to get away from home, into an environment where a clearer personal identity could be forged.

Chapter 3. Women at Work: Female Labor Force Participation and Education, 1890–1930

1. Perhaps the best overview of this process is Ellyce Rotella, *From Home to Office: U.S. Women at Work, 1870–1930* (Ann Arbor, MI: UMI Research

Press, 1981), chap. 2 and 4. Also see Margery Davies, *Woman's Place is at the Typewriter: Office Work and Office Workers, 1870–1930* (Philadelphia: Temple University Press, 1982).

2. See Rotella, *From Home to Office*, chap. 4; Davies, *Woman's Place is at the Typewriter;* Lynne Y. Weiner, *From Working Girl to Working Mother* (Chapel Hill: University of North Carolina Press, 1985), chap. 3; and Alice Kessler-Haris, *Out to Work: A History of Wage Earning Women in the United States* (New York: Oxford University Press, 1982), pp. 133–36.

Much of what follows, as in chapter 2, entails the discussion of aggregate data. Again, this raises important problems of interpretation, but it also provides a means of determining how the changing shape of women's work affected different groups of women. Before considering the interaction of work and education in any period, it is necessary to identify just what sorts of work women were doing and who was doing what. Beyond that, changes in regional patterns of female employment can be compared with some of the developments in female school participation described earlier. Similarly, the development of certain kinds of jobs, such as teaching or clerical work, can be linked with changes in women's education with the use of aggregate data. Keeping the limitations of this approach in view, it is possible to identify important patterns of association between women's work and education in this period simply by identifying general patterns in their development. Because so many of the new fields in women's work were established on the premise of women's education, their development hinged decisively on the availability of educated women. And this, it appears, helped to account for important differences in the shape of women's work from one part of the country to another.

3. Weiner, *From Working Girl to Working Mother*, chap. 3.

4. Rotella, *From Home to Office*, chap. 2, 3, and 4.

5. Davies, *Woman's Place is at the Typewriter*, chap. 3 and 4.

6. For an overview of the problem of occupational segregation for women, see Valarie Kincade Oppenheimer, *The Female Labor Force in the United States: Demographic and Economic Factors Governing its Growth and Changing Composition* (Westport, CN: Greenwood Press, 1970), chap. 3. Also see Shirley Dex, *The Sexual Division of Work: Conceptual Revolutions in the Social Sciences* (New York: St. Martins Press, 1985), pp.95–99. On the concentration of women in various white-collar occupations, see Rotella, *From Home to Office*, chap. 5 and 6; and Davies, *Woman's Place is at the Typewriter*, Appendix.

7. John L. Rury, "American School Enrollment in the Progressive Era: An Interpretive Inquiry," *History of Education* 14, no. 1 (March 1985): 58.

8. For discussion of female employment patterns in 1930, see my dissertation: John L. Rury, "Women, Cities and Schools: Education and the Development of an Urban Female Labor Force, 1890–1930," unpublished Ph.D. dissertation, University of Wisconsin, 1982, chap. 3.

9. On this point see Weiner, *From Working Girl to Working Mother*, chap. 3. Also see Part 2 of Elizabeth Baker's study, *Technology and Women's Work* (New York: Columbia University Press, 1964): "Six Decades of Change in Factory, Office and Shop" for a review of widening job opportunities for women in this period.

The problem with such observations, of course, is that they have been made at a very high level of aggregation, using national statistics. It is difficult, on the other hand, to determine just *how* women's education and women's work were associated in this period without examining them in a variety of different social and economic settings. Women in different parts of the country, after all, exhibited different patterns of labor force participation, and there were enormous differences in the organization of school systems from one region to another. In order to clearly identify the relationship between female schooling and women's work, in that case, it is necessary to consider both of these issues in a number of regional contexts.

10. See Davies, *Woman's Place is at the Typewriter*, pp. 70–75.

11. The best general account of the lives of working women in the Northeast in this period is Leslie Woodcock Tentler, *Wage Earning Women: Industrial Work and Family Life in the United States, 1900–1930* (New York: Oxford University Press, 1979).

12. David M. Katzman, *Seven Days a Week: Women and Domestic Service in Industrializing America* (New York: Oxford University Press, 1978) is one of the few books that discusses regional differences in women's work in this period (see chapter 2, "Domestic Servants," in particular). For a contemporary's account of regional differences in women's work, analytically imprecise but useful, see Annie M. Maclean, *Wage Earning Women* (New York: Macmillan, 1910).

13. For a discussion of employment patterns and women's education in the West in this period, see Harvey Kantor, *Learning to Earn: School, Work, and Vocational Reform in California, 1880–1930* (Madison, WI: University of Wisconsin Press, 1988), chap. 4 and 7.

14. For a discussion of regional differences in school enrollment at this time, and a similar characterization of enrollment patterns in the Northeast, see Rury, "American School Enrollment in the Progressive Era," pp. 56–58.

15. John G. Richardson, "Town Versus Countryside and Systems of Common Schooling," *Social Science History* 11, no. 4 (Winter 1987): 401–32; John L. Rury, "The Variable School Year: Measuring Differences in the Length of American School Terms in 1900," *Journal of Research and Development in Education* (Spring 1988): 29–36. Also see *idem*, "Urbanization and Education: Regional Patterns of Educational Development in American Cities," *Michigan Academician* 20, no. 3 (Summer 1988): 261–80; and Rury, "American School Enrollment in the Progressive Era," pp. 54–56.

16. Rury, "American School Enrollment in the Progressive Era," pp. 55–56; and Kantor, *Learning to Earn*, chap. 7.

Notes

17. For a general overview of regional differences in employment, by industries, in this period, see Harvey Perloff, Edgar S. Dunn, Eric Lampard, and Richard F. Muth, *Regions, Resources and Economic Growth* (Baltimore: Johns Hopkins University Press, 1960), chap. 13 and 17. Also see Valarie Kinkaid Oppenheimer, *The Female Labor Force in the United States*, pp. 141–90.

18. Rotella, *From Home to Office*, chap. 2 and 4.

19. For different perspectives on the relationship of education to work, see Jacob Mincer, *Schooling, Experience and Earnings* (New York: National Bureau of Economic Research, 1974); Ivor Berg, *Education and Jobs: The Great Training Robbery* (Boston: Beacon Press, 1971); and Samuel Bowles and Herbert Gintis, *Schooling in Capitalist America: Educational Reform and the Contradictions of Economic Life* (New York: Basic Books, 1976), Part 2.

20. For a discussion of ways in which education is related to job entry in recent decades, see Steven D. McLaughlin, Barbara D. Melber, John O. G. Billy, Denise M. Zimmerle, Linda D. Winges, and Terry R. Johnson, *The Changing Lives of American Women* (Chapel Hill: University of North Carolina Press, 1988), chap. 3. Figures used in this analysis are derived from the federal census. Unfortunately, the census does not permit comparison of these distributions within regions. As indicated above, however, each major region was characterized by a particular mix of female job opportunities in this period, and occupational age distributions can be compared with regional patterns of employment to identify lines of continuity.

21. Tentler, *Wage Earning Women*, pp. 93–104. Also see the discussion in John Sharpless and John Rury, "The Political Economy of Women's Work, 1900–1920," *Social Science History* 4, no. 3 (Summer 1980): 318–26. For an expression of the same problem in the thirties, see Howard M. Bell, *Youth Tell Their Story* (Washington, DC: Government Printing Office, 1938), p. 65.

22. Katzman, *Seven Days a Week*, chap. 2.

23. Susan Porter Benson, *Counter Cultures: Saleswomen, Managers, and Customers in American Department Stores, 1890–1940* (Urbana: University of Illinois Press, 1986), pp. 128–30.

24. On the ages of women in clerical and teaching jobs at this time, see Rotella, *From Home to Office*, chap. 5; and John L. Rury, "Gender, Salaries and Career: American Teachers, 1900–1910," *Issues in Education* (now *American Educational Research Journal*) 4, no. 3 (Winter 1986): 215–36.

25. Tentler, *Wage Earning Women*, p. 96.

26. For a contemporary account of the irrelevance of formal education to employment in manufacturing, see Anne MacClean, *Wage Earning Women*.

27. Benson, *Counter Cultures*, pp. 147–55; for a contemporary discussion of education for women in "salesmanship," see Albert H. Leake, *The Vocational Education of Girls and Women* (New York: Macmillan, 1918), p. 361; and

Frank V. Thompson, *Commercial Education in Public Secondary Schools* (Yonkers, NY: World Book Company, 1915), p. 143.

28. Common Schools of Cincinnati, *Fifty-Sixth Annual Report, 1885* (Cincinnati: Wilstatch, Baldwin and Co., 1886), p. 94; *Sixteenth Annual Report of the Kansas City Public Schools, 1886–87* (Kansas City, MO: Peter H. Tiernan, 1887), p. 26. Of course, the fact that women were enrolled in high schools in such large numbers in the latter nineteenth century also raised the question of what they would do with such advanced training, apart from becoming better wives and mothers. Even though the vast majority of female high school students probably had few ambitions outside of the roles traditionally given women, the sheer magnitude of female secondary school participation in this period broached the issue of women taking on new responsibilities.

29. The first quote is from Gary Cross and Peter Shergold, "'We Think We are of the Oppressed: Gender, White-Collar Work, and the Grievances of Late Nineteenth Century Women," *Labor History* 28, no. 1 (Winter 1987): 32; Ileen A. DeVault, "Sons and Daughters of Labor: Class and Clerical Work in Pittsburgh, 1870's–1910's," unpublished Ph.D. dissertation, Yale University, 1985, pp. 97 and 140; and Lisa Michele Fine, "'The Record Keepers of Property': The Making of the Female Clerical Labor Force in Chicago, 1870–1930," unpublished Ph.D. dissertation, University of Wisconsin, 1985, chap. 3. For a contemporary account, see Women's Educational and Industrial Union, *The Public Schools and Women in Office Service* (Boston: WEIU, 1914), p. 12; also see Thompson, *Commercial Education in Public Secondary Schools*, chapter 4, "Three Investigations and What They Mean for Commercial Education."

30. Mary Christine Anderson, "Gender, Class and Culture: Women Secretarial and Clerical Workers in the United States, 1925–1955," unpublished Ph.D. dissertation, Ohio State University, 1986, pp. 28–35. While Anderson does not develop the thesis that schooling provided employers with a "screen" to exclude certain kinds of applicants, her discovery of employer prejudice against various groups of women—coupled with the perception that "attitude" was often more important that technical skill in landing a job—supports this view. On the use of education as a screening device, see Richard Edwards, *Contested Terrain: The Transformation of the Workplace in the Twentieth Century* (New York: Basic Books, 1979), pp. 127 and 179–83; and Bowles and Gintis, *Schooling in Capitalist America*, chap. 4.

31. The Chicago survey is cited in Fine, "'The Record Keepers of Property," p. 175; the Charters and Whitley study is described in Anderson, " Gender, Class and Culture," pp. 50–58.

32. For a discussion of women teachers' ages and educational backgrounds, including analysis of Coffman's data on these points, see Rury, "Gender, Salaries, and Career," pp. 218–23. For a comparison of the number of teachers and clerical workers at different points in this period, see Davies, *Woman's Place is at the Typewriter*, Appendix.

33. Kessler-Harris, *Out to Work*, pp. 128–36. In 1920 there were some

7,219 women physicians, 5,464 "trained" nurses, and only 1,783 lawyers. These figures are taken from United States Census, *Fourteenth Census of the United States: 1920*, vol. 4 (Washington, DC: Government Printing Office, 1923), p. 392.

34. For a general discussion of female wage rates in this period, see Rotella, *From Home to Office*, pp. 157–62. Also see Davies, *Woman's Place is at the Typewriter*, chap. 4; DeVault, "Sons and Daughters of Labor," pp. 85–98; Fine, "'The Record Keepers of Property,'" chap. 2; Cross and Shergold, "We Think We are of the Oppressed," p. 29; and Rury, "Gender, Salaries and Career," pp. 218–23.

Occupational differences, however, were only one factor that accounted for differences in earnings. There was a good deal of variation in wages *within* occupations in this period as well. There is considerable evidence, for instance, that workers from "old" immigrant groups commanded substantially higher wages than their counterparts from southern and eastern Europe. According to a survey of industrial workers conducted by the Immigration Commission, English, German, and Irish workers were paid, on average, two to three dollars more per week than were Russian, Italian or "Slovack" workers. These differences existed, moreover, within manufacturing-related occupations. Larger numbers of the old immigrant groups worked at white-collar jobs or as entrepreneurs than did more recent arrivals, and this widened ethnic differences in income even more. For discussion of these issues and presentation of the Immigration Commission data, see Robert Higgs, "Race, Skills and Earnings: American Immigrants in 1909," *Journal of Economic History* 31, no. 2 (June 1971) 424; and Peter J. Hill, "Relative Skill and Income Levels of Native and Foreign Born Workers in the United States," *Explorations in Economic History* 12, no. 1 (Janaury 1975) 53.

35. These occupational differences in age structure and educational requirements can account for some of the inter-regional variation in both female labor force participation and enrollment levels observed above. As noted earlier, the rate of female labor force participation in the Northeast peaked in the 18-to-19 age group. And in 1930 large numbers of women age 14 to 18 were employed there as well. The Northeast, of course, was the country's principal industrial region in this period. It was the site of the nation's greatest concentration of female employment in manufacturing. The contours of female labor force participation identified with the Middle Atlantic states, in that case, probably represented a distinctive industrial pattern of female labor force participation. The same was true of school enrollment. As indicated above, women in the Northeast dropped out of school rapidly after age 14 in this period. Unskilled and poorly educated, many of these women undoubtedly found work in the area's many manufacturing firms.

In the West, on the other hand, relatively few women were employed in manufacturing. Apart from domestic service, the largest occupational categories there were clerical and professional employment. As indicated earlier, female labor force participation in the West peaked at ages 20 to 24, the age group for which white-collar employment was greatest as well. Female school participation in the western states, of course, was quite high throughout this period. As suggested earlier, female employment and school enrollment in the West appears to have followed a white-collar or service pattern of age distribution.

In the South, finally, where the largest categories of women's work were agricultural and domestic service, women appear to have entered the labor market at a gradual pace and left work even more gradually. No age group stands out as having been particularly critical for female workers in the South in 1930. This pattern of employment, of course, conforms with the image of the South as a region dominated by agriculture throughout this period, along with attendant underdevelopment of female employment in manufacturing, trade, and the rising clerical occupations. And as indicated above, school participation in the South, marked by short terms and extended teenage enrollment, also reflected the labor requirements and financial limitations of the region's agricultural economy. Female labor force participation and school enrollment were dominated by a characteristically agricultural age distribution in this period.

36. DeVault, "Sons and Daughters of Labor," chap. 2; also see Cross and Shergold, "'We Think We are of the Oppressed,'" pp. 28–37.

37. Davies, *Woman's Place is at the Typewriter*, chap. 4. A sense of this can be gained from Lisa Fine's discussion of popular images of women office workers and her analysis of a boarding house for "business women." Young women working in offices were often seen as quite independent and carefree, enjoying all the advantages of living in the city and rubbing shoulders with important businessmen. See Fine, "'The Record Keepers of Property,'" chap. 5 and 6. In their study of women in office employment, the Women's Educational and Industrial Union of Boston emphasized the importance of "social and business" customs to success in a clerical career and suggested that foreign-born women were at a distinct disadvantage in this regard. See *The Public Schools and Women in Office Service*, p. 150, in particular.

38. For an overview of the American labor force in this period, see Robert L. Heilbroner, *The Economic Transformation of America* (New York: Harcourt Brace Jovanovich, 1977), chap. 7. For a useful discussion of the relationship between ethnicity and class in this period, see Herbert Gutman, "Work, Culture and Society in Industrializing Anerica, 1815–1919" *The American Historical Review* 78, no. 3 (June 1973): 531–88; and Melvyn Dubofsky, *Industrialism and the American Worker, 1865–1920* (Arlington Heights, IL: AHM Publishing Co., 1975), pp. 1–13.

39. This approach is dictated by the limits of the data in the census that do not permit a more precise accounting of class differences in female labor force participation. Historians have studied the relationship of class backgrocund and the movement of women into white-collar—particularly clerical—jobs in specific cities. In particular, see Devault, "'Sons and Daughters of Labor'," chap. 3, 4, and 5; and Cross and Shergold, "'We Think We are of the Oppressed,'" pp. 28–38.

40. For an interesting discussion of ethnic concentration in particular fields of work and differing attitudes about women's work from one immigrant community to another in this period, see Barbara Klaczynka, "Why Women Worked: A Comparison of Different Groups—Philadelphia, 1910–1930," *Labor History* 17, no. 1 (Winter 1976): 73–87.

41. Katzman, *Seven Days a Week*, chap. 2.

42. Between 1890 and 1930 the ethnic dsitributions of women working in various occupational categories remained roughly the same. More than 90 percent of all professional and clerical women in 1890 were from native families. Forty years later their share was about the same. See my dissertation on this point: John L. Rury, "Women, Cities and Schools: Education and the Development of an Urban Female Labor Force, 1890–1930," unpublished Ph.D. dissertation, University of Wisconsin, 1982, chap. 4.

43. Davies, *Woman's Place is at the Typewriter*, chap. 4.

44. Differences in the ages of women workers in this period may also have been reflected in income differences. The best single source of information about ethnic differences in earnings is the Report of the Immigration Commission, published in 1910. Its findings are reviewed in Higgs, "Race, Skills, and Earnings: American Immigrants in 1909," 424. Beyond the issue of wages, there was the matter of occupational differences distinguishing natives and immigrants. According to the 1920 Federal Census, more than 45 percent of all native workers were employed in white-collar jobs, while fewer than 30 percent of immigrant workers were (U.S. Census, Occupations, Washington, DC, 1921, p. 342). For further discussion of skill differences between native and immigrant workers in industry, see Hill, "Relative Income Levels of Native and Foreign Born Workers in the United States," 56.

45. Report on the Condition of Women and Child Wage Earners, U.S. Senate, Sixty-First Congress, vol. 18, *Employment of Women and Children in Selected Industries* (Washington, DC: Government Printing Office, 1911) "Introduction and Summary"; also see John Sharpless and John Rury, "The Political Economy of Women's Work," p. 324. For a summary of the reasons why immigrant families sent their daughters to work, see Tentler, *Wage Earning Women*, pp. 85–89. For a contemporary account, see Caroline Manning, *The Immigrant Woman and Her Job*, Women's Bureau Bulletin, no. 74, (Washington, DC: Government Printing Office, 1930), "The Family," pp. 35–49. Also see Elizabeth Beardsly Butler, *Women and the Trades: Pittsburgh, 1907–1908* (New York: Russell Sage, 1909). Figures on the numbers of immigrant and native workers in manufacturing are taken from the *Fourteenth Census of the United States*, vol. 4, p. 342. For a discussion of the number of unskilled immigrant workers in this period and the discrimination against them, see Phillip Foner, *The Policies and Practices of the American Federation of Labor*, 1900–1909 (New York: International Publishers, 1964), p. 256.

46. Elizabeth Pleck, *Black Migration and Poverty: Boston, 1865–1900* (New

York: Academic Press, 1979), pp. 125–27. Jackie Jones, *Labor of Love, Labor of Sorrow: Black Women, Work and the Family from Slavery to the Present* (New York: Basic Books, 1985), chap. 3, 4, and 5. Also see E. Wilbur Bock, "Farmer's Daughter Effect: The Case of the Negro Female Professionals," *Phylon* 30, no. 1 (Spring 1969):17–26.

47. It is unlikely, however, that occupational differences were *entirely* responsible for different ethnic patterns of labor force participation. Black women, for instance, were employed in large numbers as domestics, and domestic service employment supported a large number of older women. But domestic service was also the largest single employment category for immigrant women in this period, and as indicated earlier, relatively few foreign-born women remained in the labor force beyond age 29. Typically, the choice of whether or not women would work rested on a combination of economic and cultural considerations. Families that chose not to send their women to work did so at a cost: forfeited income. The smaller the household budget, of course, the narrower the range of choices open to a given family. It is almost certain, for instance, that black women did not prefer working careers as domestics or laundry women to staying at home with their families. They were compelled in most cases to maintain long working careers by the racist discrimination and wage differentials that affected all black workers, male and female.

Recent research has suggested that certain groups of immigrants were willing to accept some degree of privation in order to keep their women at home, or in the labor force for minimal periods of time. Despite the poor circumstances which were not remarkably better than those of many black families, immigrant women left the labor force at a faster rate than women from other backgrounds in this period. See Virginia Yans McLaughlin, "Patterns of Work and Family Organization: Buffalo's Italians," *Journal of Interdisciplinary History* 2 (1971): 299–314; Barbara Klaczynca, "Why Women Worked: A Comparison of Different Groups Philadelphia, 1910–1930", *Labor History* 17 (Spring 1976): 73–87; Katzman, *Seven Days A Week*, p. 82; and Pleck, *Black Migration and Poverty*.

Between 70 and 75 percent of all women employed in manufacturing in this period were native-born, of either native or immigrant parentage, and the largest single block was women of native parentage, between 40 and 50 percent (computed from U.S. Census, Occupations, 1900 and 1920).

48. DeVault, "Sons and Daughters of Labor," chap. 5 and 6

49. Rotella, *From Home to Office*, pp. 157–62; The Women's Educational and Industrial Union found in a survey that children from native families were much less likely to contribute all or part of their earnings to their families than immigrant children. While nearly half of all immigrant clerical workers gave all of their paychecks to their parents, only 27 percent of native clerical workers did. The proportion of teenagers who turned none of their income over to their parents was twice as high as among immigrants. See Women's Educational and Industrial Union, *The Public School and Women in*

Office Service, p. 167. For a fascinating look at the wide variety of amusements that young working women could undertake in large cities, see Kathy Peiss, *Cheap Amusements: Working Women and Leisure in Turn-of-the-Century New York* (Philadelphia: Temple University Press, 1986).

50. For discussion of the tendency for black women to hold jobs as domestics and to work longer than other women, see Katzman, *Seven Days a Week,* pp. 79–83.

51. Between 1890 and 1930 the ethnic distributions of women working in various industries remained roughly the same. More than 90 percent of all clerical and professional women in 1890 were from native families (including second-generation immigrants). Forty years later, their share was about the same. In manufacturing and domestic service, the same was true. Native women constituted a much larger share of the entire female labor force in 1930 than they had in 1890, simply because the occupational groups they dominated, clerical and professional employment, grew most rapidly in this period. See Rotella, *From Home to Office,* chap. 2, on this point.

Chapter 4. Vocationalism Ascendant: Women and the High School Curriculum, 1890–1930

1. Lawrence Cremin, *Transformation of the School: Progressivism in American Education, 1876–1957* (New York: Alfred A. Knopf, 1961); Edward Krug, *The Shaping of the American High School, 1800–1920.* (New York: Harper and Row, 1964); and Raymond Callahan, *Education and the Cult of Efficiency* (Chicago: University of Chicago Press, 1962). For other interpretations, see Joel Spring, *Education and the Rise of the Corporate State* (Boston: Beacon Press, 1972); David B. Tyack, *The One Best System,* (Cambridge, MA: Harvard University Press, 1974); and Marvin Lazerson, *Origins of the Urban School: Public Education in Massachusetts. 1870–1915* (Cambridge, MA: Harvard University Press, 1971).

2. Perhaps the best discussion of the development of vocationalism in American education can be found in the introduction to Marvin Lazerson and W. Norton Grubb's, *American Education and Vocationalism: A Documentary History, 1870–1970,* (New York, Teachers College Press, 1974). Also see Cremin, *Transformation of the School,* chap. 2; and Lazerson, *Origins of the Urban School,* chap. 2.

3. For a discussion of this issue in the context of considering industrial education generally, see Edward Krug, *The Shaping of the American High School, 1880–1920,* p. 229; see also Lawrence Cremin, *Transformation of the School,* p. 56. There are no historical monographs on the development of the home economics curriculum itself.

4. On the early development of the home economics movement, see Emma Seifrit Weigley, "It Might Have Been Euthenics: The Lake Placid Con-

ferences and the Home Economics Movement," *American Quarterly* 27, no. 1 (Spring 1975): 79–86. On female enrollments in various subjects in nineteenth century high schools, see chapter 1 in this study.

5. Later proponents of home economics traced the roots of their cause back as far as 1789. See "Dates in the History of Home Economics," *Journal of Home Economics* (October 1911): 338. See Cremin, *Transformation of the School,* pp. 26–28, on early nonvocational purposes in manual education.

6. "The Educative Value of Cookery," *Report of the Commissioner of Education, 1888–89,* vol. 1 (Washington, DC: Government Printing Office, 1890), p. 419.

7. For an overview of this process, see Cremin, *Transformation of the School,* p. 32. Cremin emphasizes the role of organized labor and business-men's associations in promoting manual education. These organizations almost always saw manual education as male education, a point that under-scores the different purposes educators and laymen alike assigned to male and female manual training in this period. For a sample of Calvin Wood-ward's views regarding manual training, see his article "Manual, Industrial and Technical Education in the United States," in *Report of the Commissioner of Education, 1903,* vol. 1, (Washington, DC: Government Printing Office, 1904) p. 1019, a piece excerpted from the *Encyclopedia Americana.* Also see the discus-sion of Woodward's ideas in Bernice Fisher, *Industrial Education* (Madison, WI: University of Wisconsin Press, 1967), p. 76.

8. "Statistics of Manual and Industrial Training, Branches Taught," *Annual Report of Commissioner of Education, 1896–97,* (Washington, DC: Gov-ernment Printing Office, 1898) p. 2285; and "Manual and Industrial Training," *Annual Report of Commissioner of Education, 1902,* (Washington, DC: Govern-ment Printing Office, 1903) p. 1964.

9. For an elaboration of these points, see Cremin, *Transformation of the School,* chap. 2, "Education and Industry." One of the key features of this shift was the growing role of the National Association of manufacturers, followed by the American Federation of Labor, both of which threw their support behind *trade education,* or education in specific manual skills associated with certain occupational categories. Woodward and other early advocates of man-ual education were opposed to trade education because they believed it to be too skill-specific. See Fischer, *Industrial Education,* p. 73. Cremin appears to have overlooked this issue, and treats manual training and trade education as synonymous.

10. An account of the proceedings of the NSPIE convention is given in *Annual Report of the Commissioner of Education, 1909,* vol. 1, (Washington, DC: Government Printing Office, 1910) p. 194. For an overview of the discussion of women, see Bulletin No. 6, of the NSPIE, "Industrial Education of Girls." Also see Krug, *Shaping of the American High School, 1880–1920,* p. 226.

11. The quote is taken from the constitution of the AHEA, reprinted in

the *Annual Report of the Commissioner of Education, 1909*, vol. 1, p. 178. Also see "Home Economics" in the same volume, p. 9, for a discussion of home economics as a new area of study.

12. Ellen H.Richards, "The Social Significance of the Home Economics Movement," *Journal of Home Economics* 3, no. 2 (April 1911): 117, 122. Also see Bertha M. Terrill, "A Study of Household Expenditures," *Journal of Home Economics* 1, no. 4 (December 1909); Sociology and the Arts of Homemaking," *Journal of Home Economics* 3, no. 1 (February 1911): 52; David Kinley and Frank A. Fetter, "Economics and Household Science," *Journal of Home Economics* 3, no. 3 (June 1911): 259.

13. William O'Neil, *Everyone Was Brave: The Rise and Fall of Feminism in America* (New York: Quadrangle Books, 1969). Historian Mary P. Ryan also distinguishes between the nineteenth-century ideology of domesticity and the ideas of women reformers at the turn of the century, though she argues there were important continuities as well. She maintains that female reformers of the Progressive period comprised of social housekeepers who managed to create ways of utilizing domestic skills in the service of social reform. See Mary P. Ryan, *Womanhood in America: From Colonial Times to the Present* (New York: Franklin Watts, 1983), pp. 208–09. For a critique of O'Neil's perspective, see Nancy Cott, "What's in a Name? The Limits of 'Social Feminism': or, Expanding the Vocabulary of Women's History," *Journal of American History* 76, no. 3 (December 1989): 809–29.

14. Nancy Cott, *The Grounding of Modern Feminism* (New Haven: Yale University Press, 1987), pp. 20–22. On Charlotte Perkins Gilman, see her principal work on this subject, *The Home: Its Work and Influence* (New York: McClure, Phillips, 1903).

15. For a good general account of this period, even though it focuses on women's higher education, see Sheila M. Rothman, *Woman's Proper Place: A History of Changing Ideals and Practices, 1870 to the Present* (New York: Basic Books, 1978), chap. 3, "The Ideology of Educated Motherhood." For an overview of the purposes of the home economics movement, see Jane Bernard Powers, "The 'Girl' Question in Education: Vocational Training for Young Women in the Progressive Era," unpublished Ph.D. dissertation, Stanford University, 1987, chap. 2. On the link to other women's reform organizations, see Viviana A. Zelizer, *Pricing the Priceless Child: The Changing Social Value of Children* (New York: Basic Books, 1985), chap. 1.

16. See, for instance, Katherine Eggleston, "What Ought to be Done to Make the Schools Useful to our Daughters?" *Woman's Home Companion* 36, no. 9 (September 1909): 20; David Snedden, "Current Problems in Home Economics," *Journal of Home Economics* 6, no. 5 (December 1914): 430; and Anna Zalor Burdick, "The Wage-earning Girl and Home Economics," *Journal of Home Economics* 11, no. 8, (August 1919): 327.

17. Richards, "The Social Significance of the Home Economics Movement," p. 122; Elizabeth C. Condit and L. D. Harvey, "A School for Homemak-

ers," *Annual Report of the Commissioner of Education, 1911*, p. 313. Also see Elizabeth C. Condit, "Teaching Home Economics as a Profession," *Journal of Home Economics* 2, no. 6, (December 1910): 591; and "Progress in Vocational Education," *Report of the Commissioner of Education, 1913*, vol. 1, p. 252.

18. Agnes Houston Craig, "Report and Recommendations on Domestic Art Education," *Journal of Home Economics* 4, no. 3 (June 1912): 272; Frank B. Gilbreth, "Scientific Management in the Household," *Journal of Home Economics* 4, no. 5 (Nov. 1912): 438; Bertha M. Terrill, "A Study of Household Expenditures," *Journal of Home Economics* 1, no. 4 (December 1909): 399; Ellen H. Richards, "The Outlook in Home Economics," *Journal of Home Economics* 2, no. 1 (February 1910): 17.

19. Ellen H. Richards, "Wanted: A Test for 'Man Power,'" *Journal of Home Economics* 1, (February 1913): 60.

20. Mrs. Annie L. Hansen, "The Work of the Domestic Educator," in *The Education of the Immigrant Bulletin*, U.S. Bureau of Education, 1914, p. 7; Dr. Mather Sill, "Malnutrition of School Children in New York City," *Journal of Home Economics* 1, no. 3 (June 1909): 369; Mabel H. Kitteredge, "The Need of the Immigrant," *Journal of Home Economics* (October 1913), p. 315; "Methods of Americanization" (editorial), *Journal of Home Economics* 11, no. 2 (February 1919): 85.

21. See Kinley and Fetter, "Economics and Household Science," p. 255. They argue that housework ought to be socially recognized as work. Other discussions of housework as a peculiarly female vocation include *Education of the Home*, Bulletin No. 18, Bureau of Education, 1911 , p. 7; "Homemaking as a Vocation for Girls" in *Cooking in the Vocational School*, Bulletin No. 1, U.S. Bureau of Education, 1915, p. 7. Interestingly, proponents of home economics stressed its vocational value less as time wore on. In the 1920s articles in the *Journal of Home Economics* increasingly stressed such themes as good family relations and the moral value of clean living. In 1919 a survey of school principals and supervisors across the country revealed that nearly 40 percent felt that home economics was included in the curriculum primarily for cultural rather than vocational ends. The remainder felt that vocational purposes were most important. See "Manual Arts and Homemaking Subjects," *Annual Report of the Commissioner of Education, 1920*, (Washington, DC: Government Printing Office, 1921) p. 23. For an example of articles characteristic of the twenties, see Emma A. Winslow, "An Experiment in Socializing Home Economics Education," *Journal of Home Economics* 12, no. 1, (January 1920): 26; Frances Zuill, "Objectives in Home Economics for the Seventh, Eighth, and Ninth Grades," *Journal of Home Economics* 16, no. 3 (March 1924): 107; and Cora M. Winchell, "Home Economics at the Crossroads," *Journal of Home Economics* 18, no. 10 (October 1926): 553.

22. Harvey A. Kantor, *Learning to Earn: School, Work, and Vocational Reform in California, 1880–1930* (Madison: University of Wisconsin Press, 1988), pp. 59–65.

23. For discussion of the way in which educators viewed the expansion of clerical enrollments, see Janice Weiss, "Educating for Clerical Work: A History of Commercial Education in the United States, Since 1850," unpublished Ed.D. dissertation, Harvard University, 1978, p. 135. Weiss accepts the candid observation of contemporaries that commercial education was an enormous boost to overall enrollment levels. An analysis I performed elsewhere, however, indicates that enrollments rose in all different types of urban settings, independently of the type of labor markets they confronted. The rapid growth of commercial enrollments may have led some educators to believe that demand for commercial education was a driving force behind the growth of secondary education in this period, but enrollments clearly did not respond primarily to increased demand for clerical labor. See John L. Rury, "Women, Cities and Schools: Education and the Development of an Urban Female Labor Force, 1890–1930" unpublished Ph.D. dissertation, University of Wisconsin, 1982, chap. 5.

24. For a discussion of the early courses in commercial subjects in American high schools, see Krug, *The Shaping of the American High School*, p. 6.

25. For a discussion of the recruiting methods employed by Private Business schools and educators' responses to them, see Leverett S. Lyon, *Education for Business* (Chicago: University of Chicago, 1922), p. 284. Interestingly, Lyon suggests that recruiters for private business schools appealed more to female students than to males.

26. Leverett S. Lyon, *A Survey of Commercial Education in the Public High Schools of the United States* (Chicago: University of Chicago, 1919), Introduction. Also see Lyon, *Education for Business*, p. 5; and U.S. Bureau of Education, *Biennial Survey of Education, 1926–28* (Washington, DC: Government Printing Office, 1930), p. 1058.

27. Lyon, *Education for Business*. p. 5.

28. Ibid., p. 284. In his survey of the commercial course in public high schools, Lyon found that only 14 percent of the high school courses were a year or less. Most private business school courses could be completed within five or six months. Lyon, *A Survey of Commercial Education*, p. 13. On the dropout problem, also see F. V. Thompson, *Commercial Education in Public Secondary Schools* (Yonkers, NY: World Book Company, 1915), pp. 92–96; and Albert H. Leake, *The Vocational Education of Girls and Women* (New York: Macmillan, 1918), p. 354.

29. See *Business Education in the Secondary Schools*, U.S. Bureau of Education Bulletin No. 32, 1919, (Washington, DC: Government Printing Office, 1919) p. 19. This bulletin reprints the report of the Business Education Committee of the Kingsley Commission. Also see Thompson, Commercial Education in Public Secondary Schools, p. 30; Lyon, *Education for Business*, p. 170.

30. See Lyon, *A Survey of Commercial Education*, Introduction, and Leake, *Vocational Education for Girls and Women*, p. 334

31. These figures have been derived from the *Biennial Survey of Education*, Public High Schools in 1918–20 and 1928–30.

32. Lyon, *A Survey of Commercial Education*, p. 45; *idem, Education for Business*, p. 124; Thompson, *Commercial Education in Public Secondary Schools*, p. 125; *Business Education in Secondary Schools*, p. 14.

33. Lyon, *A Survey of Commercial Education*, p. 15; Thompson, *Commercial Education in Public Secondary Schools*, p. 82.

34. Lyon, *Education for Business*, p. 297; *Biennial Survey of Education*, "Public High School," 1927–1928, p. 1078.

35. Industrial courses for women were offered in cities across the country. Male enrollments in industrial training courses in 1920 were twenty times female enrollments. See, "Public High Schools," *Biennial Survey of Education*, 1920–22 (Washington, DC: Government Printing Office, 1923) In 1910, however, one-third of all pupils enrolled in manual training and industrial schools at the secondary level were female. See "Manual and Industrial Training," *Education Report, 1910*, p. 1242.

36. *Report of the Commissioner of Education, 1914*, (Washington, DC: Government Printing Office, 1915) "Progress in Vocational Education," p. 269. Also see "Types of Vocational Secondary Schools," in *Vocational Education* Bulletin, U.S. Bureau of Education, p. 33.

37. See Leake, *The Vocational Education of Girls and Women*. pp. 230–31 and 291.

38. Ibid., pp. 287–88.

39. Women dropped out of industrial schools, it appears, as rapidly as they did the comprehensive schools. See Jane Bernard Powers, "The 'Girl Question" in Education," chap. 9. Only a third of the Manhattan Trade School's 1,200 students in 1914 graduated. Another third dropped out after less than a month. See Leake, *The Vocational Education of Girls*, p. 290–91.

40. *Annual Report of the Commissioner of Education, 1901*, vol. 2, (Washington, DC: Government Printing Office, 1902) "Coeducation of the Sexes in the United States," p. 1217.

41. For an overview of the debate over coeducation in this period, see John C. Maxwell, "Should the Educations of Boys and Girls Differ? A Half Century of Debate," unpublished Ph.D. dissertation, University of Wisconsin, 1966. On developments in colleges and universities that paralleled these debates, see Barbara Miller Solomon, *In the Company of Educated Women: A History of Women and Higher Education in America* (New Haven: Yale University Press, 1985), pp. 51–62.

42. *Annual Report of the Commissioner of Education 1901*, vol. 2, (Washington, DC: Government Printing Office, 1902) "Coeducation of the Sexes in the United States," p. 1218; *Biennial Survey of Education*, 1920–22, "Public High

Schools," pp. 581–94. There is evidence that industrial education courses became more male-dominated with time. In 1910, 2.6 percent of all high school women were enrolled in such courses, along with 12 percent of all high school men. In 1920 only 1 percent of high school girls were enrolled in industrial courses, as opposed to 21 percent of all high school boys. Men were clearly moving into industrial education at a much faster rate than women.

43. See, for instance, suggestions that women be excused from math courses in *Annual Report of Commissioner of Education, 1913,* vol. 1, (Washington, DC: Government Printing Office, 1914) pp. 81–82; and *Special Features in City School Systems.* U.S. Bureau of Education Bulletin No. 31, 1913, Segregation of the Sexes," p. 52. Also see Maxwell, "Should the Education of Boys and Girls Differ?" pp. 13 and 186; and Bernard Powers, "The 'Girl' Question in Education," pp. 170–79.

44. See the discussion of this question in Bernard Powers, "The 'Girl Question' in Education," chap. 11.

45. Maxwell, "Should the Education of Boys and Girls Differ?," p. 63.

46. Figures are taken from "Public and Private High Schools," *Report of the Commissioner of Education, 1911,* vol. 11, p. 1219; and "Private High Schools," in *Biennial Survey of Education, 1928–29,* (Washington, DC: Government Printing Office, 1930) p. 793.

47. *Biennial Survey of Education, 1928–29* (Washington, DC: Government Printing Office, 1930) pp. 798–99.

48. *Report of the Commissioner of Education, 1911,* vol. 2, (Washington, DC: Government Printing Office, 1912) p. 1215; 1900 and 1920 data taken from *Report of the Commissioner of Education,* "Public and Private High Schools," 1901, and *Biennial Survey of Education, 1921–22,* p. 428. See the table in my dissertation, "Women, Cities and Schools: Education and the Development of an Urban Female Labor Force," p. 286.

49. Catholic rector quoted in "Coeducation of the Sexes in the United States," 1901, p. 8; Thomas Edward Shields, *The Education of Our Girls* (New York: Benziger Brothers, 1907), p. 25.

50. See "Coeducation of the Sexes in the United States," 1901, pp. 1219–28; *Report of the Commissioner of Education, 1908,* vol. 1, (Washington, DC: Government Printing Office, 1909) "Coeducation," p. 90.

51. Leake, The Vocational Education of Girls and Women, p. 273; Maxwell, "Should the Education of Boys and Girls Differ?" p. 177; Thompson, *Commercial Education in Public Secondary Schools,* p. 143.

52. See Maxwell, "Should the Education of Boys and Girls Differ?" Conclusion.

53. These figures reflect enrollments in home economics courses alone. The *1928 Biennial Survey of Education* included figures for courses in sewing and

cooking in addition to home economics. Since many schools offered all three courses, and it was possible for women to enroll in more than one at any time, combined figures for all the courses could artificially inflate home economics enrollments in particular states. When enrollments in cooking and sewing are considered, the regional distribution of female participation in home economic courses changes very little. These figures are presented below.

54. The figures for 1922 and 1928 are for typing only. This was chosen, again, to avoid duplication. Typing was the most basic business-related skill young women could acquire and featured the highest enrollment levels of all the commercial courses. Women enrolled in other business subjects were almost certainly enrolled in typing at some point in their high school careers.

55. Evelyn W. Allan, "Home Economics in a Girl's Commercial High School," *Journal of Home Economics* 13, no. 4, (April 1921): 148. For commentary on the rapid rate at which women enrolled in the commercial course dropped out of school, see F. V. Thompson, *Commercial Education in Public Secondary Schools*, p. 97. Also see Bernard Powers, "The 'Girl Question' in Education," pp. 219–21.

56. David Snedden, *Vocational Education* (New York: Houghton Mifflin, 1920), p. 454.

Chapter 5. Varieties of Adaptation: Local Patterns of Women's Education and Work

1. Given the limited attention devoted to these issues, no one of these discussions is intended to be exhaustive. Rather, they should be taken as exploratory forays into areas of inquiry related to the foregoing analysis of women's education and women's work at the national and regional levels. While hardly definitive, in that case, the discussion that follows offers answers to a number of important questions which can be tested and refined in yet more thorough studies in the future.

2. For discussion of this, see Stanley K. Schultz, *The Culture Factory* (New York: Oxford University Press 1973); and Carl F. Kaestle and Maris A. Vinovskis, *Education and Social Change in Nineteenth Century Massachusetts* (New York: Cambridge University Press 1980), chap. 2.

3. See Sheilds McIlwaine, *Memphis: Down in Dixie* (New York: E. P. Dutton, 1948), chap. 7 and 8; Gerald Capers, *The Biography of a River Town: Memphis, Its Heroic Age* (New Orleans: Tulane University Press, 1966), chap. 9, and William D. Miller, *Memphis During the Progressive Era* (Memphis: Memphis State University Press, 1957), chap. 1.

4. For a good treatment of regional differences in educational development, see John G. Richardson, "Town versus Countryside and Systems of Common Schooling," *Social Science History* 11, no. 4 (Winter 1987): 401–32;

also see John L. Rury, "Urbanization and Education: Regional Patterns of Educational Development in American Cities, 1900–1910," *Michigan Academician* 20, no. 2 (Summer 1988): 261–80.

5. Size was a potentially important factor in itself in determining interurban differences in educational development. See my article: John Rury, "Urban Structure and School Participation: Immigrant Women in 1900," *Social Science History* 8, no. 3 (Summer 1984): 219–41.

6. Human ecologists argue that city size and the degree of differentiation—or specialization—in local labor markets are directly related. See Amos Hawley, *Human Ecology* (New York: Ronald Press, 1971), p. 327.

7. For a general discussion of Boston's population and social structure at this time, see Stephan Thernstrom, *The Other Bostonians: Poverty and Progress in the American Metropolis, 1880–1970* (Cambridge: Harvard University Press, 1973).

For an account of the social structure in Memphis, especially as regarded the question of race, see McIlwaine, *Memphis*, particularly chap. 12.

8. On the growth of industry in Memphis at this time, see Capers, *Biography of a River Town*, chap. 9. On urban and industrial development in the South, see David R. Goldfield, *Cottonfields and Skyscrapers: Southern City and Region, 1607–1980* (Baton Rouge, LA: Louisiana State University Press, 1982). On urban-industrial development in northern cities, see David Ward, *Cities and Immigrants: A Geography of Change in Nineteenth Century America* (New York: Oxford University Press); and Allan Pred, *The Spatial Dynamics of U.S. Urban-Industrial Growth, 1800–1914: Interpretive and Theoretical Essays* (Cambridge: Harvard University Press, 1966). On Boston, see Edward C. Kirkland, *Men, Cities and Transportation: A Study in New England History* (Cambridge: Harvard University Press, 1948).

9. Davies, *Woman's Place is at the Typewriter*, chap. 3 to 5.

10. On regional differences in skill levels required of various workers, see Pred, *The Spatial Dynamics of Urban-Industrial Growth*, chap. 3. Also see Rury, "Urbanization and Education."

11. These figures are derived from statistical data from the Census of Occupations, 1900, 1920, and 1930. The existence of a large black population in Memphis and other southern cities guaranteed a ready supply of women willing to perform domestic labor for low wages. The availability of this supply of labor was doubtless a factor in the widespread use of domestics across the South in this period. For an account of the lives of black women domestics in Memphis at this time, see McIlwaine, *Memphis*, pp. 312–15.

12. Calculated from figures in the U.S. Census Occupations Volumes, 1900 and 1930.

13. These figures were calculated with the use of expenditure data provided by the Commissioner of Education Report 1900, Part 3, (Washington, DC: Government Printing Office, 1901) p.24.

14. David Moss Hilliard, *The Development of Public Education in Memphis, Tennessee, 1848–1945* (Chicago: University of Chicago, 1946), p. 172.

15. Enrollment calculations based on data on the number of teenagers in school for six months or longer taken from the Twelfth Census of the United States, *Population, vol. 1.* (Washington, DC: Government Printing Office, 1901).

16. For an overview of these developments, see William Miller, *Memphis During the Progressive Era*, p. 120; and David M. Hilliard, *The Development of Public Education in Memphis Tennessee*, p. 163.

17. These figures were derived from expenditure data collected from the Biennial Survey of Education compiled by the Office of Education in 1922. See U.S. Commissioner of Education, *Biennial Survey of Education, 1920–22*, (Washington, DC: Government Printing Office, 1922).

18. Hilliard, *The Development of Public Education in Memphis, Tennessee*, p. 163. For an indication of the popularity of the commercial course, particularly in the Northeast, see George Counts, *The Selective Character of American Secondary Education*, (Chicago: University of Chicago Press, 1921), especially p. 56.

19. For an overview of the development of vocational education in this period, see Marvin Lazerson and Norton Grubb, *Vocationalism in American Education: A Documentary History* (New York: Teachers College Press, 1974), Introduction.

20. For a useful discussion of the development of commercial education in Boston, see "Commercial Education in Retrospect," by Louis J. Fish, in *Superintendent's Report School Document No. 4, 1917* (Boston: City of Boston Printing Department, 1918), p. 43. Data on the amount of total instructional time devoted to various subjects was drawn from *Boston School Report, 1910.* (Boston: City of Boston Printing Department, 1911), Appendix 1, "Percentage of Time Given to Each Subject Taught in the High Schools."

21. Miller, *Memphis During the Progressive Era*, p. 120. Figures for enrollment in various subjects were drawn from *Tennessee State School Report, 1910* (Nashville; Brandon Printing Co., 1911), pp. 114–15; and *Tennessee State School Report, 1911*, (Nashville: Brandon Printing Co., 1912), pp. 234–35.

22. Women's Educational and Industrial Union, *The Public Schools and Women in Office Service* (Boston: WEIU, 1914), p. 13; Superintendent's Report, *Boston Public Schools Document No. 35, 1928*, (Boston: City of Boston Printing Department, 1929), p. 42, Boston Public Schools, *Annual Report of Superintendent of Schools, 1929* (Boston: City of Boston Printing Department, 1930), p. 131.

23. *Tennessee State School Report, 1913* (Nashville: Brandon Printing Co., 1913), p. 168. A bare 289 students were enrolled in typing and stenography, as opposed to 904 in home economics, 681 in Latin, and 495 in modern languages. *Tennessee State School Report, 1915* (Nashville: Brandon Printing Co., 1916), pp. 128–29; U.S. Office of Education, *The Public School System of Memphis,*

Tennessee (Washington, DC: Government Printing Office, 1920), vol. 4, "Civil Education," pp. 51–52.

24. Hilliard wrote in 1945 that the school system changed little in the two decades following 1920. "The most popular and best taught," he maintained were "the traditional academic subjects." Unfortunately, he provides no statistics on enrollments. See *The Development of Public Education in Memphis, Tennessee*, p. 173.

25. For discussion of the origins of the boys and girls Latin schools, see Schultz, *The Culture Factory*. Boston Public Schools, School Document No. 16, "Annual School Report"; School Document No. 13, "Superintendent's Report"; and School Document No. 8, "Course of Study for Girls High School of Practical Arts," 1907. In his 1910 report, the superintendent commented that the High School of Commerce was modeled on similar schools in New York and Philadelphia. *Boston Public Schools, School Document No. 10*, "Superintendent's Report," 1910, p. 37.

26. Boston Public Schools, *School Document No. 8*, "Annual School Report," 1908, (Boston: City of Boston Printing Department, 1909), pp. 49 and 55. Information on seating capacity of various Boston high schools can be found in Boston Public Schools, *School Document No. 9*, "Statistics," p. 35.

27. Boston Public Schools, *School Document No. 10*, "Superintendent's Report," 1910; Boston Public Schools, *School Document No. 3*, "Superintendent's Report," 1914, p. 62.

28. Boston Public Schools, *School Document No. 8*, "Superintendent's Report," 1914 (Boston: City of Boston Printing Department, 1915), p. 64. By 1914 cooperative arrangements with stores and a new "salesmanship" course had been established.

29. See Boston School Report, 1910, Appendix I, "Percentage of Time Given to Each Subject in the High Schools." As late as 1920, when home economics was an established feature of high schools in most areas in the country, more than 90 percent of the women enrolled in female "practical arts" classes and continuation or evening schools in Boston were enrolled in dressmaking or millinery, courses with direct application in the city's garment industry. By contrast, courses in cooking drew only thirty-six students out of more than twenty-five hundred. See *Eighty-Fifth Annual Report of the Department of Education, Massachusetts, 1920–21.* (Boston: Wright and Potter Printing Co., 1922), p. 254. Statistics on the distribution of daytime enrollments were not provided.

30. Hilliard, *The Development of Public Education in Memphis, Tennessee,* p. 173.

31. U.S. Office of Education, *The Public School System of Memphis, Tennessee,* pp. 52–53.

32. For a discussion of the influence of Booker T. Washington, particu-

larly in the South, see Louis R. Harlan, *Booker T. Washington: The Wizard of Tus-keegee, 1900–1915* (New York: Oxford University Press, 1983). Also see Horace Mann Band, *Education of the Negro in the American Social Order* (New York: Prentice Hall, 1934), p. 363; and Louis R. Harlan, *Separate and Unequal,* (Chapel Hill: University of North Carolina Press, 1958), pp. 42–43.

33. Jane Bernard-Powers, "'The Girl Question in Education': Vocational Training for Young Women in the Progressive Era," unpublished Ph.D. dissertation, Stanford University, 1987, pp. 161–65.

34. George Counts, *The Selective Character of American Secondary Education.*

35. For discussion of regional differences in American cities at this time, particularly as regarded educational issues, see Rury, "Urbanization and Education."

36. For a general discussion of urban development in this period, see Pred, *The Spatial Dynamics of U.S. Urban-Industrial Growth, 1800–1914,* chap. 1.

37. By the end of the 1930s, Seattle had the highest school participation rates in the nation for a city of its size. See Calvin F. Schmidt, *Social Trends in Seattle* (Seattle: University of Washington Press, 1944), chap. 6. For a general overview of the Seattle schools in this period, see Bryce E. Nelson, *Good Schools: The Seattle Public School System, 1901–1930* (Seattle: University of Washington Press, 1988).

38. Janice Weiss, "Educating for Clerical Work: A History of Commercial Education in the U.S. Since 1850," unpublished Ed.D. dissertation, Harvard University, 1978, p. 125.

39. Weiss, "Educating for Clerical Work," p. 191.

40. Counts, *The Selective Character of American Secondary Education,* p. 19.

41. See Schmidt, *Social Trends in Seattle,* chap. 6, for a discussion of high rates of school participation there.

42. Harvey A. Kantor, *Learning to Earn: School, Work, and Vocational Reform in California, 1880–1930* (Madison, WI: University of Wisconsin Press, 1988), chap. 7.

43. See the discussion of this point in Ileen A. DeVault, "Sons and Daughters of Labor: Class and Clerical Work in Pittsburgh, 1870's–1910's," unpublished Ph.D. dissertation, Yale University, 1985, chap. 5. For a classic treatment of the issue of status anxiety as a theme in this period, see Richard Hofstadter, *The Age of Reform: From Bryan to FDR* (New York: Alfred Knopf, 1955).

44. The clearest example of this is Weiss, "Education for Clerical Work," p. 175; also see David Hogan, "Education and the Making of the Chicago Working Class," *History of Education Quarterly* 18, no. 3 (Fall 1979);

and Miriam Cohen, "Work and School, Italian Women in New York, 1900–1950," in Milton Cantor and Bruce Laurie, eds., *Sex, Class and the Women Worker*, (Westport, CT: Greenwood Press, 1978).

45. May Allison, et. al., *The Public Schools and Women in Office Service*, Dept. of Research, Women's Educational and Industrial Union.

46. Since the WEIU survey dealt only with women in commercial courses, it cannot be used to assess the backgrounds of women across the high school curriculum.

47. DeVault, "Sons and Daughters of Labor," chap. 4.

48. On the middle-class status of skilled workers in this period, see Melvin Dubovsky, *Industrialism and the American Worker, 1865–1917* (New York: AHM Publishers, 1973), p. 12. Also see the discussion in DeVault, "Sons and Daughters of Labor," chap. 5.

49. These findings, of course, appear to contradict those of the analysis of school enrollment performed in chapter 2. The two analyses are not comparable, of course, since one is a national sample taken from census data, and the second is taken from special surveys of particular cities. Yet differences in the observed importance of social class may represent an important trend as well. A number of historians have suggested that class became a more salient factor in American life in the opening decades of the twentieth century. It is possible that ethnicity declined in importance and that social class became a more important determinant of high school enrollment over time. For dicussion of the growing importance of class, see Olivier Zunz, *The Changing Face of Inequality: Urbanization, Industrial Development and Immigrants in Detroit, 1880–1920* (Chicago: University of Chicago Press, 1982).

There are a number of studies that document the superiority of office work over other types of female labor. See *The Public Schools and Women in Office Work*, chap. 3, "Wages," or Boston Public Schools, "Superintendent's Report," 1928, p. 72, for a discussion of wages paid to female clerical workers, as well as the discussion of this point in chapter 3 of this study.

50. For a discussion of working women's wages, and using young women's earnings to support their families, see Robert Smuts, *Women and Work in America* (New York: Schocken Books, 1961), pp. 90–92. Skilled workers typically enjoyed a substantially higher standard of living than unskilled workers in this period. On this point see Dubofsky, *Industrialism and the American Worker, 1865–1914*, p. 12.

51. For a discussion of the Senate survey, see John Sharpless and John Rury, "The Political Economy of Women's Work, 1900–1920," *Social Science History* 4, no. 3 (Summer, 1980): 320–26. Results of the WEIU survey are to be found in Allison, et. al., *Women in Office Service*, p. 314.

52. Allison, et. al., *Women in Office Service*, p. 322.

53. For a moving characterization of immigrant women and their back-

grounds in this period, see Caroline Manning, "The Immigrant Woman and Her Job," *Bulletin of the Women's Bureau No. 74*, U.S. Department of Labor (Washington, DC: Government Printing Office, 1930).

54. Weiss, "Educating for Clerical Work," p. 132.

55. Harry Braverman, *Labor and Monopoly Capital* (New York: Monthly Review Press, 1974), p. 307.

Index